I0257242

FACTS AND FALSEHOODS CONCERNING THE WAR ON THE SOUTH 1861-1865

by
Elizabeth Avery Meriwether

THE CONFEDERATE
REPRINT COMPANY
☆　☆　☆　☆
WWW.CONFEDERATEREPRINT.COM

Facts and Falsehoods Concerning the
War on the South 1861-1865
by Elizabeth Avery Meriwether

Originally Published in 1904
by A. R. Taylor and Company
Memphis, Tennessee

Reprint Edition © 2014
The Confederate Reprint Company
Post Office Box 2027
Toccoa, Georgia 30577
www.confederatereprint.com

Cover and Interior Design by
Magnolia Graphic Design
www.magnoliagraphicdesign.com

ISBN-13: 978-0692331682
ISBN-10: 0692331689

PREFACE
☆ ☆ ☆ ☆

To the People of the South this little work is offered. It does not aspire to the dignity of History. It is mostly a collection of facts under one cover, which I trust will prove of use to the future historians of the South. Perhaps the fittest title to this work would be "A Protest Against Injustice" – the injustice of misrepresentation – of false charges – of lies. The feeling of injustice certainly inspired the idea of this work. The greater number of the facts herein laid before the reader were not drawn from Southern or Democratic sources, but from high Republican authorities. Part first of this work presents Abraham Lincoln to the people of this generation as his contemporaries saw and knew him. The characteristics portrayed will be a revelation to many readers. As an offset to the falsity of Republican histories of the war of the '60s, permit me to express the hope that in the near future our people will make more general use of those histories which are truthful and just to the South. For instance, the English historian, Percy Gregg's large history of the United States, might be condensed, or rather that part giving the story of the '60s could be detached, and published in one small, cheap volume, so that every family in the South can own a copy. John A. Marshall's large volume, *American Bastile*, can be used in every Southern school to rouse in the hearts of boys and girls hatred of Despotism. S.D. Carpenter's *Logic of History,* and Matthew Carey's *Democratic Handbook* should not be allowed to go out of print. Both of these books contain much that will be of great value to the future historian.

> You may fool all the people part of the time,
> You may fool some of the people all the time,
> But you can't fool all the people all the time.
>   – Abraham Lincoln.

> All lies have sentence of death written against them in Heaven's Chancery itself, and slowly or fast, advance incessantly toward their hour. – Carlyle.

> I sing the hymn of the Conquered
> who fell in the battle of life,
> The hymn of the wounded, the beaten,
> who died overwhelmed in the strife;
> Not the jubilant song of the Victors
> for whom the resounding acclaim
> Of nations was lifted in chorus,
> whose brows wore the chaplet of fame.
> While the voice of the world shouts its chorus,
> its paeon for those who have won.
> While the trumpet is sounding triumphant,
> and high to the breeze and the sun.
> Gay banners are waving,
> hands clapping and hurrying feet
> Throwing after the laurel-crowned victors,
> I stand on the field of Defeat.
> Speak History! Who are Life's victors?
> Unroll thy long annals and say,
> Are they those whom the world called the victors,
> who won the success of a day?
> The Martyrs or Nero? The Spartans who fell
> at Thermopylae's tryst
> Or the Persians and Xerxes? His judges, or Socrates?
> Pilate or Christ?
>   – W. W. Story.
>   *Blackwood's Magazine*, 1881.

AUTHORITIES

The following are cited as some of the authorities for the matters stated in the pages of this little book and here summarized for brevity:

1. *The Olive Branch* (Boston, 1814), by Matthew Carey.
2. *The Pelham Papers*, published 1796, in the Connecticut *Courant*, Hartford.
3. *The Logic of History* (Madison, 1864), by Stephen D. Carpenter, Editor Wisconsin *Patriot*.
4. *History of the United States* (New York, 1880), by John Clark Ridpath.
5. *Notes on the History of Slavery in Massachusetts* (New York, 1866), by George H. Moore.
6. *History of the Negro Race in America 1619-1880* (New York, 1883), by George W. Williams, first colored member of the Ohio Legislature, and late Judge Advocate of the Grand Army of the Republic of Ohio.
7. *Abraham Lincoln: The Man of the People* (New York, 1899), by Norman Hapgood.
8. *Life of Abraham Lincoln*, by J. G. Holland (Springfield, 1866), Editor Scribner.
9. *Life of Abraham Lincoln* (New York, 1900), by Ida Tarbell.
10. *The American Conflict: A History of the Great Rebellion* (New York, 1867), by Horace Greeley, Editor the New York *Tribune*.
11. *Life of Lincoln*, by John T. Morse (New York, 1893).
12. *Life of Oliver P. Morton, Governor of Indiana* (Indianapolis, 1899), by William Dudley Foulk.

13. *History of the United States*, by E. Benjamin Andrews (New York, 1894), President Brown University.

14. *Life and Times of Hannibal Hamlin* (Cambridge, 1899), by Charles Eugene Hamlin.

15. *The Story of the Civil War* (New York, 1894), by John Codman Ropes.

16. *Disunion and Reunion* (Chicago, 1893), by Woodrow Wilson, Professor in Princeton University, New Jersey.

17. *The Real Lincoln* (Richmond, 1901), by Charles L. C. Minor.*

18. *Abraham Lincoln and Men of the War Time* (Philadelphia, 1892), by A. K. McClure.

19. *Our Presidents and How We Make Them* (New York, 1900), by A. K. McClure.

20. *Abraham Lincoln: A History* (New York, 1890), by John G. Nicolay and John Hay.

21. *American Bastile* (Philadelphia, 1882), by John A. Marshall.*

22. *History of the United States* (New York, 1893), by James Ford Rhodes.

23. *My Diary, North and South*, by William Howard Russell, published originally in the London *Times* during the War.

24. *Personal Memoirs of U. S. Grant* (New York, 1885).

25. *The Great Conspiracy* (New York, 1886), by John A. Logan.

26. *Memories of Men Who Saved the Union* (New York, 1887), by General Donn Piatt.

27. *Butler's Book* (Boston, 1892), by Benjamin F. Butler.

28. *Executive Power* (Boston, 1862), by Benjamin R. Curtis, Judge United States Supreme Court.

29. *Lalor's Encyclopedia* (New York, 1881), edited by John J. Lalor.

30. *The Life of William H. Seward* (New York, 1900), by Frederick Bancroft.

31. *Abraham Lincoln: The True Story of a Great Life* (Chicago, 1889), by William H. Herndon and Jesse William Weik.

32. *Democratic Speaker's Handbook* (Cincinnati, 1868), by Matthew Carey, Jr..*

33. *Life of Abraham Lincoln* (New York, 1902), by Joseph Barrett and Charles W. Brown.

34. *Nullification and Secession in the United States* (New York, 1897), by E.P. Powell.

35. *Life of Abraham Lincoln*, by William H. Herndon, published and suppressed soon after Lincoln's death.

36. *Life of Abraham Lincoln* (Boston, 1872), by Ward H. Lamon.

37. *Story of the Great March* (New York, 1865), by George W. Nichols, Aid de Camp to General Sherman.

38. *Southern Historical Papers* (Richmond).*

* These sources are Southern and Democratic. All the others are Northern and Republican.

Elizabeth Avery Meriwether in 1882
(age 58)

CONTENTS
☆ ☆ ☆ ☆

PART I

CHAPTER ONE 15
A Republican newspaper's estimate of Abraham Lincoln.

CHAPTER TWO 19
A glance over the country's situation at the moment of Lincoln's death. Republicans drunk with joy. Their vindictive policy. They fear and distrust Andrew Johnson.

CHAPTER THREE 23
The apotheosis of Abraham Lincoln; its cause and effect.

CHAPTER FOUR 27
The estimate Republican leaders held of the living Lincoln.

CHAPTER FIVE 33
Wendell Phillips' estimate of Lincoln. Secretary of War Stanton's opinion. The Wade and Winter Davis manifesto. Stanton's first interview with Lincoln. His insulting treatment of Lincoln. General McClellan's letters to his wife. Lincoln reads Artemas Ward at Cabinet meeting. Chase's disgust. Lincoln's hilarity. Why did Lincoln appoint Stanton Cabinet Minister? Seward on United States Constitution.

CHAPTER SIX 41
A Western Republican paper propounds the true Republican doctrine.

CHAPTER SEVEN 49
Grant and Washburn defy Lincoln's authority. Washburn bullies Lincoln. A United States Senator bullies Lincoln. Senator Wade storms at him.. Senator Hale assails him. Congress distrusts him. Rev. M. Fuller's opinion of Lincoln. Lincoln's trickery.

CHAPTER EIGHT 55
Herndon's Pen Portrait of Abraham Lincoln. A Springfield lawyer's pen portrait. General Piatt on "pious lies." The "real Lincoln Disappears From

Human Knowledge." *Herndon's Life of Lincoln. Why Suppressed. Extracts From the Suppressed Book.*

CHAPTER NINE 65
Lincoln's jealousy. His passion for horse races, cock fights and fist fights. Holland's comment thereon. Lincoln the "soul of honesty." He passes off counterfeit money. His "tender heartedness." He sews up hogs' eyes. "The Old Huzzy." A great fight. "I am the big buck of the lick."

CHAPTER TEN 75
Mr. Lincoln hates and despises Christianity. He goes to church to mock and deride "pious lies." Holland's strange story. Other Republican leaders despise Christianity. The four Ws.

CHAPTER ELEVEN 85
Lincoln's singular treatment of the lady he four times asked to marry him. His curious letter about that lady. His cruel treatment of Miss Todd. His home a hell on earth.

CHAPTER TWELVE 93
Mr. Lincoln's passion for indecent stories. Holland's comment thereon. The "foulest in stories of any other man." Governor Andrews' disgust. Lincoln writes indecent things. He dislikes ladies' society.

CHAPTER THIRTEEN 99
Lincoln and Lamon visit Antietam battlefield. Lincoln calls for comic songs; Lamon sings "Picayune Butler." General McClellan shocked. The Perkins' letter. Mr. Lincoln's reply.

CHAPTER FOURTEEN 105
The true and the false. Apotheosizing writers. Miss Tarbell takes the lead. Why Lincoln's father left Kentucky. Apotheosis twaddle. Two little girls in the White House. More twaddle. A study of Lincoln's character.

CHAPTER FIFTEEN 115
A brief mention of the two policies. President Johnson and the Republican leaders.

PART II

CHAPTER SIXTEEN 123
Antagonistic principles. The great American monarchist. Federalists fear and hate Democracy. War on the South began in 1796. The Olive Branch. The Pelham papers. New England begins work for disunion and secession in 1796.

CONCERNING THE WAR ON THE SOUTH 11

CHAPTER SEVENTEEN 133
Republicans cover up the real cause of the war. New England secessionists. Their determination to dissolve the Union. Early and universal belief in the right of secession.

CHAPTER EIGHTEEN 141
New England's effort to secede in 1812, 1814. and 1815.

CHAPTER NINETEEN 161
More evidence of New England's disunion and secession work.

CHAPTER TWENTY 167
New England's three hates still active. The Republican party organized 1854. Ambassador Choate bears false witness.

CHAPTER TWENTY-ONE 173
Save the Union, free the slaves, the pretext, not the purpose, of the war on the South. Real cause, hatred of Democracy.

CHAPTER TWENTY-TWO 189
Republicans ascend to power. Lincoln and Seward make ambiguous speeches. Webster Davis on the carnage of the War. Seward's remarkable letter to Lincoln. Nicolay and Hay's comment on Seward's letter. A moral pervert.

CHAPTER TWENTY-THREE 199
Seward's falsehoods. Treachery blacker than Benedict Arnold's. Lincoln confesses that he, at Medill's demand, made war on the South.

CHAPTER TWENTY-FOUR 203
Greeley opposes war. He declares the right of the South to independence and the right of secession. Why Lincoln did not sooner begin the war. Why Buchanan did not begin it.

CHAPTER TWENTY-FIVE 209
Almost universal opposition to war in the Northern States. Indiana longs for peace. Morton's "desperate fidelity." "I am the State." Congressman Cameron's bosh on the "life of the nation." Nicolay and Hay's bosh on treason.

CHAPTER TWENTY-SIX 223
Why Grant refused to exchange prisoners. Grant compares Northern and Southern soldiers. Desertions from the Union Army. Riots. Arbitrary arrests. "Suspects." Thirty-eight thousand men and women locked up in Northern jails. Civil law overthrown. Lincoln disliked and distrusted. The peoples'

indictment in 1864. Judiciary opposes Lincoln.

CHAPTER TWENTY-SEVEN 231
What a battle meant to Lincoln. Greeley prays Lincoln for peace. Rosecrans and Halleck on the peoples' hatred of the war. Soldiers dislike Lincoln. Judge Curtis on Lincoln's usurpation of power. Republican writers, Rhodes, Moore, Hapgood, Bancroft and others, laud despotism.

CHAPTER TWENTY-EIGHT 243
Lincoln's eagerness for re-election. His unlawful use of the United States Army. Butler and Dana testify. Lincoln's crime against the ballot box and American freedom. Republican writers unfit teachers of American boys.

CHAPTER TWENTY-NINE 255
Mr. Vallandingham's case. Unhappy condition of Northern Democracy under despotism. Lincoln lays down the lines of despotism.

CHAPTER THIRTY 263
Was the war waged to free slaves? Lincoln on the negro. Van Buren. Lamon's evidence. Wendell Phillips. Lincoln's letter to Greeley. Seward's indifference to the negroes' fate. Grant's opinion. Conway's letter.

CHAPTER THIRTY-ONE 267
The reconstruction period. Hate and cruelty.

CHAPTER THIRTY-TWO 277
Republican Hate.

CHAPTER THIRTY-THREE 315
New England's strange malady of the mind.

PART I

CHAPTER ONE

A Republican Newspaper's Estimate of Abraham Lincoln

"Abraham Lincoln has long since entered the sublime realm of apotheosis. Where now is the man so rash as to warmly criticise Abraham Lincoln?" (St. Louis *Globe-Democrat*, March 6, 1898).

The above sentence from one of the ablest Republican newspapers in the country is perhaps a little terser and stronger than the usual statement regarding the position Republicans are determined Lincoln shall hold in the minds of men, but truly represents the reverential attitude which is held toward Lincoln, not only by Republicans, but by men of all political parties. He has "entered the realm of apotheosis" – to criticise him unfavorably is resented by Republicans as sacrilegious, and of every hundred, ninety and nine either believe that Lincoln is the demi-god he is said to be, or they pretend to believe it, and go their way, thus giving their sanction to the apotheosis referred to by the *Globe-Democrat*. Even in the South the real Lincoln is lost sight of in the rush and bustle of our modern life, and many Southerners accept the opinion of Lincoln that is furnished them ready made by writers who are either ignorant, or else who purposely falsify plain facts of history. To such extent has this proneness to accept fiction for fact gone, this proneness to take ready-made opinions from others, that even in Mississippi the proposition has been seriously made to place a portrait of Lincoln in the halls of the State Capitol. No doubt the Mississippi legislator who proposed the Lincoln portrait flatters himself that he was displaying a broad and liberal spirit; ignorant of the facts, he believed Lincoln was a man of pure and lofty spirit, a patriot moved by a noble impulse to serve and save his country, therefore worthy of Southern as well as

Northern admiration. Certainly no right thinking man would erect a statue or put a portrait in their legislative hall of a self-seeking, cunning, coarse-minded politician, a man scorned by his own official family and by the most powerful and prominent of his Republican contemporaries. Amid the universal din of praise that it has become the fashion to sing of Lincoln, only the student remembers the real facts, only the student knows not only that the Lincoln of the popular imagination of today bears little or no resemblance to the real Lincoln, but that the deification of Lincoln was planned and carried out by the members of his own party, by men who but a few short hours before Booth's bullet did its deadly work at Ford's theater, were reviling him as a buffoon, a coarse, vulgar jester. History affords no stranger spectacle than this, that today, nearly forty years after his death, the American people, North and South, have come to regard almost as a god a man who, when living, and up to the very hour of his death, was looked upon with contempt by nearly every man of his own party who intimately knew him, even by members of his Cabinet, by Senators, Congressmen, preachers and plain citizens. The unthinking, who do not care to correct mistaken views of historical characters, may as well throw this book aside, but those who prefer Facts to Falsehoods will, the author believes, feel repaid by reading on to the end. Nearly every statement will be substantiated by high Republican authority, the great part made by the closest friends of Mr. Lincoln, men who cannot be deemed prejudiced against him. In another issue, the *Globe-Democrat* says, "One thing is certain, Lincoln was apotheosized after his death. Had he lived 4000 years ago his name would now be enrolled among the gods of Greece and Rome."

  The first part of this announcement is true. The ceremony of Lincoln's apotheosis *was* performed soon after his death. The second part may be doubted. The men of ancient Greece and Rome whom their fellow mortals enrolled among the gods, were given that honor, either for some bold, bad, or good achievement. History affords no instance of any mortal having gained godship as Lincoln did. The men who bestowed that honor upon Lincoln, though of his own party, though having known him well during his Presidential life, had during that period openly disliked, despised, and distrusted him, and had persistently lavished upon him the most "venomous detractions" the English language afforded. These facts will be proved by indisputable evidence. Why the Republican leaders who had always "venomously vituperated" the living Lincoln, the hour after his death made frantic haste to perform the apotheosis ceremony, and hoist their dead President up to the sublime realm of the gods, it is the purpose of the writer to show. We entreat the reader not to make the mistake of supposing that the apotheosis ceremony was a mere holiday affair gotten up to amuse or astonish the public. Its conception was a flash of genius. It was the last act of the dreadful tragedy of war, and the prelude of political plans of deep and far-reaching importance. The apotheosis ceremony and its successful upholding during all the years (thirty-eight) since Lincoln's death, has done more to prolong the power of the Republican party than its victories and conquest of the South. The old saying that "facts are stranger than fiction" is as true as it is trite. The most fertile fictionist earth ever produced has never created so unique, so incongruous, so unparalleled a character as was Abraham Lincoln, mentally, morally and physically, nor has the most inventive ever thought out so unexampled a career as was his from cradle to coffin bed. Nor could the most ingenious romancer, delving in his closet, have devised so original, so daring a scheme and so successfully carried it out as that apotheosis ceremony, planned on the spur of the moment by the Republican leaders, confused, confounded, alarmed as they were by the sudden taking-off of their first President. Although the writer of this has no authentic account of any secret caucus held by the Republican leaders in Washington City at the time of Mr. Lincoln's death, their entire unity of action in the unexpected emergency that confronted them is presumptive evidence that a caucus was held, almost before Mr. Lincoln's body was cold; that plans were made and secret instructions sent forth to the foremost men of the party, advising them of the course necessary to pursue, the tone, the attitude, it was the duty of every man to assume toward their dead President. The men composing the caucus saw as by a flash of lightning the vital necessity of concealing from the world the opinions they and their whole party had held of the living Lincoln. The preservation of party power was their first thought. They saw the black gulf into which their triumphant party would sink unless swift measures were taken. They realized the fact that if their President were known to the world as they knew him, the glory of their victory would fade; as he stood, so their party would stand. If he was despised, they and their party would be despised. If made public, every venomous word they had flung on the living Lincoln would rebound on their party. To exalt the dead President became the vital necessity of the hour. The passion of the Republican heart is to possess power. They had won power through seas of blood;

to lose it now would be anguish to their very souls. To exalt to the high realm of godship the dead man they had in life despised as the dirt under their feet, was the first thought that darted on their agitated brains. To bury with their dead President's body every mental and physical quality which had so prominently distinguished him from his kind, and which had provoked from them so many gibes and jeers and contemptuous flings, was the first duty they saw before them; the next was to manufacture an effigy of their dead President, clothe it from head to heels in attributes the very reverse of those the living President had been clothed in, and then boldly, under the wide light of the Nineteenth Century, start that effigy, that fake of their own creation, down the ages, labeled, "Abraham Lincoln, First President of the Republican party, the greatest, wisest, godliest man that has appeared on earth since Christ."

The reader is warned not to commit the grievous mistake of dismissing this statement as a fairy tale, or the mistake of fancying that its truth or falsity is of small moment. After a close and critical study of the case, the writer of this believes that the Republican party, from the death of Lincoln to this day, is chiefly supported by the fictions put forth in that apotheosis ceremony. These fictions, told and retold so often, have become almost the faith of the world. The writer holds that belief in falsehood is always injurious to humanity, and that the highest duty we owe to humanity is to put truth in the place of lies. When the apotheosis theory ceases to govern historians, and the real facts of the war of the '60s are laid before the world, Republican history of the war will sink out of sight as worthless rubbish.

CHAPTER TWO

A Glance over the Country's Situation at the Moment of Lincoln's Death. The Republicans' Drunken Joy. Their Vindictive Policy. They Fear and Distrust Andrew Johnson.

The awful war was ended; the South had surrendered her arms and lay prostrate at her conqueror's feet, bleeding at every pore. Her soldiers (those not buried on battlefields) were slowly wending their way over their devastated country toward their devastated homes, shoeless, ragged, hungry, as they had so often been while bravely fronting and fighting the foe; they trudged onward and Southward sadder than night itself. How different their conquerors! These were feeding themselves fat at the grand feast of success; were quaffing deep of the wine of victory. Lamon, the constant companion of Lincoln, has left on record the story of Lincoln's joy. Lamon says, "Everybody was happy; the President's spirits rose to a height rarely witnessed: he was unable to restrain himself."

So unable, the irascible Stanton called him to order, with a severe reprimand, as will be related later on. Lamon says:

> An informal Cabinet meeting was held, and how to dispose of the traitors was discussed. Most of the members were for hanging them. Lincoln was then asked for his opinion and replied by relating a story.
>
> I once [said Lincoln] saw a boy holding a coon by a string. "What have you got?" I asked.
>
> "It's a coon," replied the boy. "Last night Dad cotched six coons. He killed them all but this poor little cuss. Dad

told me to hold him till he got back, and I'm afeared he's going to kill this one too. Oh, I do wish he'd get away."

"Why don't you let him loose?" I asked.

"If I let him loose Dad'll give me hell," said the boy.

"Now," said Lincoln, "if Jeff Davis and the other fellows will only get away themselves it will be all right, but if I catch them and let them loose, Dad'll give me hell."

It was Lincoln's nature to make light of the crudest tragedies, to find amusement in the awfulest horrors. The anguish, the agonies of the four years' war, the slaughter of 700,000 men who wore the blue, and more than half as many who wore the gray, Lincoln could jovialy liken to catching six coons, the killing of five, and the captivity of one. Not one particle of pity went out to the condition of the conquered. On the contrary, their thoughts and energies were at work devising plans to still further make wretched their conquered foe. In all the long and woeful history of man's inhumanity to man, I know of nothing to equal the virulence, the vindictiveness of hate manifested by Republican leaders after the South's surrender.

"We've got 'em down at last!" was the exultant boast.

"What next?"

"They are ours by the law of conquest," said another, "Ours to rule as conquerors rule."

"We'll grind them down to the very mire of degradation," said another.

"We'll crush every atom of rebel spirit from their rebel hearts. We'll wipe out their State lines and make territories under military rulers; we'll confiscate their land, cut it up into forty-acre lots, and give it to the negroes. We'll enfranchise the blacks, disfranchise the whites, and set ex-slaves masters over ex-masters."

"But," said another, "I've heard it whispered that the President means to be merciful to the Rebs."

"The President!" was the sinister rejoinder. "In the future, as in the past, our will, not his, be done."

Even as they spoke the sound of Booth's bullet smote upon their ears and for a moment they were dumb. True, they had never loved their first President. True, they had scorned him and reviled him, but they knew him, knew how far they could move him to go their way. They never forgot that before his election to the Presidency he had in a speech in Congress declared the right of secession, the right of the South to independence, and they knew how the imperialists of their party had easily induced him to recede from secession and State rights, and take up the imperial idea that secession is a monstrous political crime, to punish which war was inaugurated and the whole Southland drenched in blood. This pliable President was dead; how would it be with his successor? Could they put the bit in *his* mouth and guide him the way they intended to go? Andrew Johnson was to them an unknown quantity. Would *he* be willing to wipe out State lines in the South and set over the people military rulers. Would *he* adopt the policy of confiscation? Would *he* see the utility of sinking the white men and women of the South into a deeper degradation than the yellow race on the Pacific coast are held in by the white? Putting a proud people, accustomed to dominance and freedom, under the black heels of savages from Africa would be a feat of such supreme and unspeakable despotism as neither pagan or Christian conquerors ever before attempted. This feat they were determined to accomplish. They knew that Andrew Johnson was a renegade from the South. They knew that he had been born and reared in the school of Democracy, which they hated and despised. They knew he had played traitor to the State of his birth, to the party which had honored him with the highest office in the State. They knew in the awful time which tried the souls of his people he had been false to them, false to kith and kin and blood, had fled northward and thrown himself into the arms of their deadliest foes. They knew when their first President let slip the bloody dogs of war, the triple traitor from Tennessee had sicced on those dogs, shouting as they leaped southward: "On, Lion! On, Wolf! On, Tiger! Catch! Tear! Devour!"

They well knew Johnson's treachery to his own people had left a gulf between him and them, a gruesome gulf filled with the blood and bones of slaughtered men. Could any bridge span a gulf like that? Would not that gulf forever hold the traitor from Tennessee away from his own people, his own country? Why then did fear steal upon their souls? They had heard it said that "the teachings of childhood are never wholly obliterated." What, if in some secret recess of Johnson's heart one spark, one single spark of Democracy's fire was left? What if that spark should revive? Should glow with life? Should break into flame? Should flare backward over the four years of Republican rule? Backward, shedding a lurid light over the horrors, the agonies, the anguish of the thousand battlefields, and the rivers of blood? Over the moans and groans of the wounded and dying? All these lay along the track of the four years of war. Added to these were the outrages to freedom, free speech stifled, the press choked breathless, the Constitution kicked into the Capitol cellar, habeas corpus bound hand and foot, the Supreme Court set aside as naught, the old Bourbon infamy, *letres de cachet* resurrected from the ruins of the Bourbon Bastile, and brought to this country to rule in the North as it ruled in France 300 years ago; 38,000 of its victims yet lay in dungeon cells. What if these sights and sounds should stir the heart of that traitor from Tennessee and he should come to feel that blood is thicker than water, and his strong right arm should strike forth commandingly, and his strident voice say to them, the conquerors, "It is enough! Stay now thine hand."

Could they bear this from the renegade Democrat of Tennessee? Was not the South *theirs* by the law of conquest? *Theirs* by the decree of the god of war? Before their excited minds flashed the possibility of many things. What if speech and press should be again freed? What if the words of contempt, the vituperations, the abusive epithets they had so viciously hurled upon their President while he was alive, with which the air in and around Washington was thick, should be seized by a freed press, pilloried in a thousand columns and sent broadcast over the world? Would not *their* party shrivel under the exposure? It is said in the face of great danger Thought acts with lightning speed. Hardly had those alarmed Republicans asked of one another, "How escape the avalanche of calamities that threaten us?" ere the road to safety was lumined before their eyes. The apotheosis project was devised and so successfully carried out, even Democrats of the South and of the North are taken in by its falsehoods and often join Republicans in singing praises to the man whom in life his own party scorned and derided.

CHAPTER THREE

The Apotheosis of Abraham Lincoln. Its Cause and Effect.

McClure and other Republican writers inform us that two men, Mr. William H. Herndon and Ward H. Lamon, from youth up, were the closest friends to Mr. Lincoln, were trusted friends in the days of Lincoln's poverty and insignificance, devoted, grateful friends in the days of his power and high fortune. Both Herndon and Lamon wrote a biography of the man they loved.

The highest Republican authorities testify that these two men produced by far the best story of Lincoln's life ever published. Not a man has ever denied or doubted the honesty, fairness or truth of these two writers. I am particular in this matter, as I shall quote liberally from these authors. McClure's *Lincoln*, page 46, has this: "Lamon was selected by Mr. Lincoln to accompany him to Washington City, as a protector from assassination. Mr. Lincoln appointed Mr. Lamon United States Marshal of the District of Columbia, that he might always have him at hand."

Schouler (good Republican authority) in his *History* says, "Lamon, as Marshal, made himself the bodyguard of the man he loved."

During his stay in Washington City, Lamon was Mr. Lincoln's closest friend; into his ears Lincoln poured all his little and big troubles. Lamon has left an account of the curious proceedings which took place immediately after Lincoln's death. We extract the following:

> The ceremony of Mr. Lincoln's apotheosis was planned and executed by men who were unfriendly to him while he lived. The deification took place with showy magnificence; men who had exhausted the resources of their skill

and ingenuity in venomous detractions of the living Lincoln were the first, after his death, to undertake the task of guarding his memory, not as a human being, but as a god.

On another page Lamon gives specimens of the "venomous detractions" which the apotheosizers of the dead Lincoln had lavished on the living. Members of the Cabinet were in the habit of referring to President Lincoln as "the baboon at the other end of the avenue." Senators referred to him as "that damned idiot in the White House." Other specimens of "venomous detractions" will be given later on.

Of the apotheosis ceremony, Lamon continues thus:

> There was the fiercest rivalry as to who should canonize Mr. Lincoln in the most solemn words; who should compare him to the most sacred character in all history. He was prophet, priest and king, he was Washington, he was Moses, he was likened to Christ the Redeemer, he was likened unto God. After that came the ceremony of apotheosis.

And this was the work of men who never spoke of the living Lincoln except with jeers and contempt. Lamon says this "venomous detraction" was known to Mr. Lincoln; the detractors took no pains to conceal it until after Lincoln's death, when it became a political necessity to pose him as the "greatest, wisest, godliest man that ever lived." Of the way such detractions wounded Mr. Lincoln's feelings, Lamon speaks as follows:

> Mr. Lincoln was so outraged by the obloquies, so stung by the disparagements, his existence was rendered so unhappy, that his life became almost a burden to him. I went one day to his office and found him lying on the sofa, greatly distressed. Jumping to his feet, he said: "You know, Lamon, better than any living man, that from my boyhood up my ambition was to be President, but look at me; I wish I had never been born! I would rather be dead than as President thus abused in the house of my friends." The tragic death of Mr. Lincoln brought a more fearful panic to his traducers than to his friends.

The reason of this is plain. The few true friends about Mr. Lincoln were not politicians. Lamon loved Lincoln for himself, faults and all, and possibly for the favors bestowed upon him. The Republican politicians about him detested Lincoln personally and had little or no respect for his mental ability, but the moment after Lincoln's death they saw how disastrous it would be for their party and themselves should the public come to know of the low estimate in which they had held their first President.

Continuing the apotheosis subject, Lamon makes the following remarkable statement:

> For days and nights after the President's death it was considered treason to be seen in public with a smile on your face. Men who ventured to doubt the ineffable purity and saintliness of Lincoln's character, were pursued by mobs of men, beaten to death with paving stones, or strung up by the neck to lamp posts until dead.

Who were the men back of these crimes? Who were they who in secret conclave decreed that a smile on the face should be punished as high treason? Who were they whose fine diplomatic art contrived to gather mobs on the street and then stirred them up to the madness of beating men to death with paving stones or hanging them on lamp posts until dead? For what object were these desperate measures resorted to? The Republican writers inform us that almost without exception, every Republican who knew Mr. Lincoln personally, not only failed to see his greatness, but were so impressed by his littleness as to be anxious to depose him, and put a dictator in his place. B.F. Butler, in his book, says several men were talked of for the dictatorship. Edwin Stanton more than once proposed to General McClellan to seize the reins of government and make himself dictator. Butler says:

> There was a crop of dictators; each party wanted the man. The zealous abolitionists wanted Fremont. The property men of the country wanted a property man. The New York *Times*, in an elaborate editorial, proposed that George Law, an extensive manufacturer of New York, should be dictator.

Lamon says Lincoln was well posted as to these dictator plots. So widespread was the dissatisfaction with Lincoln, so high and influential were the men engaged in the plots, no man at the time offered any objection, no man, no Republican paper (that we can learn of) denounced the project as treason, or the projectors as traitors. No man urged, in opposition, the ability and fitness of Mr. Lincoln. At that time, as all through the dreadful four years' war, the word "traitor" was by Republicans only applied to men who did not advocate the war of conquest on the South. The slightest word indicating a belief that the war was not just or was unnecessarily cruel, was enough to brand a man as a traitor deserving a dungeon cell. Among the distinguished men who distrusted Lincoln's ability, who scorned and reviled him, were Secretary of the Treasury Salmon P. Chase. Secretary of War Edwin Stanton, Vice President Hannibal Hamlin, Secretary of State Seward, Fremont, Senators Sumner, Trumbull, Ben Wade, of Ohio, Henry Wilson, of Massachusetts, Thaddeus Stevens, Henry Ward Beecher, Wendell Phillips, Winter Davis, Horace Greeley. Chandler of Michigan, and hosts of others. Yet all of these (with the exception of Greeley) immediately after the apotheosis ceremony deemed it for the good of their party and themselves to bury out of sight every "venomous detraction" they had lavished on the living President and forthwith to put themselves into a reverential attitude toward the dead man and force upon the world the belief that Lincoln had been their wise and trusted ruler, their guide, their head, their Moses who had led them out of the awful Wilderness of War. So far as I can discover, Greeley was the only Republican who did not make a sudden jump from distrust and contempt to adoration.

Zack Chandler, of Michigan, who had much to do with pushing Lincoln on to coercion, was among the number who were eager to depose Lincoln and put a dictator in his place. It was Chandler, who, before it became evident that Lincoln was determined on war, while more than two-thirds of the people in the Northern States denounced the bare idea of coercion, wrote these sinister words: "This Union will not be worth a curse without a little blood-letting."

Although Lincoln had gratified Chandler by letting the blood, and day by day was still letting it from thousands of brave young hearts, Chandler was dissatisfied and wanted Lincoln removed and a dictator put in his place.

CHAPTER FOUR

The Estimate Republican Leaders Held of the Living Lincoln.

In his *History of the United States*, Vol. IV, page 520, Rhodes makes the sweeping assertion that "Lincoln's contemporaries failed to perceive his greatness."

Other Republican writers make the same statement. Yet none attempted to explain why those who best knew Mr. Lincoln failed to esteem or respect him. Chase, while in his Cabinet, had every opportunity to know Lincoln well. Tarbell says, "Mr. Chase was never able to realize Mr. Lincoln's greatness."

McClure says, "Chase was the most irritating fly in the Lincoln ointment."

In their voluminous life of Lincoln, Nicolay and Hay have this:

> Even to complete strangers Chase could not write without speaking slightingly of President Lincoln. He kept up this habit till the end of Lincoln's life. Chase's attitude toward the President varied between the limits of active brutality and benevolent contempt.

Yet Nicolay and Hay, and all other Republican writers, rate Mr. Chase very high as a man of honesty, talent, and patriotism. The reader must bear in mind that every Republican writer since the year 1860 uses the word "patriotism" in a perverted sense, not as meaning love of country, but meaning approbation of the war made on the South. To a Republican, opposition to that war was treason, support of it was patriotism. The worst scoundrel that ever lived, if he eulogized that war, was patriotic. Had St. Peter himself returned to earth and even hinted that war was cruel and unnecessary, he would have been called a traitor and confined in a dungeon cell. Of a bill to create offices in 1864. Chase wrote in his diary, "If this bill becomes a law, Lincoln will most certainly put men in office from political considerations."

On this, page 448, Rhodes comments thus: "A President who selected unfit generals for the reason that they represented phases of public opinion, would hardly hesitate to name postmasters and collectors who could be relied upon as a personal following." This is as near as Rhodes dare come in adverse criticism of the apotheosized man.

Rhodes further says, "In conversation, in private correspondence, in the confidence of his diary, Chase dealt censure unrestrained on Lincoln's conduct of the war."

Morse says, "Many distinguished men of his own party distrusted Mr. Lincoln's character."

On an official visit to Washington, February 23, 1863, Richard H. Dana wrote Thomas Lathrop as follows:

> I see no hope but in the army; the lack of respect for the President in all parties is unconcealed. The most striking thing is the absence of personal loyalty to the President. It does not exist. He has no admirers. If a convention were held tomorrow he would not get the vote of a single State. He does not act or talk or feel like the ruler of an empire. He seems to be fonder of details than of principles, fonder of personal questions than of weightier matters of empire. He likes rather to talk and tell stories with all sorts of people who come to him for all sorts of purposes, than to give his mind to the many duties of his great post. This is the feeling of his Cabinet. He has a kind of shrewd common sense, slip-shod, low-leveled honesty that made him a good Western lawyer, but he is an unutterable calamity to us where he is. Only the army can save us.

This was the way Mr. Dana and many other Republicans saw Mr. Lincoln before the apotheosis ceremony. After that ceremony the Honorable S.E. Crittenden expressed deep regret that "The men whose acquaintance with Mr. Lincoln was intimate enough to form any just estimate of his character did not more fully appreciate his statesmanship and other great qualities. They did not recognize him as the greatest statesman and writer of the times." Is it not a little singular that neither Crittenden or any other Republican writer has made any attempt to explain the phenomenon, that despite Mr. Lincoln's greatness and goodness not one, so far as I can discover, of his contemporaries perceived those qualities while he lived? The New York *Independent*, a strong Republican journal, in its issue of August 9th, 1862, thus commented on Lincoln's state papers:

> Compare the state papers, messages, proclamations, orders, documents, which preceded or accompanied the War of Independence, with those of President Lincoln's papers. These are cold, lifeless, dead. There has not been a line in any government paper that might not have been issued by the Czar of Russia or by Louis Napoleon of France.

The state papers of the War of Independence were inspired by the highest, the most generous emotion of the human heart-love of freedom. The state papers of President Lincoln were inspired by the meanest, the most selfish – the passion for conquest. Is it strange that in tone and spirit, Lincoln's state papers should resemble those of the Czar of Russia? Both men stood on a despot's platform.

"Our state papers," continues the New York *Independent*, "during this eventful period [the war of conquest on the South] are void of genius and enthusiasm for the great doctrine on which this government was founded. Faith in human rights is dead in Washington." Never spoke journal a more lamentable truth. Faith in human rights was not only dead in Washington, but the Government in Washington was using all the machinery in its power to trample down that faith deep in bloody mire on a hundred battlefields. The Washington Government had gone back a hundred years to the old monarchic doctrines of George III., and was doing its utmost to quell and kill the patriotic spirit of '76, which had rescued the Colonies from kingly rule. Dunning, President of Columbia University, in one of his essays on the Civil War (the war of conquest on the South), says, page 39:

> President Lincoln's proclamation of September 24th, 1862, was a perfect plat for a military despotism. The very demonstrative resistance of the people to the government only made military arrests more frequent. Lincoln asserted the existence of military law throughout the United States.

The President of Columbia University might have gone a little farther back and found that the plat Lincoln made for a military despotism was when he called for 75,000 armed men to invade and conquer the States of the South. The Rev. Robert Collier, a distinguished divine of Chicago, was on a visit to Washington City. Says Lamon:

> The Rev. Mr. Collier, sharing the prevailing sentiment in regard to the incapacity and inefficiency of Lincoln's government, chanced to pass through the White House grounds. Casting a glance at the Executive Mansion, he saw three pairs of feet resting on the ledge of an open window on the second floor. Calmly surveying the grotesque spectacle, Mr. Collier asked a man at work about the grounds "What that meant?" pointing to the six feet in the window. "You old fool!" retorted the man, that's the Cabinet a settin' and them big feet is old Abe's."

Some time after, in a lecture at Boston, Mr. Collier described the scene and commented on the imbecility of the Lincoln government: "Projecting their feet out of a window and jabbering away is about all they're good for in Washington," said the great preacher.

The reader will observe the first line of this quotation: *"Mr. Collier, sharing the prevailing sentiment in regard to Mr. Lincoln's incapacity."* This sentiment prevailed up to the hour of Lincoln's death. As soon as the apotheosis ceremony was performed, the Rev. Collier made haste to assume toward Lincoln an attitude of reverence and admiration. "I abused poor Lincoln like the fool the man called me," said Mr. Collier.

Charles Francis Adams wrote of the living Lincoln: "When Lincoln first entered upon his functions as President, he filled with dismay all those brought in contact with him." The dismay did not abate as the years went by; on the contrary, the opposition to Lincoln, the distrust, the disgust, increased from day to day to the hour of his death. In 1873 ex-Minister Adams made an address to the Legislature of New York on the occasion of Seward's death. On page 48 Adams said, "When Lincoln entered upon his duties as President he displayed moral, intellectual and executive incompetency." So far as I can discover, not during Lincoln's life did any noted Republican state that he displayed anything else.

June 20th Richard H. Dana, in the New York *World*, wrote thus:

> I have had several interviews with Lincoln, Seward, Blair, Stanton, Wells and Chase. They all say dreadful things of each other, all except Seward. They are all at sixes and sevens. I cannot describe Lincoln. He was sobered in his talk; told no extreme stories. You feel for him a kind of pity, feeling that he has some qualities of great value, yet fearing his weak points may make him wreck something.

CHAPTER FIVE

Wendell Phillips' Estimate of Lincoln. Secretary of War Stanton's Opinion. The Wade and Winter Davis Manifesto. Stanton's First Interview With Lincoln. His Insulting Treatment of Lincoln. McClellan's Letters to His Wife. Lincoln Reads Artemus Ward at Cabinet Meeting. Chase's Disgust. Lincoln's Hilarity. Why Did Lincoln Appoint Stanton Cabinet Minister? Seward on United States Constitution. Stanton Bullies Lincoln.

Not only in private life but in public speeches did Wendell Phillips speak of President Lincoln in the most uncomplimentary terms. On August 1, 1862, Wendell Phillips said to his audience:

> As long as you keep the present turtle [Lincoln] at the head of affairs you make a pit with one hand and fill it with the other. I know Mr. Lincoln. I have been to Washington and taken his measure. He is a first-rate second-rate man; that is all of him. He is a mere convenience and is waiting, like any other broomstick, to be used.

In a speech made at Music Hall, New Haven, 1863, Philips said, "Lincoln was badgered into emancipation. After he issued it he said it was the greatest folly of his life. It was like the Pope's bull against the comet."

In a speech in Tremont Temple, Boston, Wendell Phillips said to his large audience, "With a *man* for President we should have put down the rebellion in ninety days" (*Logic of History*, page 12). At a Republican meeting in Boston he called to express disgust at the conduct of the Government, said, "President Lincoln, with senile, lick-spittle haste, runs before he is bidden, to revoke the Hunter proclamation. The President and the Cabinet are treasonable. The President and the Secretary of War should be impeached."

In 1864, in a speech at Cooper Institute, Phillips denounced Lincoln's despotic acts in the strongest possible terms. He said:

> I judge Mr. Lincoln by his acts, his violation of the law, his overthrow of liberty in the Northern States. I judge Mr. Lincoln by his words and deeds, and so judging, I am unwilling to trust Abraham Lincoln with the future of this country. Mr. Lincoln is a politician; politicians are like the bones of a horse's fore shoulder; not a straight one in it. I am a citizen watchful of constitutional liberty. Are you willing to sacrifice the constitutional rights of seventy years? A man in the field [the army] said, "The re-election of Lincoln will be a national disaster." Another said, "The re-election of Lincoln will be national destruction." I want free speech. Let Abraham Lincoln know that we are stronger than Abraham Lincoln; that he is the servant to obey us.

August 5, 1864, Henry Winter Davis and Senator Wade of Ohio issued a very bitter manifesto against President Lincoln, charging him with "a more studied outrage on the legislative authority of the people than was ever before perpetrated."

When Lincoln was asked if he had seen this speech of Phillips and the Winter Davis-Wade manifesto against him, he replied, "I have seen enough to satisfy me that I am a failure, not only in the opinion of the people in the rebellion, but of many distinguished politicians of my own party" (Lamon's *Recollections*, page 187). This occurred only a short time before Lincoln's death. Of all Mr. Lincoln's "venomous detractors," Stanton was the most venomous. It seems that Stanton first met Lincoln in Cincinnati, in 1858. Stanton and Lincoln both gave an account of that meeting. Stanton told the story to General Donn Piatt who relates it as follows:

> "A few minutes," said Stanton, "before I went to the trial of the McCormack case I met Mr. Lincoln for the first time. He had been retained to assist in the case and called on me. I saw a long, lank creature. He wore a dirty linen duster for a coat, on the back of which the perspiration from his arm-

pits had splotched two wide stains, which met at the center and resembled a dirty map of the continent. "I said," snorted Stanton, "that if that giraffe appeared in the case I would throw up my brief and leave."

Lamon gives the story as Lincoln gave it to him:

> "On first meeting Stanton," Lincoln said, "he treated me so rudely I went out of the room; saw McCormack and told him I should have to withdraw as his counsel in the case, stating the reasons therefor. McCormack went in and remonstrated with Stanton. "I will not," said Stanton, scornfully, "associate with such a damned gawky, long-armed ape. If I can't have a *man* who is a gentleman in appearance I will abandon the case."

Lincoln was in the next room and heard every word. When McCormack returned, Lincoln refunded his fee and left for Urbana, Illinois, where he related the occurrence to his brother lawyers. Stanton's disgust toward Lincoln never abated during Lincoln's life. He never referred to him except as "that gorilla at the White House," or "that ourang outang at the other end of the avenue." Before Stanton was appointed to the Cabinet, he was in the habit of visiting General McClellan. In McClellan's *Life* a number of letters to his wife are published, in which McClellan speaks of Stanton's visits. In one he wrote thus: "The most disagreeable thing about Stanton is the extreme virulence of his abuse of President Lincoln, his whole administration, as well of all the Republican party. I am often shocked."

In another, McClellan writes, "Stanton never speaks of the President in any way other than as "that original gorilla." He often says, "DuChaillie was a fool to wander all the way to Africa in search of what he could have found in Springfield, Illinois."

In another, McClellan writes:

> Nothing can be more bitter than Stanton's words and manner when speaking of the President and his administration. He gives them no credit for honesty of purpose or patriotism, and very seldom for ability. He often advises the propriety of my seizing the government and taking power in my own hands.

In another letter McClellan writes, "Stanton often speaks of the painful imbecility of the President."

In McClure's *Life of Lincoln*, page 150, is this:

> Before Stanton was appointed Secretary of War he was an open and malignant opponent of the Lincoln administration. He often spoke to public men, military and civil, with withering sneers of Lincoln. I have heard him speak thus of Lincoln, and several times to him in the same way.
>
> After Stanton left Buchanan's Cabinet he maintained close confidential relations with Buchanan, kept up a correspondence, and in some of his letters he expressed the utmost contempt for Lincoln. In some of his letters, published in Curtis' *Life of Buchanan*, Stanton speaks freely of the "painful imbecility of Lincoln, of the venality and corruption that ran riot in the Government." It is an open secret that Stanton advised the overthrow of the Lincoln Government, to be replaced by McClellan as a military dictator. These letters published by Curtis, bad as they are, are not the worst letters written by Stanton to Buchanan. Some of them are so violent in expression against Lincoln they have been charitably withheld from the public" (See Minor's *Real Lincoln*).

In *On Circuit With Lincoln*, page 428, Whitney tells of these suppressed letters. Hapgood's *Lincoln*, page 164, refers to Stanton's brutal absence of decent personal feeling towards Lincoln, and tells of his insulting behavior when they met five years earlier, of which meeting Stanton said, "I met Lincoln at the bar and found him a low, cunning clown."

McClure says Stanton had little respect for Lincoln's fitness for the Presidency, yet to Mr. Buchanan during his Presidency Stanton showed an excess of deference. Mr. Buchanan, in a letter to his niece, Miss Harriet Lane, complained that Stanton, when in his Cabinet, "was always on my side and flattered me *ad nauseum*" (See Minor's *Real Lincoln*). Yet in the very teeth of all this evidence showing how the foremost Republicans indulged in "grotesque descriptions" of Lincoln's person, some of his historians have the gall to charge such descriptions to Southern people. "Grotesque descriptions," says the truthful (?) Morse, "of Mr. Lincoln had long been rife among the Southerners, as if he had been a Caliban in education, manners and aspect, whose conversation would be redolent of the barn yard and pigsty."

If such descriptions were rife in the South they were borrowed from Republican sources. Was it a Southern man who always referred to President Lincoln as "the gorilla in the White House"? or "that baboon at the other end of the avenue"? Was it any man in the South who called Lincoln "that long-armed ape"? and refused to act with him in a law case? Was it any man in the South who talked of "Lincoln's painful imbecility"? Was it the governor of a Southern or New England State who said that "Lincoln retailed stories so obscene he left his presence in disgust"? Was it a Northern or Southern minister who left the East Room, after interviewing Lincoln, "with a sickening sensation of despair that such a man was in such a position"?

Is it not time Republican writers should pay a *little* regard to truth? They know well that the men of the South had little or no opportunity to know Lincoln personally. Was Mr. Morse really ignorant on this subject? Had he never heard of the "venomous detractions" lavished on the living Lincoln by men of his own party? Or did he know, but, to carry out the apotheosis scheme, think it his duty to charge those detractions to Southern people? The most revolting story told of Lincoln (with the exception of the comic song he called for on the field of battle) is related by General Piatt, who had it direct from Chase. It is known that the Emancipation Proclamation was finally put forth as a war measure. The days were very dark for the Union army. The Southern chiefs were still victorious on every field. Rivers of human blood continued to flow on battlefields. The hospitals in Washington were crowded with mutilated, wounded, dying Union soldiers. At this juncture Lincoln hoped the issue of an Emancipation proclamation would put new life into the Union army, would turn the tide of disaster and bring victory to his troops. The proclamation was written. The Cabinet was called to hear and consider it. The members met in solemn conclave. President Lincoln entered; in his hand *not* the proclamation, but a copy of Artemus Ward's latest "funny book." Mr. Lincoln opened at the first page and read on and on, almost to the very last, amid roars of laughter from every Cabinet minister except Chase, who sat silent, with solemn, reproving visage. Now and then Mr. Lincoln would look up from Ward's "funny page" at Chase's solemn face and break into louder guffaws of hilarity, followed by the boisterous guffaws of all his Cabinet advisers except Chase. General Piatt says that "Chase's inveterate dislike of Lincoln's jokes and stories was a source of great amusement to Mr. Lincoln and the other members of his Cabinet, and that Lincoln seldom lost an opportunity to entertain himself and them in that direction."

"Both Stanton and Chase," says General Piatt, "described these occasions to me: Chase with an aggrieved tone, Stanton with hilarious laughter. The reader may judge of their sort when I state that scarcely one of Lincoln's stories would bear printing."

On a previous page we have shown Stanton's angry disgust on seeing Lincoln's dirty linen duster. Soap and water can wash dust away; no amount of soap and water will wash away mental and moral foulness. Stanton turned up his nose at the dust, but laughed hilariously at Lincoln's moral foulness. Lincoln's appointment of his bitterest enemy, and the bitter enemy of the Republican party, to the high office of Cabinet Minister not only astonished, it angered Republicans. It was well known that Stanton all his life had called himself a Democrat, had served the Democratic party as Cabinet Minister during President Buchanan's administration, and had always professed to be a pro-slavery man. While in Mr. Buchanan's Cabinet, Stanton had accepted the opinion expressed by President Buchanan and his constitutional advisers, that neither the President or Congress had any constitutional right to coerce seceding States. Knowing such were the opinions Stanton professed, why did Lincoln put him in his Cabinet? This was the question of the hour. Hapgood says of Stanton's appointment:

> No man not a Southern rebel had less right to expect office from Lincoln than Stanton. Most men who had expressed the opinions held by Stanton would have had scruples of delicacy about coming in close relationship of confidential adviser with the object of their contempt. No scruple delayed Stanton: his acceptance was prompt.

Stanton accepted office because he wanted place and power; he had no principles to stand in his way. Always eager to eulogize the man his party had deified, Hapgood calls Lincoln's appointment of Stanton "brilliant magnanimity." This, however, is only apotheosis twaddle to which Republican writers resort to support the theory of Lincoln's divinity. Those who knew Mr. Lincoln's mental and moral peculiarities explain the real reasons which made him show more favors to enemies than to those who had faithfully worked for him. The following is

Herndon's explanation:

> Lincoln always gave more to his enemies than to his friends. In the close calculations of attaching the factions to himself he counted on the affection of his friends to serve him and tried to appease his enemies by gifts. There was always truth in the charge of his friends that he failed to reciprocate their devotion with favors; adhesion to his interests was what Lincoln wanted. If he got adhesion gratuitously he never wasted his gifts paying for it.

Herndon bluntly says in his suppressed *Life of Lincoln*, "Lincoln had no gratitude. He accepted the services of his friends as his due, and never thought of making any returns."

Morse, Vol. I, page 327, says, "Stanton carried his revilings of the President to the point of coarse, personal insults." On another page Morse speaks of Stanton's "habitual insults." Lincoln knew of these insults, yet when it was determined that Cameron should vacate the Cabinet, Lincoln said to Chase, "I know that Stanton dislikes me, but I wish to see him. Ask him to call and see me."

Stanton called, and after some talk, Lincoln said, "The office of Secretary of War will soon be vacant. Will you accept it?"

Stanton was dumfounded. This "long-armed ape," this "gorilla," this "baboon," whom he had so bitterly scorned and reviled, offered him one of the highest offices in his gift. On recovering his breath, Stanton did not, like the surprised maiden, blush and say, "This is so sudden," but he said something very like it: "You take me by surprise. Will you give me a day to consider it?"

Hapgood says he promptly accepted. General Piatt, who well knew Stanton, was so astonished, he said to him, "How can you reconcile your contempt for Lincoln, and your widely different views on politics, with service under him?"

Stanton evaded reply, but Piatt, who worshiped Stanton's success, as it was his nature to worship successful men and successful measures, and who believed that God had called Stanton, as well as Lincoln, to the front, undertakes to explain why an old Democrat, who, under Buchanan, had believed the South had a right to independence, was now willing to serve a President and party which, as was declared a thousand times during the war, were determined to "crush, conquer, kill or annihilate" the whole people of the South on the ground that they had no right to leave the Union.

"Stanton," said Piatt, "saw the absurdity of holding the Union by the rotten rail of a Virginia abstraction."

The "Virginia abstraction" meant the United States Constitution, concerning which Seward had given Piatt a lesson: "We are bound to the tail of a paper kite," said Seward to Piatt, "called the Constitution. A written Constitution is dangerous to us of the North. The South is using it as a shield."

The Constitution was dangerous to "us [the Republican party] of the North." It stood in the way of that party's imperial policy of conquest. The Republican party kicked the Constitution into the Capitol cellar to clear the way for conquest.

CHAPTER SIX
☆ ☆ ☆ ☆

*A Western Republican Paper Propounds the
True Republican Doctrine.*

The Lemars (Ia.) *Sentinel,* 1879, fearlessly propounded Republican doctrines:

> No reasonable man will say that President Buchanan was wrong when he said that the North had no constitutional right to coerce seceding States, but what of that? Up jumped Abraham Lincoln, the rail-splitter, and kicked the Constitution into the Capitol cellar, and called for 75,000 armed men to march down and conquer the South, and when the 75,000 proved not enough, the rail-splitter called for more, and more, until he had over 2,000,000 armed men, and he sent them down to burn and pillage, to kill, conquer or annihilate traitors to our glorious Union, the Constitution all the while in the Capitol cellar.

Although every intelligent man in the Republican party knows that their party despised the Constitution, still as the great body of the North's people had not lost love and reverence for it, few Republicans openly denounced it. Wendell Philips, Lloyd Garrison, and other bold men, time and again, had publicly denounced the Constitution and shouted aloud their desire to tear it in pieces. Beecher, from his pulpit, contemptuously called the Constitution a "sheep skin" government deserving no respect.

If the Republicans were puzzled to understand why Lincoln passed by staunch men of his own party to favor Stanton, they were at no loss to understand why Stanton accepted office from the man he despised. Piatt says, "Stanton and Seward rioted in the use of power." The souls of both these men were filled with the evil passion for power. Before Stanton's accession to office, why did he so assiduously pay court to General McClellan? Why use his utmost endeavor to inspire McClellan with scorn and contempt for Lincoln and his government? Why insidiously flatter McClellan? Why urge him to seize in his own hands the reins of Government and make himself supreme dictator? In this dictator scheme did Stanton see a chance for himself to achieve power? Certain it is, Stanton's frequent visits to McClellan, his confidential outpourings, his flatteries, his desire to see McClellan make himself dictator, all stopped short the very day Stanton accepted place and power from Lincoln. From that day Stanton turned the cold shoulder on McClellan and reveled in the power his office gave him.

In Lamon's *Recollections of Lincoln*, page 198, is this: "It was generally believed that President Lincoln abjectly endured the almost insulting domination of Secretary of War Stanton." On page 233 Lamon says, "There was a prevailing opinion that Stanton at times arbitrarily refused to obey or carry out President Lincoln's orders."

Lamon so loved Lincoln, anything detracting from his glory annoyed him. He denies that Lincoln was governed by Stanton, yet, being of a garrulous turn of mind, and honestly believing that the whole world is interested in any and every incident of Lincoln's life, Lamon often relates incidents which directly contradict his own previous assertions. The following story, to the ordinary understanding, goes to show that Stanton played the master over Lincoln:

> On the night of March 3rd, 1865 Mr. Lincoln, with several members of his Cabinet, was at the Capitol waiting the final passage of bills by Congress in order that the President should sign them. Everybody seemed happy at the prospect of peace. A dispatch from General Grant was handed to Stanton, who read it, and handed it to the President. The telegram advised Stanton that Grant had just received a letter from General Lee, requesting an interview, with a view to re-establishing peace between the sections. The dispatch was read by others of the party. Mr. Lincoln's spirits rose to a height rarely witnessed. He was unable to restrain himself from giving expression to the natural impulse of his heart. He

was in favor of granting lenient and generous terms to the defeated foe. Mr. Stanton fell into a towering rage; he also could not restrain himself. Turning on the President, his eyes flashing fire, he cried angrily, "Mr. President, you are losing sight of the consideration at this juncture, how and by whom is this war to be closed? Tomorrow is inauguration day. Read again that dispatch. Don't you appreciate its significance? If you are not to be President of an obedient and loyal people, you ought not to take the oath of office. You are not a proper person to be empowered to so high a trust. You should not consent to act in the capacity of a mere figurehead. If terms of peace do not emanate from you, and do not imply that you are supreme head of the Nation, you are not needed. By doing thus you will scandalize every friend you possess."

How did the President of the United States receive this severe castigation? This insolent bullying from his Cabinet member? Did he freeze him with cold displeasure? Did he resent with grave dignity? Did he break out in hot anger? Nothing of the sort. President Lincoln accepted his inferior officer's scolding with the submissiveness which comes from an inferior to a superior.

Lamon concludes the story thus:

> Mr. Lincoln sat silent at the table for a few minutes, then he said: "Stanton, you are right. The dispatch did not strike me at first as I now consider it." Then taking pen and paper Mr. Lincoln wrote a dispatch, handed it to Stanton, requesting him to sign, date and send it to Grant.

In this scene which man played the part of a snubbed and scolded school-boy? Which the part of an irascible school-master who had caught the boy misbehaving himself? Yet poor Lamon's judgment was so befogged, his eyes so bedazzled by the glare of Lincoln's wonderful success, he could neither think nor see straight. On one page he tells his readers that his friend, his "benefactor, Lincoln," was always the masterful and guiding spirit, that even the bad-tempered Secretary of War was submissive and reverential to Lincoln. A page or two after he gives us a picture of his great man in the character of a whipped school-boy.

It has been said a hundred times that the untimely taking off of Mr. Lincoln was a woeful misfortune to the Southern people; that had Lincoln lived through a second term the South would have been spared the horrors of the reconstruction period. This has been told so often, many North and South have come to believe it. It is quite possible that Mr. Lincoln would have been satisfied with the return of peace and the entire surrender of the Southern army. There is nothing in Lincoln's history to show that his heart had become gangrened with hate of Southern people, as was the case with some others. He had longed for victory, for peace, for a second term – these three things had come to him and filled his heart with joy. But, would *these* have satisfied the men who would have been around Lincoln? Andrew Johnson attempted to carry out the policy it was supposed that Lincoln had decided on, but the foremost men of the Republican party opposed that policy. Johnson's persistence came near losing him his office and his life as well. The great body of Republican leaders came to hate Johnson because of his more merciful policy full as intensely as they hated Jefferson Davis. The question is, was it Lincoln's nature to have successfully resisted the pressure the leading men of his own party would have brought to bear on him? Could they not easily have forced Lincoln to yield and adopt their cruel policy of treating the South? When we consider how the leaders felt toward Mr. Lincoln, how little respect and esteem they entertained for him. how imbecile and inferior they believed him to be, it does not seem at all probable that *they* would have yielded their opinions to his. Though not wantonly cruel, though not of a nature to seek pleasure by causing human suffering. Lincoln had little or no pity for pain. Unlike B. F. Butler and Sherman, Lincoln did not find gleeful delight in the power to humiliate, torment, and torture the men and women of the South who were utterly at his mercy. It does not appear that by nature Grant was despotic or unusually cruel, yet to serve his ambition he became the tool of others who were cruel. The reader must have noticed these lines in Lamon's story of Lincoln and Stanton, just related:

> Lincoln's spirit rose to a height rarely witnessed; he was unable to restrain himself from giving expression to the natural impulse of his heart. He was in favor of granting lenient and generous terms to the defeated foe. *Mr. Stanton fell info a towering rage: he could not restrain himself; turning*

on the President, his eyes flashing fire, he said, etc.

What so angered Stanton? Stanton was not only a savage, ill-tempered man, but he delighted in cruelty. Did he fall into that towering rage because Lincoln was in favor of granting lenient and generous terms to the South? Was it of this leniency that Lincoln so swiftly repented and submitted himself to the dominance of the savage and cruel Stanton? If this was not the cause of Stanton's sudden anger, it might possibly have sprung from pure irritability. The reader may remember Stanton's unnecessary fit of ill temper on seeing Lincoln arrayed in a dusty linen coat. Lamon says, "Lincoln was unable to restrain himself; his spirits rose to a height rarely witnessed." The actions of a very uncouth man, even under happy excitement, may be very rasping to the irritable nerves of a cross, savage tempered man. Was it something of this sort that threw Stanton into that towering rage? Illustrative of the oddities of Lincoln's character, and the curious effect joy sometimes produced upon him, we offer a little story taken from *Butler's Book*.

After Fort Hatteras was captured by the Union forces General Butler was so eager to be the first to carry the good news to Lincoln, he set off for Washington City and arrived there late at night. Accompanied by Assistant Secretary of the Navy Mr. Fox, they drove rapidly to the White House, roused the night watchman, sent a servant to rouse Mr. Lincoln, and the two men, Fox and Butler, went into the Cabinet room to await his coming. Mr. Lincoln did not take time to dress. He entered in his night gown, barefooted. Butler concludes the story as follows:

> Everybody knows how tall Lincoln was [six feet four inches]; he seemed much taller in that night shirt. [Fox was five feet nothing.] Fox told the joyous story, whereupon he and Lincoln fell into each other's arms; that is, Fox threw his arms around Lincoln about as high as the hips. Lincoln reached down over Fox until his long arms were nearly to the floor; thus holding each other they began a waltz, flying round and round; the night shirt-tail was so agitated it fluttered in the breeze like a flag of joy. I was so overcome by the spectacle I lay back on the sofa and roared with laughter.

The reader may remember Herndon's description of the night gowns Lincoln usually wore: "Long, narrow, yellow flannel things which struck him just above his knobby knees. A young lawyer," says Herndon, "on seeing Mr. Lincoln for the first time in one of those yellow flannel gowns was almost paralyzed."

Morse wants it believed that Lincoln appointed Stanton to office because of his peculiar fitness. There is not the least evidence that Stanton had ever manifested such fitness, unless, indeed, Lincoln fancied Stanton's scorn and contempt for him, his Cabinet, and party were signs of fitness. Morse (page 328) thus describes Stanton's ability for the office Lincoln gave him:

> Stanton's abilities command some respect, though his character never excited either liking or respect. In his dealings with men he was capable of much duplicity; he was arbitrary, harsh and bad-tempered. He often committed acts of injustice and cruelty for which he rarely made amends, and still more rarely seemed disturbed by any remorse or regret. These traits bore hard on individuals, but ready and unscrupulous cruelty was supposed to be useful in war. Lincoln is the only ruler in history who could for years have co-operated with such a man as Stanton.

What an admission is this! *"Ready and unscrupulous cruelty supposed to be useful."* Was it Pope's, Sherman's, Sheridan's, Brownlow's, Butler's "ready, unscrupulous cruelty" which recommended them to Lincoln's favor? Was it McClellan's less cruel nature which lost him the favor of Lincoln, of Seward, and Stanton? McClellan's orders show that he wanted to observe the customs of war as established by civilized peoples. The above named army officers, except McClellan, reveled in cruelty.

Morse (page 376) continues: "From Stanton's snug personal safety [in his office, supposed to be very dear to him] he delivered gross insults to the highest generals in the Union army."

In Gen. Donn Piatt's *Men Who Saved the Union*, he says:

> Without an exception Stanton was more subject to personal likes and dislikes than any man ever called to public station. Both Stanton and Seward were drunk with lust of power. They fairly rioted in its enjoyment. Stanton used the fearful power of the Government to crush those he hated, and used the same to elevate those he loved. His official business

became a personal affair.

Rosecrans unintentionally offended the ego of this despot in the Cabinet and Stanton's spite followed him through the whole war. Piatt says Stanton gave Rosecrans first neglect and then cruel punishment and abuse:

> Stanton grew furious almost to insanity over the failure of his generals. Stanton was impatient, tyrannical and often unjust. Stanton left few friends in the administration; his unfortunate manner offended the officers of the army and irritated the politicians. General Grant hated him and tried to put Stanton on record as an imbecile.

Notwithstanding Stanton's dislike and scorn of Lincoln up to the hour of his death, Republicans relate that Stanton stood by the dying Lincoln, and after the last breath left his body Stanton reverentially turned his eyes up to heaven as he solemnly said: "He now belongs to the ages."

CHAPTER SEVEN
☆ ☆ ☆ ☆

*Grant and Washburn Defy Lincoln's Authority.
Washburn Bullies Lincoln. A United States Senator
Bullies Mr. Lincoln. Senator Wade Storms at Him.
Hale in the Senate Assails Him. Rev. Mr. Fuller's
Unfavorable Opinions of Lincoln. Lincoln's Trickery.*

Lamon says:

Lincoln had given to Mr. Joseph Mattox and to General Singleton permits and passes through the line to bring cotton and other Southern products from Virginia. Washburn heard of it, called immediately on the President and threatened to have General Grant countermand the permits if Lincoln would not revoke them. Mr. Lincoln replied: "I do not believe Grant would take upon himself the responsibility of such an act."

"I will show you, sir," cried Washburn, excitedly. "I will show you whether Grant will do it or not." Washburn abruptly withdrew and by the next boat left Washington for Grant's headquarters, and soon returned, and so likewise did Mattox and Singleton. Grant had countermanded the permits. This was a source of exultation to Mr. Washburn and his friends and of corresponding surprise and mortification to the President. "I wonder," said he "when General Grant changed his mind on this subject? Grant was the first man to give permits for the passage, and to his own father."

Sometime after Mr. Lincoln referred to the matter and said: "It made me feel my insignificance keenly for the moment, but if my friends Washburn, Henry Wilson and others derived any pleasure from a victory over me, let them enjoy it."

Does this story indicate that the men in his own party respected or feared Mr. Lincoln? How would Washington or Jackson or any other President have borne disrespectful treatment from inferior officers? On page 239 of Lamon's *Recollections* he tells another anecdote showing how little Lincoln's contemporaries respected and esteemed him:

> After the war ended a United States Senator called on President Lincoln to give his idea as to how the conquered South should be treated. As Mr. Lincoln did not readily accept the suggestions, the Senator burst out angrily, "Mr. President, it does appear to some of your friends, myself included, as if you had taken leave of your senses." The Senator strode out in a rage; meeting on the avenue a Congressman, his wrath exploded in words: "Lincoln is a damned idiot!" he blurted out. "He has no spirit. He's as weak as an old woman. He never was fitted for the position he holds."

"He is not fitted for the office he holds," had been the cry of nearly every Republican of distinction from the first day Lincoln was seen in Washington, and that cry was kept up to the last day of his life. The apotheosis ceremony served notice on the whole Republican party that that cry must be forever silenced, that from that hour Lincoln must be viewed as a deified man, as one having entered the "sublime realm of the gods."

Lamon has another story showing how little Lincoln's contemporaries esteemed or respected him:

> A short time before the fall of Vicksburg, Mr. Lincoln said to me, "I feel I have made Senator Wade my enemy for life."   "How?" I asked.
>
> "Wade," he replied, "was here urging me to dismiss Grant."
>
> I said, "Senator, that reminds me of a story."
>
> "Yes! Yes!" he petulantly interrupted, "with you, sir, it is all story, story. story! You are the father of every military blunder since the war begun! You are on your way to hell, sir! and with this Government. You are not half a mile

off this minute!" Wade was very angry; grabbing up his hat and cane he went off.

Certain it is, had not Vicksburg been speedily captured, Lincoln would have been deposed.

Lamon speaks of the "aggressive spirit of Congress toward President Lincoln," and of the "small respect and less love Congressmen and Senators bore to the living Lincoln."

Senator Hale, one of the foremost Republican leaders, from the Senate floor assailed Lincoln. "Senators," said Hale, "we must not strike too high or too low, but between wind and weather. The Marshal is the man to hit." Marshal Lamon being Lincoln's closest personal friend, Hale proposed to strike the President over Lamon's shoulders.

Lincoln himself told Lamon that Hale was hitting at him. "This opposition to Lincoln," says Lamon, "became more and more offensive. The leaders resorted to every means in their power to thwart him. This opposition lasted to the end of Mr. Lincoln's life."

These men habitually referred to the Chief Magistrate of the Republic as "that hideous baboon at the other end of the avenue."

McClure's *Life of Lincoln* shows the hostile attitude toward Lincoln of the leading members of the Cabinet, and adds:

> Outside of the Cabinet, the leaders were quite as distrustful of President Lincoln's ability to fill the great office he held. Senators Trumbull, Wade, Chandler, Winter Davis, and the men of the new political power did not conceal their distrust of Lincoln. Lincoln had little support from them at any time during his administration.

The reader should bear in mind the fact that it is the unanimous testimony of Republican writers that two-thirds of the people of the Northern States, from the very beginning of his administration, opposed Lincoln's war on the South, and continued openly to oppose until the strong machinery of the Lincoln Government suppressed free speech and strangled the once free press. In the face of this fact the reader will notice that McClure, as other Republican writers of today, glibly and presumptuously call the small minority of Republicans who supported Lincoln's and Seward's war measures "the Nation." McClure, Morse and other writers tell their readers that two-thirds of the people opposed Lincoln, yet in the next breath tell them, "The men [Republican war men] to whom the Nation turned," etc. This is on its face false. The word Nation implies the great body of the people. The two-thirds of the people have more right to be called "the Nation" than the one-third. As two-thirds of the people made the Nation, and these two-thirds strongly opposed the war measures which Trumbull, Wade, Chandler and others who were waging the cruel and bloody war which *they*, the two-thirds, *they* the Nation, bitterly opposed, it follows that they, the two-thirds, "the Nation," could not and did not turn to those war Republicans for any purpose whatever except to condemn and deplore their evil work of blood. The custom of ignoring the great body of the people as if they had no existence is common in kingly countries, but was not in vogue in this Republic until shortly after Seward and Lincoln changed a free Republic into an imperial government. Observing Americans in England may have noticed this custom as seen in the London papers. When Parliament adjourns and royalty and the high fashionable few leave the city, as they always do when the society season is over, the London newspapers calmly announce that "London is empty." And one high society man will say to another, "There isn't a soul in the city." One may often see this expression in English novels coming from the mouth of some high society man or woman.

Some Republican papers of America are so imbued with the imperial spirit they also use the insulting phrase. The *Globe-Democrat*, a Republican paper of St. Louis, in big head lines over an article concerning the recent crowning of the English King, made the following announcement:

Exodus From London.
The City Practically Deserted Since the Coronation.

"Practically deserted," when four or five million souls were still in the city. These unconscious insults to the million working people in London come from the worship of royalty and the nobility. In America it comes from the worship of wealth and men in high office. In both cases the basic cause is the prevalence of monarchic principles.

The Rev. R. Fuller, a Baptist minister from Baltimore, who was spokesman for the young Christians, wrote Chase from Baltimore on April 23, 1861 of his interview with President Lincoln, as follows:

From Mr. Lincoln nothing is to be expected except as you can influence him. Five associations, representing thousands of our best young men, sent a delegation of thirty to Washington yesterday and asked me to go along as chairman. We were cordially received. I marked the President closely; he is constitutionally gay and jovial, but he is wholly inaccessible to Christian appeals. His egotism will forever prevent his comprehending what patriotism means (See Rhode's *History of the United States* and Chase's *M. S. Papers*).

Rhodes states that Lincoln clearly said to the young Christian delegates: "I have no desire to invade the South, but I must have troops to defend this capital." This was pure trickery on Lincoln's part. In the second part of this work will be found indisputable evidence to prove the fact that before Lincoln entered on the Presidency, certainly during the first month of his incumbency, he and Seward determined on war. and determined to make the Northern people believe the South began it. Lincoln well knew his capital was in no particle of danger until after he himself began the war.

CHAPTER EIGHT

Herndon's Pen Portrait of Abraham Lincoln.
A Springfield Lawyer's Pen Portrait. Gen. Piatt on "Pious Lies."
The "Real Lincoln Disappeared from Human Knowledge."
Herndon's Life of Lincoln. Why Suppressed.
Extracts From the Suppressed Work.

It is known that the outside form of man or beast, the shape of his head, his body, the expression of his eyes, the tone of his voice, are indices of his mental and moral character. Few may be able to interpret these indices; nevertheless they are signs stamped by the Creator himself. For this reason I shall lay before my readers two pen portraits of Mr. Lincoln, drawn by two men who knew him in Springfield – both drawn soon after Mr. Lincoln's death, and before his burial, as he lay in his costly catafalque. Both of these portraits are taken from Herndon's suppressed *Life of Lincoln*; both are reproduced in Mr. Weik's *True Story of a Great Life*, purporting to have been written by Herndon.

Herndon's pen portrait of Mr. Lincoln:

> Abraham Lincoln was six feet four inches high. He was thin in the chest, wiry, sinewy, raw-boned, and narrow across the shoulders. His legs were unnaturally long and out of proportion to his body. His forehead was high and narrow, his jaws long, his nose long, large and blunt at the tip, ruddy and turned awry toward the right. A few hairs here and there sprouted on his face. His chin projected far and sharp and turned up to meet a thick, material, down-hanging lip. His

cheeks were flabby, the loose skin in folds or wrinkles. His hair was brown, stiff and unkempt. His complexion very dark, his skin yellow, shriveled and leathery. His whole aspect was cadaverous and woe-struck. His ears were large and stood out at almost right angles from his head. He had no dignity of manner, and was extremely ungainly and awkward. His voice was shrill and piping. He usually wore an old hat and a faded brown coat which hung baggy on his long, gaunt frame. His breeches were usually six inches too short, showing his big, bony shins; his sleeves were six inches too short, showing his big, bony hands. His body was shrunk and shriveled. He usually slept in a long, coarse, yellow flannel nightgown, which struck him just below his knobby knees, showing his long, lanky legs and big feet. [A young lawyer first seeing him in this costume was almost paralyzed.] The first impression of a stranger on seeing Mr. Lincoln walk, was that he was a tricky man: his walk implied shrewdness.

If the reader wishes to study the strange character of Mr. Lincoln, he must bear in mind the above description of his person. When we present the salient features of Mr. Lincoln's mental and moral nature, the analytical reader can compare them with his physical, especially should the reader hold in memory these words: "The first impression of a stranger on seeing Mr. Lincoln walk was that he was a tricky man."

If there ever was a tricky man born on earth, it was Abraham Lincoln. Side by side of his own pen portrait of Lincoln. Herndon places another, drawn by a Springfield lawyer, who did not wish his name given:

> I am particularly requested to write out my opinion of the man, Abraham Lincoln, late President of the United States. I consent to do this without any other motive than to comply with the request of a brother lawyer. While Mr. Lincoln and I were good friends, I believe myself wholly indifferent to the future of his memory. My opinion of him was formed by a personal and professional acquaintance of over ten years, and has not been altered or influenced by any of his promotions in public life. The adulation by base multitudes

of a living and the pageantry surrounding a dead President do not shake my well-settled convictions of the man's mental calibre. Phrenologically and physiologically, the man was a sort of monstrosity. His frame was large, bony and muscular. His head was small and disproportionately shaped. He had large, square jaws, a large, heavy nose, a small, lascivious mouth, soft, tender, bluish eyes. I would say he was a cross between a Venus and a Hercules. I believe it to be inconsistent with the law of human organization for any such creature to possess a mind capable of anything great. The man's mind partook of the incongruities of his body. It was the peculiarities of his mental and the oddity of his physical structure, as well as his head, that singled him out from the mass of men.

Lamon says of Herndon:

> He was a lifelong abolitionist, devoted to public philanthropy and disinterested political labors. Herndon was a fierce zealot and gloried in being called fanatic. He said fanaticism at all times was the salt of the earth, with the power to save it. He was hot-blooded morally and physically. He had determined to make an abolitionist out of Lincoln when the proper time came, and he knew that time would only be when Lincoln could change front and come out without detriment to his personal aspirations.

Herndon's work of converting Mr. Lincoln to the abolition cause was slow. Lincoln had not in him one particle of the stuff martyrs are made of. Abolition at that time was unpopular in Illinois. Lincoln was afraid to take it up and did not commit himself to it until 1858, two years before his nomination for the Presidency.

General Donn Piatt, an officer in the Union Army, a man of some culture and literary attainment, who knew Mr. Lincoln personally and greatly admired him, made a study of his character. In *Men Who Saved the Union*, Piatt expresses the belief that God especially called Lincoln to office to do the work he did.

Piatt, as well as Herndon and Lamon, did not approve of apotheosizing Mr. Lincoln. These three men were anxious to have the real Lincoln known to the world. On this subject Piatt wrote thus:

> With us when a leader dies, all good men [meaning stanch Republicans] go to lying about him. From the monument that covers his remains to the last echo of the rural press, in speeches, in sermons, eulogies, reminiscences, we hear nothing but pious lies.

Piatt refers to the lies told about Lincoln, but he makes the mistake of calling those lies "pious." That word is usually applied to praise bestowed on the dead to please living friends and relations. The lies told about Lincoln were told wholly and solely for political effect, for the purpose of supporting the Republican party. Neither Herndon, Lamon or Piatt seemed to understand this. They wanted the truth to be known, but they did not seem to perceive that the truth about Lincoln would injure the party, would belittle and disgrace it, would put a thousand clubs into the hands of Democrats to beat the party down and out of office. Politicians saw this, and determined that the real Lincoln should never be known.

"Abraham Lincoln," continued General Piatt, "has al- most disappeared from human knowledge. I hear of him, I read of him in eulogies and biographies, but I fail to recognize the man I knew in life."

Both Herndon and Lamon failed to recognize in the eulogies and biographies the man they knew in life. The thing they saw was not the portrait of the real Lincoln. It was the effigy which Republican leaders had hastily manufactured, after their apotheosis ceremony, and had started down the ages labeled "Abraham Lincoln, the first President of the Republican party, the greatest, wisest, purest man who ever trod the earth since Jesus of Nazareth." No man who will look at the facts of history can doubt the truth of this.

At the time of Mr. Lincoln's death, 1865, his close and loving friend, Lamon, determined to write his life:

> But [says Lamon], I soon learned that Mr. William H. Herndon was similarly engaged. There could be no rivalry between us. The supreme object of both was to make the real history and character of Mr. Lincoln as well known to the public as they were to us. Mr. Herndon, as I, deplored the many publications pretending to be biographies of Lincoln, which teemed from the press so long as there was hope of

gain. Out of the mass of these works, of only *one* is it possible to speak with any degree of respect.

And that one (Holland's) was falsified and whitewashed.

For the above reason Lamon gave up his intention of writing Lincoln's biography, leaving the task to Herndon. Herndon's *Life of Lincoln* was published soon after Lincoln's death. Its reception by Republicans was peculiar. Not a man at that time, so far as I can discover, denied or expressed a doubt of its honesty, its friendliness to Lincoln or of its veracity. Certain Republican journals wondered why Herndon thought it necessary to tell this and that concerning his friend's life. One or two made favorable comments. The *Globe-Democrat*, of St. Louis, as late as 1897, had this: "Herndon's Biography of Lincoln is, in many respects, the best that has yet been written. There is no doubt that his account is wholly trustworthy, and there is nothing more interesting in all the output of Lincoln literature."

The editor of the *Globe-Democrat* was an officer in the Union Army. In another issue of the *Globe-Democrat* we find this:

> There is no doubt that Herndon's account of Lincoln is entirely trustworthy. Herndon and Lincoln were practically in daily contact for over twenty years and their relations were entirely amicable. Life went hard with Herndon in late years (after Lincoln's death); he fell heir to a farm near Springfield, dropped the law and went into fancy stock-raising, which soon resulted disastrously. Then he took to hard drinking and not long afterward died in poverty. He was Lincoln's law partner and closest friend for over sixteen years. His biography of Lincoln, in many respects, is the best one that ever has been written.

Hapgood, in 1899, wrote an apotheosizing work called *Abraham Lincoln*. Hapgood says, "Herndon has told President Lincoln's life with the most refreshing honesty and with more information than any one else."

Such being the character of Herndon's *Life of Lincoln*, the reader may be surprised to learn that this work is not now to be had for love or money. Why? For the one and sole reason that it did not coincide with the apotheosis ceremony. It did not portray the character of Abraham Lincoln as the Republican leaders wished it to be portrayed.

It pictured the *real* Lincoln, not the effigy which had been hurriedly gotten up by the apotheosizers. For these reasons, certain Republicans resolved to spirit out of existence every copy they could get. Agents were sent on a still hunt and every book they could find was destroyed; even the publisher's plates were obtained and broken to pieces. A near relative of Herndon, in a position to know, is responsible for this statement. This relative further states the reason was that "Mr. Herndon had told too many truths about Lincoln." Truth did not harmonize with the apotheosis ceremony.

When, in 1869, Lamon realized that his friend Herndon's work was passing out of existence, driven out by Republican politicians, he returned to his intention of writing Lincoln's life. Lamon and Herndon well understood that Republican politicians did not want the real Lincoln shown to the world, but did not seem to know that those politicians looked upon it as a vital necessity to the prosperity of their party to present Mr. Lincoln to the world, not as he was in life, not as they had known him, but as a deified being of unparalleled greatness, wisdom and virtue. Being either ignorant or indifferent on this matter, Lamon was as anxious as Herndon had been to show the public his hero and friend, exactly as he and his contemporaries in Illinois had known him. The "venomous detractions" of politicians in Washington City had not in the least shaken Lamon's and Herndon's love for Lincoln. They scouted and despised the deification twaddle which these detractors put in play, even before the real Lincoln was cold in his coffin. In this spirit Lamon set to work, 1869, to write the true story of Lincoln to take the place of the suppressed work of Herndon. Poor Herndon was bitterly disappointed at the unmerited fate of his book. He had spent a deal of money, time and labor in gathering materials – "rich materials" – had traveled far and wide seeking and interviewing the early friends and relatives of Lincoln. He had hoped not only to make money by his labor of love, but to win fame as the writer of the best biography of the greatest man extant. Lamon paid Herndon $3,000 for the privilege of using his "rich materials." In 1872 Lamon's *Life of Lincoln* was published. It certainly is the best yet written, except Herndon's, but if my information is correct, the same influences which swept Herndon's book out of existence are at work secretly to destroy Lamon's. At this writing, February 12, 1903, it is hardly possible to obtain even a second-hand copy of Lamon. Herndon's work was the better, inasmuch as it was terser and made no effort to whitewash a single act of its hero. Lamon had lived more in the world than Herndon, and felt the necessity of trimming and softening somewhat to suit polite society. Meanwhile, as Lamon put it, the press continued to teem with "pretended lives of Lincoln, not one of which deserved one particle of respect." These pretended biographies are fostered and praised and cherished by Republicans. The falser they are, the higher the praise. A short time ago a Republican paper stated that 800 different lives of Lincoln had been published.

As time passed inquiries were made for Herndon's work. To allay curiosity as well as to impose another life on the public, in 1889, twenty-four years after Lincoln's death, a three volume book was published by Bedford, Clark & Company, in Chicago, entitled:

> The True Story of a Great Life:
> The History of Abraham Lincoln
> by
> William H. Herndon,
> For Twenty Years His Friend and Law Partner,
> and
> Jesse William Weik, A. M.

If anyone who has ever read Mr. Herndon's suppressed *Life of Lincoln* will compare it with this three-volume affair, he will know that this last was not written by Herndon. The preface, without doubt, is Herndon's. The body of the work shows that Mr. Weik (as Lamon) had access to Herndon's "rich materials." But the object of the three men, Herndon, Lamon and Weik, was not the same. The two first really aimed to paint Lincoln as he was. Mr. Weik wished to please the Republican party. Herndon's preface shows that the purpose which dominated him in 1866, when he wrote the first life of Lincoln, was unshaken. He still, 1889, believed the truth, *all* the truth, about Lincoln should be told, and although his first book had been driven out of existence because it told the truth twenty-four years later, Herndon still wanted the truth told, and had a hope the truth would be told, and might live and put to flight the mass of lies that flooded the country. At this time, twenty-four years after Lincoln's death, misfortune had overtaken Herndon. Disappointment, poverty, drink, had broken down the stern old fanatic who had labored so many years to convert Lincoln to the abolition cause. Weik's intention, it seems, was to concoct a book which would just give enough truth to interest, and not enough to offend the Republican apotheosizers.

In his preface to Mr. Weik's three volumes, Herndon makes the following statement: "Over twenty years ago I began this book, but an active life at the bar caused its postponement. Being now advanced in years, I feel unable to carry out the undertaking, and am assisted by Mr. Weik." Being advanced in years, weakened by drink and misfortunes, it can be easily believed that Mr. J.W. Weik financially remunerated Mr. Herndon for concealing the fact that not only had he (Herndon) *begun* to write Lincoln's life over twenty years previous, but had written and published it, and had witnessed its destruction by those he had imagined would set a high value on it.

Weik, no doubt, fancied his book would sell better if it were thought to be the only life of Lincoln Herndon had written. In the preface to this Weik book, Herndon makes the following statement of intentions which are not fulfilled in the book itself:

> With a view to throwing light on some attributes of Mr. Lincoln's character heretofore obscure, these volumes are given to the world. The whole truth concerning Mr, Lincoln should be known. The truth will at last come out, and no man need hope to evade it. Some persons will doubtless object to the narrative of certain facts which they contend should be assigned to the tomb. Their pretense is that no good can come from such ghastly exposures. My answer is, that *these facts are indispensable to a full knowledge of Mr. Lincoln. We must have all the facts concerning him. We must be prepared to take Mr. Lincoln as he was. He rose from a lower depth than any other great man did – from a stagnant, putrid pool.* I should be remiss in my duty if I did not throw light on this part of the picture. Mr. Lincoln was my warm, devoted friend. I always loved him. I revere his name to this day. My purpose to tell the truth about him need occasion no apprehension. *God's naked truth cannot injure his fame. The world should be told what the skeleton was with Lincoln, what cancer he had inside.*

Thus wrote the honest old fanatic; though broken in health, though reduced to poverty, he was the same man who loved truth and only truth. But the promises made by Herndon in the above preface are

CONCERNING THE WAR ON THE SOUTH

not kept in the body of the so-called "Herndon and Weik's Story of Lincoln." No *ghastly exposures* are made. The "cancer inside" is not spoken of. The "lower depths, the *stagnant, putrid pool*," are not mentioned. On the contrary, the larger part of this three-volume work plainly bears the apotheosis stamp, but it tells some things of Lincoln's early life which Republicans wish to bury out of sight. Consequently, even this so-called *"True Story of Lincoln"* is under the ban, and almost out of existence. I am told that Appleton has just brought out these three volumes in one, and that certain facts incompatible with the apotheosis plan are left entirely out. I am not anxious to show my readers *"stagnant, putrid pools,"* or *"ghastly exposures"* or *"inside cancers"* which have no direct bearing on Mr, Lincoln's public acts, but the character, the deeds, showing the moral qualities of the man our boys are urged to emulate and revere, are matters of vital concern to all Christian parents. For this reason I shall reproduce from Herndon's suppressed *Life of Lincoln* extracts showing what manner of man was the real Lincoln.

Extracts from Herndon's suppressed *Life of Lincoln* found scattered over the pages of that work, which was brought out soon after Lincoln's death:

1. "Mr. Lincoln possessed inordinate desire to rise in the world: to hold high positions in high offices."

2. "Mr. Lincoln always craved office."

3. "Mr. Lincoln coveted honor and was eager for power. He was impatient of any interference that delayed or obstructed his progress."

4. "Mr. Lincoln was a shrewd and by no means an unselfish politician. When battling for a principle, it was after a discreet fashion. When he was running for the Legislature his speeches were calculated to make fair weather with all sides. When running for the United States Senate, he was willing to make a sacrifice of opinion to further his own aspirations."

5. "When Lovejoy, the zealous abolitionist, came to Springfield to speak against slavery, Lincoln left town to avoid taking sides either for or against abolition. This course practically saved Lincoln, as the people did not know whether he was an abolitionist or not."

6. "Lincoln believed in protective tariff, yet when urged to write a letter for the public saying so, he refused, on the ground that it would do him no good."

7. "Until Mr. Lincoln's 'house divided against itself' speech, in 1858, he was very cautious in his anti-slavery expressions. Even after the Bloomington convention he continued to pick his way to the front with wary steps. He did not take his stand with the boldest agitators until just in time to take Seward's place on the Presidential ticket of 1860."

8. "To be popular was to Lincoln the greatest good in life." Yet Republicans call him "The Martyr President." Do martyrs crave popularity?

9. "Lincoln made simplicity and candor a mask to hide his true self."

10. "Lincoln was extremely fond of discussing politics. He disliked work. He detested science and literature. No man can put his finger on any book written in the last or present century [Nineteenth] that Lincoln read through. He read but little."

11. "If ever," said Lincoln, "the American society of the United States are demoralized and overthrown, it will come from the voracious desire for office, the wriggle to live without work, toil or labor, from which I am not free myself."

12. "Lincoln had no gratitude. He forgot the devotion of his warmest friends and partisans as soon as the occasion of their service had passed.'"

13. "Lincoln seldom praised anyone; never a rival."

14. "Lincoln never permitted himself to be influenced by the claims of individual men. When he was a candidate himself he thought the whole canvass ought to be conducted with reference to his success. He would say to a man. 'Your continuance in the field injures *me*,' and be quite sure he had given a perfect reason for the man's withdrawal. He would have no obstacle in his way."

15. "Lincoln was intensely cautious. He revealed just enough of his plans to allure support and not enough to expose him to personal opposition."

16. "When first a candidate for the United States Senate Lincoln was willing to sacrifice his own opinion to further his aspirations for the Presidency."

17. "Notwithstanding Lincoln's over-weening ambition, and the breathless eagerness with which he pursued the object of it, he had not a particle of sympathy with any of his fellow-citizens who were engaged in a similar scramble for place and power."

CHAPTER NINE

Lincoln's Jealousy. Lincoln's Passion for Cock-fights and Fist Fights. Holland's Comment Thereon. Lincoln the "Soul of Honesty." He Passes off Counterfeit Money. Lincoln Sewed up Hogs' Eyes. The "Old Huzzy" Kicks Lincoln Senseless. A Great Fight. "I Am the Big Buck of the Lick."

Lamon gives the same account of Lincoln's political character. Lamon speaks of Lincoln's "burning ambition for distinction," which never abated, never ceased till life ceased. Yet neither Herndon or Lamon even hint that any higher, less selfish motive than desire to lift himself in the world inspired Lincoln's struggle for office. We are not told that Lincoln had plans or dreamed dreams that if he attained high place he would use it for the benefit of unfortunate humanity, of the downtrodden.

Since Lincoln's death his apotheosizers attribute high motives to him, but there is no proof. Those who best knew him saw no such motives, and, in fact, themselves did not seem to know such motives were desirable or expected. Modern Republicans call Lincoln the "martyr" President, and say "he fell a martyr in the cause of negro freedom." Those who well knew him assert he was wholly indifferent to the fate of the negroes. Piatt testifies that Lincoln "had no more sympathy for the negro race than he had for the horse he worked or the hog he killed."

In all history I know of no public man who possessed less of the stuff martyrs are made of than Lincoln. Was ever a martyr "eager for worldly honors?" Did any man with three drops of martyr blood in his heart deem "popularity the greatest good in life?" Would any man, zealous in the cause of negro freedom, run out of the town to avoid speaking on the subject? Self-seeking politicians are too common for one to wonder at Mr. Lincoln's self-seeking nature; such traits might be passed quietly by but for the fact that he is held up before the youth of this country as the model man whom they must emulate and revere. The very writers who record the ignoble traits of Mr. Lincoln's character themselves seem to be unconscious of the mean nature of such traits. Herndon and Lamon both picture the scene in which Mr. Lincoln stands up the central figure in a rowdy crowd of men, swinging about his head a bottle of whiskey, vaunting himself, shouting out, "I am the big buck of the lick! If any man wants to fight, let him come on and whet his horns!" Yet neither of these lovers of Mr. Lincoln seem to see the scene as any ordinary man of refinement must see it.

On page 341 of Lamon's *Life of Lincoln* we find this:

> Mr. Douglas' great success in obtaining place and distinction (in advance of Mr. Lincoln) was a standing offense to Mr. Lincoln's self-love and individual ambition. He was intensely jealous of Douglas and longed to pull him down and outstrip him in the race for popular favor, which both considered the chief end of man.

If this be true, and I have found nothing in any history of Mr. Lincoln's life (except unsupported assertions) to contradict its truth, it shows a man of mean and selfish nature. Jealousy is a feeling born of selfishness. No generous, large-minded man or woman can be jealous of another's success. In the case of Lincoln and Douglas, it appears that neither man was inspired by any feeling higher than the desire for his own individual success; neither seems to have cherished the hope of serving his fellow-men. Since the apotheosis ceremony, Republican writers and politicians assert and re-assert the fiction that from boyhood up the great ambition of Lincoln's heart was to free slaves. This is false, as those few who knew Lincoln well have stated time and again. The foregoing extracts from Herndon throw some light on Mr. Lincoln's political character. I will now give extracts from Herndon and Lamon, showing Mr. Lincoln's every day social life – the amusements and the companions he was fond of.

Herndon says:

> Lincoln's highest delight was to be in the midst of a crowd of rowdy men, engaged in a fist fight with some man,

while the crowd betted on the result. Money, whiskey, knives, tobacco, all sorts of small properties were at stake. Lincoln was uncommonly muscular. It is related that he could lift a barrel of whiskey and drink out of its bung hole. Lincoln's next highest delight was in talking over these fist fights.

Lamon and Herndon both say:

> Lincoln was extremely fond of horse races and cock fights, and had a passion to spin yarns on street corners or in grocery stores [dram shops] to a crowd of boys. Yarns always too vulgar to be repeated. These yarns Lincoln would tell in the presence of preachers. He could not realize the offense of telling a vulgar yarn if a preacher was present.

It is to be hoped the great majority of self-respecting men will not tell vulgar yarns in anybody's presence.

Hapgood calls Lincoln's passion for fist fights, cock fights and horse races "an innocent sporting tendency." Is there a Christian mother or father in America who would not be pained to know their sons indulged in "innocent sporting tendencies" of this sort?

Mr. Holland boldly says of this period of Lincoln's life: "He was a man after God's own pattern."

Holland makes this remarkable statement: "Living among the roughest men, many addicted to the coarsest vices, Lincoln never acquired a vice. There was no taint on his moral character. No stimulant ever entered his lips. No profanity ever came from them."

Lamon, Herndon, Dennis Hanks (Lincoln's cousin, brought up in the same town with Lincoln, as intimate as a brother), and others testify that Lincoln drank whiskey drams, but he was not a drunkard. Lamon says Lincoln always took his dram when asked, and played seven-up at night and made a good game. Holland admits Lincoln's passion for telling "vulgar stories, too indecent to be printed." To many persons this passion appears to be a very serious vice – a vice if indulged in by sons or daughters would deeply pain any decent parent.

Mr. Hay, present Secretary of State, said of Lincoln, "He was the finest character since Christ." It is hardly possible that Mr. Hay was ignorant of Lincoln's real character. It is hardly possible that he did not know the opinions which Lincoln's contemporaries in Washington City held of him during his life. Yet in support of the apotheosis ceremony,

Mr. Hay thinks it necessary to talk twaddle about Mr. Lincoln.

> Abe [says Lamon, page 56] never liked ardent spirits, but he took his dram as others did. He was a natural politician, extremely ambitious and anxious to be popular. For this reason, and this alone, he drank with the boys. If he could have avoided drinking without giving offense, he gladly would have done it. But he coveted the applause of his pot-companions, and because he could not get it otherwise, he made pretense of enjoying his liquor as they did. The people drank, and Abe was always for doing what the people did. Abe was often at the Gentryville grocery, and would stay long at night, telling stories and cracking jokes.

"*Pot-companions,*" and this is the man Republicans tell our boys was like unto Christ. Do these men wish to make infidels of American boys? How can any boy reverence Jesus of Nazareth if he believes He was like Abraham Lincoln who drank drams and told indecent stories to his "pot-companions"?

Mr. Herndon's suppressed *Life of Lincoln* says, "Lincoln disliked the society of ladies. He wriggled and squirmed when in their presence, anxious to get away."

Some of Lincoln's biographies, written according to the apotheosis plan, boldly assert that Lincoln was very fond of the society of *refined* ladies. Refined ladies were the sort Lincoln most disliked – he felt restrained in their presence. No man who knew Lincoln said he was fond of ladies' society.

Herndon says, "Lincoln was the soul of honesty, he was called Honest Abe Lincoln." "Honesty was Lincoln's polar star."

Mr. Lincoln appears not to have possessed what is called the "money grip." He cared little for money. He never made exorbitant charges for his law services. Money was not his passion. His instincts did not lead him into crooked ways to get money, or into mean ways to keep it. Politics was Lincoln's passion. Was he honest in politics? Both Lamon and Herndon testify that he deceived and used trickery to gain votes. Is it not as dishonest to gain votes by false pretense as to gain money? Are American boys to be taught that political dishonesty is honorable? But, on money matters, as on other questions, Mr. Lincoln's biographers have hazy ideas of honesty. Instance the following story *ap-*

plaudingly related by Lamon and other biographers: When Lincoln was nineteen years old he hired to Mr. Gentry to go with his young son, Allen Gentry, on a flatboat down the Mississippi River on a trading trip. The boat was loaded with produce to be sold to farmers settled on the river bank. Lincoln's duty was to help row the boat and help sell the produce, for which he was paid eight dollars per month. In the course of his business, young Gentry received a quantity of counterfeit money. "Never mind," said Lincoln, "I will pass it off on some other fellow," which he did. Of this transaction. Lamon says, "The trip of young Gentry and Lincoln was a very profitable one. Abe displayed his genius for mercantile affairs by handsomely passing off on the innocent folks along the river some counterfeit money which had been imposed on young Gentry."

Shall the youth of this country be taught that to "pass counterfeit money on innocent folks" displays "genius for mercantile affairs?" To applaud dishonesty is to teach dishonesty.

After relating the counterfeit money story, Lamon put the following note at the bottom of the page: "It must be remembered that counterfeit money was the principal currency along the river at that period." This is not true. It has always been in this country a penitentiary offense to pass counterfeit money. The settlers along the river were neither fools nor savages. Many were educated men and women, emigrants from the Atlantic States. They well knew the danger and dishonesty of passing counterfeit money. I have talked on this subject with old men who lived on the river bank at that time. They assure me it was always known to be as dishonest to pass counterfeit money as to steal, and men caught so doing were tried and sent to the penitentiary, as the law commanded.

"Lincoln," says Herndon, "was tender-hearted." Many of Lincoln's biographers dwell on this tender-hearted virtue. Donn Piatt made a study of Lincoln's character and says he was not tender-hearted. On the contrary, he was callous and unfeeling. Of this, more anon. After stating that his friend Lincoln was tender-hearted, Herndon relates the following:

> When about twenty-one years old. Lincoln hired for $8 per month to work on a flatboat going to New Orleans with a load of grain and live stock. He and two other men undertook to drive a drove of hogs on the boat. The animals

would not walk the plank leading from the land to the boat. They would run past the plank. Lincoln suggested that they should blind the hogs by sewing their eyes up. Being very strong, Lincoln caught the hogs one by one, held their heads tightly. A second man held the feet, while the third man, with needle and thread, sewed up the animals' eyelids so they could not see. This device did not succeed. The hogs still refused to walk the plank. Then the strong Lincoln again seized the hogs one by one. carried them on the boat, held their heads as in a vice while another man cut the stitches and restored vision to the animals.

Was this tender-heartedness? Biographers give anecdotes like the above, apparently blind to their repulsive nature. The following is also related by Herndon, who was told the story by Mr. Lincoln, as he (Lincoln) said, "to illustrate a scientific fact."

It was Lincoln's duty, when a youth in his father's house, to put a sack of corn on the old mare, ride to the mill and grind it. Each man's animal was expected to work the mill machinery, and each man made his animal do the work. As the old Lincoln mare plodded round and round, Lincoln applied the lash, and with every lash, to hurry her into faster movements, Lincoln yelled out, "Get up, you old huzzy!"

Even an old "huzzy" resents injustice. After the old mare had patiently borne many lashes, just as young Lincoln said "get up" for the fiftieth time, her patience gave out, she lifted her hind foot and landed it square between Lincoln's eyes, and he fell insensible and lay insensible all night. On coming to consciousness he finished the sentence cut short by the mare's heels, shouting "you old huzzy!"

Is it insanity or pure mendacity to liken a man of this nature to the gentle and loving Nazarene? Who for an instant can imagine Jesus swinging a bottle of whiskey around his head, swearing to the rowdy crowd that he was the "big buck of the lick?" Or with a whip in his hand, lashing a faithful old slave at every round of her labor? Who can imagine Jesus sewing up hogs' eyes? What act of Lincoln's life betrays tender-heartedness? Was he tender-hearted when he made medicine contraband of war? When he punished women caught with a bottle of quinine going South? The laws of war of all civilized people exempt surgeons' and hospital supplies from capture or intent of harm. Not only did Lincoln prevent medicine from going South, but when the whole South was devastated, when she was unable, properly, to feed and medicine the Union soldiers in her prisons, the Southerners paroled a Federal prisoner and sent him with a message to Lincoln, informing him of the South's condition in that respect, and telling him if he would send his own surgeons with medical supplies they would be allowed to minister to the needs of the Union men in prison. Lincoln refused. Was this tender-hearted? When Greeley implored Lincoln not to inaugurate war on the South, and told him if he "rushed on carnage" he would clearly put himself in the wrong, was it tender-hearted to despise Greeley's prayer, rush on carnage, and for four years drench the whole Southland with human blood? And when Lincoln's legions were devastating the South, when with wanton cruelty, at the point of the bayonet, Sherman drove 15,000 women and children of Atlanta, Georgia, out of their homes, out of the city, to wander in the woods, shelterless, foodless, and then laid the whole city in ashes, did Lincoln give one thought to the sufferings of those innocent women and children? Did he once, during the four years of the cruel war, utter or write one kind word of the people on whom *he* had brought such unspeakable misery?

When some of the South's naval men were captured, and Lincoln ordered that they should be hanged as pirates, and threw them in loathsome dungeon cells to await hanging, was that tender-hearted? In the last war between Germany and France, how much more humanely did the conquering Germans treat the conquered French? When Butler, sometimes called "the beast," in public speeches made in Northern cities, in newspapers, in legends, put up in big letters in his office, defamed and denounced the women of New Orleans as "she adders" and "she devils," and issued Order 28, which shocked all the civilized people of earth (except Russians and the Republican party), did Lincoln say one kind word of those so basely wronged women of New Orleans? In Butler's *Book* he boasts that Lincoln, and every other Republican, approved his course in New Orleans (including his abuse and falsehoods about the women of that city), and the infamous Order 28, which licensed his soldiery to insult and assault women at their pleasure. When, befouled all over by that foul order, Butler went from New Orleans to Washington City, not one of the foreign ministers called on Butler except the Russian. In his history of the United States, Rhodes virtually charges Butler with telling falsehoods about a certain transaction between him and Grant, but when Butler basely defames and lies outright on every woman in New Orleans, Rhodes is ready enough to accept his lies as gospel truths, without any attempt at investigation. Such is the justice of Republican writers. The customs of civilized people forbid, in wars, the destruction of growing vines and crops, and the wanton burning of private homes. These customs or laws were trampled under foot by the Republican party and its invading legions, and Lincoln exultantly congratulated his generals for the cruel work they did. The generals of the army were expressly ordered to destroy everything, to make the Southland a desert waste. While Sheridan was engaged in this remorseless work, Grant telegraphed him. "Do all the damage you can. Destroy the crops. We want the Shenandoah Valley a barren waste. We want Virginia clear and clean, so that a crow flying over it will have to carry his ration or starve to death."

For one whole month Sheridan and his legions carried on this cruel work, and at last when the valley indeed was a desert waste, and thousands of women and children wandered in the woods and fields, homeless and hungry, Lincoln, the tender-hearted (God save the mark!) gleefully sent a telegram of congratulation to Sheridan. "I tender you and your brave army my thanks," said Lincoln, "and the thanks of the Nation, and my personal admiration for your month's operation in Shenandoah Valley, and especially for the splendid work." The "especially splendid work" that pleased Lincoln was the cruel work of burning homes and turning women and children out into the devastated fields to starve and die.

Lincoln took it upon himself, as all despots do, to speak for the Nation. If by the "Nation" is meant the great body of people, the large majority, Mr. Lincoln had no right to assume that the Northern Nation thanked Sheridan for his remorseless work. The Nation's sympathies at that time were with the South. On page 47 of the Weik's and Herndon *Story of a Great Life* is the following story:

> In the noted fight between Abraham Lincoln's stepbrother and William Grigsby, John Johnson (the stepbrother), William Grigsby and Abe himself played a stirring part. Taylor's brother was the second for Johnson; William White was Grigsby's second. They had a terrible fight. It soon became apparent that Grigsby was too much for Lincoln's man, Johnson. It had been agreed that no one was

to break the ring, but when Abe saw that his man was getting the worst of the fight he burst through the ring, caught Grigsby, threw him off some feet distant: then up stood Lincoln, proud as Lucifer, swinging a bottle of liquor over his head and swearing aloud. "I am the big buck of the lick!" he shouted. "If anybody doubts it let them come on and whet his horns."

A general fight followed this challenge, at the end of which the field was cleared, the wounded retired amid the exultant shouts of the victors. In Lamon's *Life of Lincoln* the story is related thus:

> The ground for the fight was one mile and a half from Gentryville. The bullies for twenty miles around attended; the friends of both parties were present in force; excitement ran high. When Abe's man, Johnson, was down and Bill Grigsby was on top, and all the spectators swearing and cheering, crowded up to the edge of the ring. Abe burst out of the crowd into the ring, seized Grigsby by the heels and threw him off; then he swung a bottle of whisky over his head and swore he was the big buck of the lick. Not one in the large crowd cared to encounter the long sweep of Abe's muscular arms, and so he remained master of the lick. Not content, however, with this triumph, he vaunted himself in the most offensive manner, made hostile demonstrations toward Grigsby, declaring he could whip him then and there. Grigsby meekly replied he did not doubt it, but if Abe would make things even, and fight with pistols, he would willingly give him a fight. Abe replied: "I am not going to fool away my life on a single shot."

Is this a man American youths should be taught to reverence and emulate? Is this a picture to present for the admiration of our sons and daughters? Yet of this man apotheosizing writers dare to say, "He as nearly resembles Christ as human nature can."

CHAPTER TEN

Mr. Lincoln Hates and Despises Christianity. He Goes to Church to Mock and Deride. "Pious Lies." Holland's Strange Story. Other Republican Leaders Deride Christianity. The Four Ws.

    It is quite possible that many true and trustworthy men have been unbelievers in the Bible as the word of God. Many men have doubted and denied the divinity of Christ. Good men have claimed that Jesus was only a good man whose sublime moral teachings brought on Him the wrath of rulers. Mr. Lincoln's unbelief was more aggressive than the ordinary infidel's; he disliked and despised Christianity as if it were an enemy to humanity. He had no appreciation for the sublime truths taught by Jesus of Nazareth. Since the apotheosis ceremony, and especially since the contemporaries of Mr. Lincoln have nearly all passed away, it has become the custom of biographers to show up Mr. Lincoln as a very religious man. Mr. Holland, Noah Brooks and Miss Tarbell take the lead of all romancers on this subject. These writers throw facts to the wind, and, as Gen. Piatt puts it, fill their pages with "pious lies." Pious lies of this nature greatly annoyed Herndon and Lamon. Both Herndon and Lamon took time and labor trying to kill these pious lies, but after Herndon's and Lamon's death pious lies became more numerous, bold and audacious than ever. In his suppressed *Life of Lincoln* Herndon says:

    Lincoln was a deep-grounded infidel. He disliked and despised churches. He never entered a church except to scoff and ridicule. On coming from a church he would mimic the preacher. Before running for any office he wrote a book against Christianity and the Bible. He showed it to some friends and read extracts. A man named Hill was greatly shocked and urged Lincoln not to publish it. Urged it would kill him politically. Hill got this book in his hands, opened the stove door, and it went up in flames and ashes. After that, Lincoln became more discreet, and when running for office often used words and phrases to make it appear that he was a Christian. He never changed on this subject. He lived and died a deep-grounded infidel.

Lamon, who was very intimate with Lincoln during the latter's Presidency, as well as before, says he never changed. Nicolay and Hay say the same. Yet since Lincoln's deification nearly every eulogist, lecturer and biographer of Lincoln asserts that he was a sincere Christian. Many of Lincoln's relations and friends testify that he scoffed and derided religion and the Bible.

On the subject of Mr. Lincoln's religious ideas, Lamon, who, during Lincoln's four years in the White House, was closer to him than any other man, wrote as follows in 1872:

> No phase of Mr. Lincoln's character has been so persistently misrepresented as this of his religious belief. Not that the conclusive testimony of many of his intimate associates and relations relative to his frequent expressions on such subjects have ever been wanting, but his great prominence in history, his extremely general expressions of religious faith called forth by the exigencies of his public life, or indulged in on occasion of private condolence have been distorted out of relation to their real significance or meaning to suit the opinion or tickle the fancy of individuals or parties.

Mr. Lamon might have added to the above the fact that after the Republican leaders had performed the apotheosis ceremony they deemed it best for the honor and maintenance of their party to bury out of sight Mr. Lincoln's real character, and to pose him before the world as the greatest and purest man born since Christ, and at the same time they decreed that from the hour of Mr. Lincoln's death, he was to be pictured as a sincere and true Christian. If Lamon knew that the Republicans thought it for the interest of their party that Mr. Lincoln should be represented as a Christian, he dared to differ from them and did his best to down falsehoods on this subject. Some biographers assert that "when a boy, Lincoln was of a grave and religious nature; that he often retired from company and read the Bible, on his knees, and otherwise manifested a reverential and religious turn of mind." Herndon says Lincoln was deficient in reverence for any thing or person. Lincoln's stepmother denied that he "ever went into a corner to ponder the sacred writings and wet the pages with his tears of penitence."

Dennis Hanks is clear on this point. He denied that his cousin Abe was ever reverential, and denied that he liked sacred songs, and testifies that the songs Lincoln was fond of were of a very questionable character:

> When Lincoln went to church [say Lamon and Hanks], he went to mock and came away to mimic. When he went to New Salem he consorted with free thinkers and joined with them in deriding the gospel story of Jesus. He wrote a labored book on this subject, which his friend Hill put in the stove and burned up. Not until after Mr. Lincoln's death were these facts denied (See Lamon's *Life of Lincoln*).

In the face of abundant and unimpeachable evidence proving that Lincoln was a deep-grounded infidel, unscrupulous biographers continue to assert that he was a true Christian. Nicolay, who was Mr. Lincoln's private secretary during his Presidency, said on this subject: "Mr. Lincoln did not, to my knowledge, in any way change his religious views or beliefs from the time he left Springfield till his death."

Herndon, the most faithful friend of Lincoln, was so outraged at the falsehoods put forth about Lincoln's piety in the "pretended biographies" of his life that in 1870 he wrote a letter to Lamon, from which the following is taken:

> In New Salem Mr. Lincoln lived with a class of men, moved with them, had his being with them. They were scoffers of religion, made loud protests against the followers of Christianity. They declared that Jesus was an illegitimate child. On all occasions that offered they debated on the various forms of Christianity. They ridiculed old divines, and not infrequently made those very divines skeptics by their logic; made them disbelievers as bad as themselves.
>
> In 1835 Lincoln wrote a book on infidelity and in-

tended to have it published. The book was an attack on the idea that Jesus was Christ. Lincoln read the book to his friend Hill. Hill tried to persuade him not to publish it. Lincoln said it should be published. Hill, believing that if the book was published it would kill Lincoln forever as a politician, seized it and thrust it in the stove. It went up in smoke and ashes before Lincoln could get it out. When Mr. Lincoln was candidate for the Legislature he was accused of being an infidel, and of having said that Jesus was an illegitimate child. He never denied it, never flinched from his views on religion.

In 1854 he made me erase the name of God from a speech I was about to make. He did this to one of his friends in Washington City. In the year 1847 Mr. Lincoln ran for Congress against the Rev. Peter Cartright. He was accused of being an infidel; he never denied it. He knew it could and would be proved on him. I know when he left Springfield for Washington he had undergone no change in his opinion on religion. He held many of the Christian ideas in abhorrence. He held that God could not forgive sinners.

The idea that Mr. Lincoln carried a Bible in his bosom or in his boots to draw on his opponent is ridiculous.

Lincoln's cousin, Dennis Hanks, testifies:

> At an early age Abe began to attend the preachings around about, but mostly at the Pigeon Creek Church, with a view to catching anything that might be ludicrous in the preaching, in the manner or matter, and making it a subject of mimicry as soon as he could collect a crowd of idle boys and men to hear him. He frequently reproduced a sermon with nasal twang, rolling his eyes, and all sorts of droll aggravations, to the great delight of the wild fellows assembled. Sometimes he broke out with stories passably humorous and invariably vulgar.

In Lamon's *Life of Lincoln*, page 55, he says:

> It is important that this question should be finally settled. The names of some of Mr. Lincoln's nearest friends are given below, followed by clear and decisive statements for

which they are responsible, and all of them of high character, men who had the best opportunities to form a correct opinion as to Mr. Lincoln's religious ideas.

The following are samples of evidence on this subject. Mr. Jesse E. Fall reluctantly testifies:

> Mr. Lincoln's friends were not a little surprised at finding in some biographies statements of his religious opinions so utterly at variance with his known sentiments. Lincoln held opinions utterly at variance with what are taught in the churches.

William H. Herndon testifies: "Mr. Lincoln told me a thousand times that he did not believe that the Bible was any revelation from God. I assert this of my own knowledge; others will confirm what I say."

After Lincoln's death his wife wrote Lamon: "Mr. Lincoln had no hope and no faith in Christianity." Lamon testifies that "Lincoln never changed his opinions of the Christian religion, but he became discreet in talking of them."

John Matthews testifies as follows:

> I knew Mr. Lincoln as early as 1834; knew he was an infidel. He attacked the Bible and the New Testament; he talked infidelity, ridiculed both Bible and Testament. He often shocked me, he went so far. He often came into the clerk's office, where I and other young men were writing. He brought a Bible with him, read a chapter and argued against it. He wrote a book on infidelity. I was his personal and political friend. I never heard that he changed his views.

On page 497 Lamon says:

> While it is clear that Mr. Lincoln was at all times an infidel, it is also very clear that he was not at all times equally willing that everybody should know it. He never offered to purge or recant; he was a wily politician and did not disdain to regulate his religious manifestations with reference to his political interest. He saw the immense and augmenting power

of the churches, and in times past had felt it. The charge of infidelity had seriously injured him in several of his earlier political campaigns. Aspiring to lead religious communities, he saw he must not appear as an enemy within their gates. He saw no reason for changing his convictions, but he saw many good and cogent reasons for not making them public.

In 1865 Mr. Holland wrote (to borrow Lamon's words) a "pretended Life of Lincoln," which shows lamentable disregard for truth and lamentable perversion of the moral sense. Having fully accepted the apotheosis decree regarding the dead President, Mr. Holland very much desired to present to the public Mr. Lincoln as being a good and true Christian. To do this, in the face of strong evidence to the contrary, also in the face of the fact that hundreds of friends and relatives of Mr. Lincoln were still living, who could and would contradict misstatements, was the problem Mr. Holland had to contend with. After thinking the matter over, Mr. Holland finally inserted in his *Life of Lincoln* the best story he could find to prove that Mr. Lincoln was a devout Christian. If this story be true, it would show Mr. Lincoln to have been more infamous than any open and avowed infidel the world knows of. We give the story as given in Mr. Holland's *Life of Lincoln*. The reader must judge for himself:

> During one of Mr. Lincoln's political campaigns, a few days before the election, he took a book containing a careful canvass of the city of Springfield, showing the candidates for whom each citizen had declared his intention to vote, and called Mr. Newton Bateman into his office to a seat by his side, carefully locking the door. "Let us look over this book," said Lincoln. "I particularly wish to see how the ministers of the churches are going to vote." Newton Bateman was Superintendent of Public Instruction for the State of Illinois. Turning over the leaves one by one, Lincoln counted up the names; then with a face full of sadness said: "Here are twenty-three ministers of different denominations, and all of them are against me, and here are a great many prominent members of the churches, a very large majority of whom are against me. I don't understand this. I am not a Christian. God knows I would be one."

Drawing from his bosom a pocket Testament, his cheeks wet with tears, with a trembling voice he quoted it (the Testament) against his political opponents, especially against Douglas. He said the opinions adopted by him (Lincoln) and his party were derived from the teachings of Christ, and asserted that Christ was God. The Testament he carried in his bosom he called "The rock on which I stand."

Mr. Bateman, himself a Christian, said: "Mr. Lincoln, I had not supposed that you were accustomed to think so much on this subject; certainly, your friends are ignorant of the sentiments you have expressed to me."

"I know it," he replied promptly. "I know they are. I am obliged to appear different to them. I am willing *you* should know the truth."

On this story Mr. Holland makes the following curious comment:

Why Mr. Lincoln should say he was obliged to appear an infidel to others does not appear. It is more than probable that on leaving Mr. Bateman, Lincoln met some of his old friends, and by a single bound from his tearful and sublime religious passion he told them some jest that filled his heart with mirth and awoke convulsions of laughter.

"Tearful and sublime religious passion!" What apotheosis twaddle is this! Of this Holland story Lamon says:

If Mr. Lincoln told Bateman that he did not understand why the Christian ministers and the other religious men refused to vote for him, he spoke falsely. Mr. Lincoln well knew they opposed him because he was an open and avowed infidel; one who blatantly strove to make converts of young Christian men.

Both Bateman and Holland were professed Christians. If one or both together concocted this story for the purpose of lifting from Mr. Lincoln the stigma of infidelity, their moral sense must have been singularly perverted not to see that the story they told would cover Mr. Lincoln with blacker infamy than any unbelief in Christianity could possibly do. I can conceive of no greater baseness than the acts this Holland-Bateman story attributes to Mr. Lincoln. That man must be utterly conscienceless, not to say fiendishly malignant, who, himself convinced of the truth, the saving grace of Christianity, uses his power of logic, his power of sarcasm, his gift of eloquence, to turn Christian men and youths against the faith he himself believed to be divine! Unimpeachable evidence proves that Mr. Lincoln often seized occasions to "go into offices where young men were writing, with a Bible in his pocket, from which he would read chapters and verses and then denounce, deride and argue against the Bible and Christianity."

It is proved that Mr. Lincoln, with others of like nature, would get together and scoff at the Christian faith, calling Jesus an impostor, a bastard child, and other opprobious epithets. Yet Mr. Holland would have his readers believe that all the time Lincoln was doing his best to bring contempt on Christianity he himself was a devoutly religious man. Some biographers ignore all evidence and serenely persist in the assertion that Mr. Lincoln was a fervent Christian and was "often seen on his knees before an open Bible, praying, while the tears streamed down his face." Biographers of this sort write under the full glare of the apotheosis ceremony, which blinds the vision of all faithful Republicans.

In Mr. Holland's "pretended" *Life of Lincoln* is the following:

> Mr. Lincoln will always be remembered as eminently a Christian President. Conscience, not popular applause, not love of power, was the ruling motive of Lincoln's life. There was no taint to Lincoln's moral character. No stimulant ever entered his mouth; no profanity ever came from his lips.

Lamon says:

> The people all drank; even the women drank whiskey toddies. The men took whiskey straight. Abe was always for doing what the people did, right or wrong. Dennis Hanks, Lincoln's cousin, brought up with him, wrote to Herndon, who was then writing Lincoln's *Life*, saying: "Go the whole hog; keep nothing back about Lincoln." Hanks was opposed to whitewashing.

Hapgood, page 183, says: "All the clergy in Springfield voted against Lincoln."

Other great Republican leaders in that cruel period not only had no faith in Christianity, but so hated it they never missed a chance to cast scorn and gibes at its founder. The Lancaster (Pa.) *Intelligencer*, published at the home of Thaddeus Stevens, said of him:

> During all his lifetime Thaddeus Stevens has openly scoffed at the Christian religion. Some years before the war, while trying a case in another part of the State, one of the lawyers quoted from the Bible. "Oh," retorted Stevens, "the Bible is nothing but obsolete history of a barbarous people."

In a speech made during the impeachment proceedings, Stevens referred to the Savior as that "individual Judas Iscariot betrayed."

Carl Schurz was a reviler of Christianity. Schurz thought it fine wit to refer to Jesus of Nazareth as "that ideal gentleman beyond the skies called by some people God." Some of those leaders not only cast aside religious restraints, but cut themselves loose from the ordinary rules of decency. Senator McDonald boasted that he had planted his feet on the platform of the four Ws, "Wine, Whiskey, Women, War."

Thaddeus Stevens was so pleased with this he boasted that his feet also stood on that platform.

The cruel and utterly unjust war waged on the South by the Republican party in the '60s seems to have obliterated every vestige of moral conscience, and all sense of right and wrong in some of the politicians of that party. Instance the following paragraph, cut from a Republican journal, the *Globe-Democrat* of St. Louis, October 17, 1897. The *Globe-Democrat* editor, discussing which of two courses his party should pursue, complacently remarks: "It matters not which we do, but we must all do the same. *'Which is our scoundrel?'* asked Thaddeus Stevens, in one of the controversies growing out of the reconstruction policy, *'that we may all defend him.'*"

To defend their party's dead or living scoundrels is the highest duty of Republicans. Thad Stevens' proposition was worthy of him and of the hellish policy he was discussing.

CHAPTER ELEVEN

Lincoln's Singular Treatment of the Lady He Four Times Asked to Marry Him. His Curious Letter About That Lady. His Cruel Treatment of Miss Todd. His Home a Hell on Earth.

Herndon and Lamon both say that Mr. Lincoln proposed marriage to three women. The first was Miss Rutledge, who was already engaged to a man whom she truly loved, who had gone East and remained so long her family, thinking he had forgotten his engagement, persuaded her to accept Lincoln's offer. Herndon, in his suppressed *Life of Lincoln*, says that Miss Rutledge could not love Lincoln, and before marriage pined and died in the belief that her first and only love had forgotten her. This was an error; the lover had suffered a long and tedious illness and returned to find the girl dead. The second woman Lincoln courted was a Miss Owens of Kentucky. Herndon describes Miss Owens as a handsome, well-educated, bright young woman, just one year older than Lincoln, weighing 150 pounds, and having some fortune. Lincoln was twenty-eight. Miss Owens twenty-nine years old. The age and weight of this lady cut an important figure in this affair, and should be borne in mind by the reader. Lincoln himself tells the story of his courtship of Miss Owens in a letter to his friend, Mrs. Browning. Both Lamon and Herndon insert this letter verbatim in their story of Lincoln's life. Lamon introduces it by the following remarks:

> If this letter could be withheld and the act decently reconciled to the conscience of the biographer professing to be honest and candid, this letter never should see the light in these pages. Its coarse exaggeration in describing the person the writer was willing to marry, its imputation of "toothless,

weather-beaten old age," to a really young and handsome lady, its utter lack of delicacy, its defective orthography, all this it would be more agreeable to suppress than to publish. But if we begin to mutilate a document which throws a broad light on one phase of Mr. Lincoln's character, why may we not do the like as fast and as often as the temptation may arise?

Mutilations of this nature were precisely what Republican writers were expected to make in obedience to the decree of the apotheosizing Republican politicians.

In Weik's and Herndon's *Story of a Great Life* this letter is published entire under the heading, "A Most Amusing Courtship." The letter itself Weik calls "a most ludicrous letter." Herndon makes no such comments in his suppressed *Life of Lincoln*. Should the son of any honorable man or woman write such a letter about the lady he had tried long and hard to get for a wife, had proposed to her four times, had never by her been deceived by word or act, had been told from the first that she could not marry him, that father and mother would weep tears of shame and sorrow over such a letter. They would be unable to see in it anything "amusing," anything "ludicrous."

Nicolay and Hay, who dedicated their ten volumes called the *Life of Lincoln* to Mr. Lincoln's son Robert, and who, of course, always held in mind the purpose of pleasing not only the son, but the Republican party, comment on the letter as follows:

> This letter has been published and severely criticised as showing a lack of gentlemanly feeling, but those who take this view forget that Lincoln was writing to an intimate friend, that he mentioned no names, and that twenty-five years after, when a biographer wanted to publish the letter, Mr. Lincoln refused consent for the reason, as he stated, *"there is too much truth in it for print."*

Nicolay and Hay seek to excuse the writing of this letter on the score of youth. Lincoln was twenty-eight. If a man is ever to possess gentlemanly feeling, surely he is old enough at twenty-eight. But even this excuse is nullified by the fact that twenty-five years after writing the letter Lincoln exhibited no regret, no shame, no sense of the gross impropriety of writing such a letter. He refused to have the letter given to the public, *not* because he regretted having written it, but because *"there was too much truth in it."* Yet in that letter was as vile a slur as man can make at an honorable woman. Mark the sentence: "I knew she was called an *'old maid,'* and I felt no doubt of the truth of at least *one-half* of the appellation."

Is not this intimating a doubt of the chastity of the woman he had four times asked to be his wife? Had the parties concerned lived in the South, had the lady been blessed with a big brother or a fiery father, had either the one or the other chanced to see that letter, Mr. Lincoln would not have lived long enough to become the first President of the Republican party. The following is a copy of the letter:

Springfield, April 1st, 1838.

Mrs. O. H. Browning:

Dear Madam – Without apologizing for being egotistical, I shall make the history of so much of my life as has elapsed since I saw you, the subject of this letter. And I now discover that in order to give you a full and intelligible account of the things I have done and suffered since I saw you, I shall have to relate some that happened before. It was in the autumn of 1836 that a married lady of my acquaintance, a great friend of mine, being about to pay a visit to her father and relations residing in Kentucky, proposed to me that on her return she would bring a sister of her's with her if I would agree to become her brother-in-law with all convenient dispatch. I, of course, accepted the proposal, for you know I could not have done otherwise had I really been averse to it, but privately, between you and me, I was most confoundedly well pleased with the project. I had seen the said sister some three years ago. and thought her intelligent and agreeable, and saw no good objection to plodding life through hand in hand with her. Time passed, the lady took her journey, and in due time returned, sister in company, sure enough. This astonished me a little, for it appeared that her coming so readily showed she was a trifle too willing, but on reflection it occurred to me that she might have been prevailed on by her married sister to come without anything concerning me having been mentioned to her, and so I concluded that if no other objection presented itself I would consent to waive this. All this occurred to me on hearing of her arrival in the neighborhood, for be it remembered I had not seen her except about three years previous to the above mentioned. In a few days we had an interview and although I had seen her before, she did not look as my imagination had pictured her. I knew she was over size, but now she appeared a fair match for Falstaff. I knew she was called an *old maid*, and I felt no doubt of the truth of at least *half* of the appellation. But now, when I beheld her, I could not for my life avoid thinking of my mother, and this not from withered features, for her skin was too full of fat to permit of its contracting into wrinkles, but from want of teeth and weather-beaten appearance in general, and from a kind of notion running through my head that nothing could have commenced at the size of infancy and reached her present bulk at less than thirty-five or forty years; in short, I was not at all pleased with her. But what could I do? I had told her sister I would take her for better or for worse, and I made a point of honor and conscience in all things to stick to my word, especially if others had been induced to act on it, which in this case I had no doubt they had done, for I was fully convinced that no other man on earth would have her, and hence the conclusion that they were bent on holding me to my bargain. Well, thought I, I have said it, and be the consequences what they may, it shall not be my fault if I fail to do it. At once I determined to consider her my wife, and this done, all my powers of discovery were put to work in search of perfections in her which might be fairly set off against her defects. I tried to imagine her handsome, which but for her corpulence was actually true. Exclusive of this, no woman I have ever seen had a finer face. I also tried to convince myself that the mind was much more to be valued than the person, and in this she was not inferior, as I could discover, to any with whom I had been acquainted. Shortly after this, without coming to any understanding with her, I set out for Vandalia, where you first saw me. During my stay there I had letters from her which did not change my opinion either of her intellect or intention, but, on the contrary, confirmed it in both. All this while, though I was fixed firm as the surge-repelling rock in my resolution, I found I was continually repenting the rashness which had led me to make it. Through life I have been in no bondage, either real or imaginary, from the thralldom of which I so much desired to be free. After my return home I saw nothing in her to make me change my opinion of her in any respect. I now spent my time in planning how I might get along through life after my contemplated change of circumstances should have taken place,, and how I might procrastinate the evil for a time, which I really dreaded as much, perhaps more, than the Irishman does the halter. After all my suffering on this deeply interesting subject, here I am wholly, unexpectedly, completely out of the scrape, and now I want to know if you can guess how I got out of it. Clear, in every sense of the term; no violation of word, honor or conscience. I don't believe you can guess, so I may as well tell you at once. As the lawyer says, it was done in the manner following, to-wit: After I had delayed the matter as long as I thought I could in honor do (which, by the way, had brought me around to the last of fall), I concluded I might as well bring it to a consummation without further delay, and so I mustered up my resolution and made the proposal to her direct, but, shocking to relate, she said "No." At first I thought she did it through an affectation of modesty, which I thought but ill became her, under the peculiar circumstances of her case, but on my renewal of the charge I found she repeated it with greater firmness than ever. I tried again and again, but with the same success, or, rather, the same want of success. I finally was forced to give it up, at which I very unexpectedly found myself mortified almost beyond endurance. I was mortified, it seemed to me, in a hundred different ways. My vanity was deeply wounded by the reflection that I had been too stupid to discover her intentions, and at the same time never doubting that I understood them perfectly, and that she whom I had taught myself to believe nobody else would have, had actually rejected me, with all my fancied greatness. And to cap the whole thing, I had then for the first time begun to suspect that I was really a little in love with her. But let it all go; I'll try and outlive it. Others have been made fools of by the girls, but this can never with truth be said of me. I most emphatically in this instance made a fool of myself. I have now come to the conclusion of never again to think of marrying, and for this reason I can never be satisfied with any one who would be blockheaded enough to have me.

Your sincere friend,
A. Lincoln.

If this appears rough treatment of the lady who refused to marry Mr. Lincoln, what will be thought of his treatment of the lady who consented to marry him? After Miss Owens, Lincoln courted Miss Todd, who is described by Herndon and Lamon as a handsome, well-educated young lady of a fine old Kentucky family. Like Miss Owens, Miss Todd was in Springfield on a visit to a married sister. The day was set for the marriage, or rather the night of January 1st, 1841. The guests were invited and duly arrived; the feast was spread, the bride was arrayed in all her beauty and finery. They waited the coming of the bridegroom. But he came not. A strange uneasiness arose, runners were sent out in search, but they found him not. When all hope was over the disappointed, chagrined, unhappy bride retired to her chamber to hide her grief and shame. The guests departed, amazed and astounded. Next day the bride returned to her Kentucky home. When morning came Lincoln's friends found him and demanded an explanation of his extraordinary conduct.

"I found," replied Lincoln, "that I do not love Miss Todd enough to make her my wife."

When his friends made Lincoln understand how his conduct would be viewed he was greatly troubled. "Popularity to him was the greatest good in life." To lose popularity would indeed be a great loss to Lincoln. He was an ambitious politician. Lincoln's friends urged him to leave town until the excitement blew over. He went to Speed's paternal home, near Louisville, Ky., and there remained three weeks, the guest of Speed's father. Modern biographers excuse Lincoln on the ground of insanity. Herndon, in his suppressed *Life of Lincoln*, says "Lincoln was not insane, but much depressed." Speed's brother, who saw Lincoln while at his father's house, says he was not insane. Joshua Speed, Lincoln's close friend, says, "Lincoln was not insane, but was depressed, and *almost* contemplated suicide."

The apotheosizing biographers either make no mention of the

occurrence or declare he was insane. Hapgood boldly says: "When Lincoln was found next day he was as crazy as a loon." On whose authority Hapgood bases this assertion does not appear. Apotheosizing writers care very little for authority. No writer during Lamon's or Herndon's life dared assail the veracity of either of these men. Miss Tarbell, who wrote her so-called *Life of Lincoln* long after his two true friends, Herndon and Lamon, had passed away, attacked Herndon's veracity, and makes a lame attempt to deny the whole story. At the end of a year Miss Todd again visited her sister in Springfield, Ill. Mr. Lincoln, wishing to atone, again proposed marriage, and was again accepted. Herndon says that the little boy of the house, on seeing Mr. Lincoln dressing for his marriage, asked where he was going. "To hell," was Mr. Lincoln's gloomy reply.

In his suppressed *Life of Lincoln*, Herndon says:

> It literally was a hell to which Mr. Lincoln went. Miss Todd lost all love for Mr. Lincoln that night he inflicted upon her so grievous a wrong. She married for revenge, and got it in good weight. To me it has always seemed plain that Mr. Lincoln married Miss Todd to save his honor. He sacrificed his domestic peace; he chose honor, and with it years of torture, sacrificial pangs and the loss forever of a happy home. As to Miss Todd, until that fatal night, January 1st, 1841, she may have loved Lincoln, but his action on that night forfeited her affection. He had crushed her proud spirit. She felt degraded in the eyes of the world. Love fled at the approach of revenge. She led her husband a wild dance. She unchained the bitterness of a disappointed and outraged nature. Mary Todd had kept back all the unattractive traits of her character. Lincoln's married life is a curious history; facts long chained down are slowly coming to the surface. It often happened that Lincoln would get up in the dead of night, and go out of his own house to escape his wife. He often went to his law office to sleep on the old horsehair sofa there. Mrs. Lincoln's temper was something fearful.

Illustrating Mrs. Lincoln's violent temper, in the *True Story of a Great Life* is the following story: A girl in the employ of Mrs. Lincoln was discharged. The girl's uncle called on Mrs. Lincoln to learn the cause of such treatment. Mrs. Lincoln met the man at the door and was so infuriated and violent the man was glad to get safely away. But he went at once to Lincoln's office to exact from him proper satisfaction. Lincoln listened to the uncle's story, then sadly said: "My friend, I regret to hear this, but in all candor I ask you, can't you endure for a few moments what I have had as my daily portion for the last fifteen years?" The uncle was disarmed. Lincoln's look of distress so excited his sympathy he warmly shook his hand, and from that day became Lincoln's good friend. See *True Story of a Great Life*, Vol. III, p. 430.

Nicolay and Hay, of Lincoln's marriage to Miss Todd, say:

> This episode shows the almost abnormal development of conscience in Mr. Lincoln, who was ready to enter a marriage which he dreaded because he thought he had given the lady reason to think he had intended marriage. We can but wonder at the nobleness of the character to which it was possible.

Holland and other apotheosizing writers make no denial of the story. They simply tell of Lincoln's marriage in 1842. Hapgood calls Lincoln's marriage to Miss Todd "a mysterious marriage." There was no mystery; the facts are plain enough. But if Lincoln did not wish to marry Miss Todd, why did he not break it off in a less painful way?

CHAPTER TWELVE

Mr. Lincoln's Passion for Indecent Stories. Mr. Holland on This Habit. Lincoln "the Foulest in Stories of Any Other Man." Gov. Andrews' Disgust. Lincoln Writes Indecent Things. He Dislikes Ladies' Society.

Mr. Lincoln's passion for indecent stories would be passed over in silence were it not for the fact that Republican writers and politicians persist in proclaiming to the youth of this country that Mr. Lincoln is the man whose character they should emulate and revere: that he was the purest and the noblest man that ever lived; that he was a "servant and follower of Christ," "a pure Christian." Only a short while ago a speaker said: "Abraham Lincoln was the first of all men who have walked the earth since the Nazarene." Another speaker recently told his hearers that "They should give up all hope of heaven if Lincoln was excluded." Are these men insincere or ignorant? If sincere, they commit a great wrong by indorsing, as they do, a man the youth of this country should not be taught to revere or emulate.

In Charles L.C. Minor's *Real Lincoln*, published in 1901, is this:

> A mistaken estimate of Abraham Lincoln has been spread far and wide. Even in the South an editorial in a very respectable religious paper lately said as follows: "Our country has more than once been singularly fortunate in the moral character and admirable personality of its popular heroes. Washington, Lincoln and Lee have been the type of characters that it is safe to hold up to the admiration of their own

age and to the imitation of succeeding generations."

If this Southern editor had known the real character of Lincoln he would have put his pen and paper in the fire before giving such bad advice to Southern boys. In 1866 Mr. Holland wrote his *Life of Lincoln* under the full glare of the apotheosis ceremony. Although presenting Mr. Lincoln to the public, closely resembling the effigy the apotheosizers had made, still Mr. Holland did not go so far as to deny all the facts he would have been glad to conceal. The whole country was full of Mr. Lincoln's "indecent yarns," which many persons then living had heard him retail. Mr. Holland did not dare to deny the facts, or to remain silent on the subject. He says:

> It is useless for Mr. Lincoln's biographers to ignore this habit. The whole West, if not the whole country, is full of these stories, and there is no doubt at all that he indulged in them. Men who knew Mr. Lincoln throughout all his professional and political life have said that "he was the foulest in his jests and stories of any man in the country."

F.B. Carpenter, the artist who painted Lincoln's portrait, did not venture to deny the obscene stories, but was vexed at Holland for mentioning them. "I regret," wrote the amiable artist, desiring to maintain the theory of Lincoln's deification, "that Dr. Holland has thought it worth while to notice the stories going about of Mr. Lincoln's habitual indulgence in telling objectionable stories."

Holland attempts to excuse Mr. Lincoln's passion for vulgar yarns on the ground that "Mr. Lincoln's experience and connection with lawyers necessarily induced familiarity with the foulest phases of human life." Lawyers will be no little astonished to hear that the legal profession "necessarily befouls" the minds of its practitioners. Coming of a family of lawyers, and from a long and wide acquaintance with members of the bar, the present writer denies Mr. Holland's assertion that the "practice of law and association with lawyers have a tendency to lead the mind to obscenity." Lawyers will compare favorably with the medical profession; indeed, with any of the learned professions, hardly excepting the clerical.

Herndon says: "Lincoln could never realize the impropriety of telling vulgar yarns in the presence of a minister of the gospel." Will a gentleman tell vulgar yarns in anybody's presence? Rhodes, page 471, relates the following:

> A leading member of one of the greatest religious organizations (June 20th, 1864), which had been passing resolutions and sending deputations to the White House, and was entrusted with the speech-making part of the business, publicly described the demeanor of Mr. Lincoln on that occasion as follows: "Lincoln is a buffoon, a gawk; he is disgracefully unfit for the high office to which he again aspires. I departed from the East Room with a sickening sensation of the helplessness of our cause."

Lamon says: "Mr. Lincoln's habit of relating vulgar yarns (not one of which will bear printing) was restrained by no presence and no occasion." General Don Piatt writes of having heard Lincoln relate stories "not one of which could appear in print." In Vol. IV, p. 518, of Rhodes' *History of the United States*, is this: "Governor Andrew of Massachusetts, in an interview with President Lincoln on a matter he had at heart, was put off by Lincoln telling a smutty story, turning the Governor's subject into ridicule. Governor Andrew was filled with disgust."

Herndon says: "Lincoln's highest delight was to get a rowdy crowd in groceries (dram-shops) or on street corners and retail vulgar yarns too coarse to put in print." On page 63 of Lamon's *Life of Lincoln* we have this:

> Abe wrote many satires which are only remembered in fragments, but if we had them in full they were too indecent for publication; such, at least, is the character of a piece touching a church trial wherein Brother Harper and Sister Gordon were parties seeking judgment. It was very coarse, but it served to raise a laugh in the groceries at the expense of the church.

Do the Christian parents of this country want their boys taught to imitate a man who sought to "raise laughter in dramshops at the expense of the churches?"

Mr. A.Y. Ellis, friend of Mr. Lincoln, says: "On electioneering trips Mr. Lincoln told stories which drew the boys after him. I remember them, but modesty forbids me to repeat them." Dennis Hanks, Lincoln's cousin, said: "Abe had a great passion for vulgar yarns."

On p. 478, Lamon's *Life of Lincoln*, is this:

> Telling and hearing ridiculous stories was one of Lincoln's ruling passions. He would go a long way out of his road to tell a grave, sedate man a broad story or propound to him a conundrum not remarkable for delicacy. If he happened to hear of a man who was known to have something "fresh" in this line, he would hunt him up and swap jokes with him. This was so in Indiana, in New Salem, in the Black Hawk war, on the circuit, on the stump, everywhere. When court adjourned from village to village, the taverns, the groceries left behind, were filled with the sorry echoes of "Abe's Best." Men carried home with them select budgets of his stories, to be related to itching ears as "Old Abe's Last."
>
> His humor was not of a delicate quality; it was chiefly exercised in telling and hearing stories of the grossest sort. He was restrained by no presence and no occasion. He seemed to make boon companions of the coarsest men, of low, vulgar creatures; he enjoyed them, extracted from them whatever service they were capable of, then discarded and forgot them; he used them as tools to feed his desires. If one of them, presuming on the past, followed him to Washington, Mr. Lincoln would take him to his private office, lock the door, revel in reminiscences, new stories and old, an entire evening, and then dismiss him.

I know of no more repulsive characteristics than the above portray. I know of nothing more contemptible than for a man to go out of his way to "find fresh indecency;" out of his way to hunt up and "swap indecency" with some other obscene creature. That a man occupying the highest office in America, a husband and father, should find his chief delight in hearing and relating to "itching ears" vulgar stories; that he should take his indecent visitors into a private room of the White House, lock the door and "revel an entire evening in obscene reminiscences of old and new stories," is something for all America to be ashamed of. Yet this foul-minded and foul-mouthed man is held up by Republicans as a model for American boys to revere and emulate. While writing Lincoln's *Life*, Herndon inquired of his cousin, Dennis

CONCERNING THE WAR ON THE SOUTH 97

Hanks, what songs Lincoln most liked when he was a young man. Dennis replied: "Religious songs did not suit him at all. One of his favorite songs began: 'Hail Columbia, happy land! If you ain't drunk I'll be damned.'" This song, Mr. Hanks modestly said, "should only be warbled in the fields."

Another favorite of Abe's began: "There was a Romish lady brought up in Popery." "Other little songs I won't say anything about; they would not look well in print," said Mr. Hanks.

Lamon says:

> Abe was much in demand in hog-killing time; he butchered hogs for the neighbors around for thirty-one cents a day. There was only one man in the neighborhood whom Abe strongly disliked, and that was Joshua Crawford. Crawford made him pay for a book he had lent him which Abe had left where it was rained on and ruined. As Abe had no money, Crawford made him pull fodder for three days. This so angered Lincoln he determined on revenge. He wrote satires on Crawford's nose, which was deformed, being very big and bumpy at the end. This caused Crawford much mortification, grief and anguish of spirit. The Chronicles were written by Lincoln to bring the churches into ridicule. They were gotten up in Scriptural style. Sister Gordon and Brother Harper, and Crawford's nose, were served up fresh and gross for the amusement of the grocery boys. A well-to-do man named Grigsby failed to invite Lincoln to the feast and dance he gave in honor of the marriage of his two sons. This made Abe very mad; in revenge he wrote the "Chronicle of Reuben." It was very venomous in spirit. Mrs. Crawford attempted to repeat the verses in these Chronicles to Mr. Herndon, but soon stopped, turned red and said she could not; they were too indecent. These verses were written out by Mrs. Crawford's son-in-law and sent to Herndon, but though much curtailed by Mrs. Crawford's modesty, it is still impossible to transcribe them.

In *The Story of a Great Life*, p. 534, Mr. Weik makes quite an original comment on Mr. Lincoln's passion for obscenity. "Almost any man," says Weik, "that will tell a vulgar story has, in a degree, a vulgar mind. It was not so with Mr. Lincoln." Can a spring which continually pours out muddy water be itself clear? Can a mind which continually pours out foulness not itself be foul? Mr. Weik adds to his comment the sage reflection that Mr. Lincoln had no ability to discern or note the difference between the vulgar and the refined. The whiskey drinker knows the difference between whiskey and water, but he craves whiskey and turns from water as insipid.

Mr. Lincoln's passion for indecent stories never left him; it was born with him, it never weakened, never died until it died with him that fatal night in Ford's Theater. In his boyhood it was eager, curious; in his manhood bold, audacious. It made itself a factor to further his political desires; it pandered to the low, animal instincts of the rowdy class; it fed itself fat on their applause. It traveled with him on his electioneering trips over the State, drawing crowds of the base-minded around him, whose hilarity at its antics delighted Lincoln's heart. Wherever he went a trail of foulness was left in his wake; the village taverns, the village groceries were full of the foul odors from his soul. He carried it with him to Washington City; it entered the White House, it abode with him there for four years. It was his pet; he kept it warm in his bosom, he fondled it, he cuddled it. He carried it with him to Cabinet meetings; he let it loose on the Cabinet Ministers, who roared with laughter at its caperings (Chase excepted). A few days after the dreadful battle of Antietam, while all America, North and South, were mourning over the slaughtered braves, with *it* in his bosom, and Lamon by his side, President Lincoln drove out to survey the fatal field. Not even *there* in the presence of the sad-hearted commanding General, *there* amid so many fresh-made graves, did it remain quiescent. Bold, shameless, grotesquely gleesome, out it jumped from its warm nest in Lincoln's bosom, and to the horror of the Commanding General, in whose ears still reverberated the cannon's roar, still sounded the groans and moans of the wounded, the dying, it called for comic songs, and Lamon, who never failed to dance to Lincoln's piping, sang the songs.

And this is the man American youths are continually told they should revere and emulate! The story of the comic singing on Antietam's battlefield will be given in the next chapter.

CHAPTER THIRTEEN

Lincoln and Lamon Visit Antietam Battlefield. Lincoln Calls for a Comic Song. Lamon Sings Picayune Butler. General McClellan Shocked. The Perkins Letter. Mr. Lincoln's Reply.

In 1862 a damaging story appeared in the newspapers which caused much talk. From that time until Lincoln's death, in 1865, newspapers continued to relate the story, and to challenge denial, but denial was never made until long after Mr. Lincoln's death. The Sussex (N.J.) *Statesman* told the story in 1862, as follows:

Lincoln on the Battlefield.

We see that in any papers are referring to the fact that Lincoln ordered a comic song to be sung upon the battlefield. We have known the facts of the transaction for some time, but have refrained from speaking about them. As the newspapers are stating some of the facts, we will give the whole.

Soon after one of the most desperate and sanguinary battles, Mr. Lincoln visited the Commanding General, who, with his staff, took him over the field, and explained to him the plan of the battle, and the particular places where the battle was most fierce. At one point the Commanding General said: "Here on this side of the road five hundred of our brave fellows were killed, and just on the other side of the road four hundred and fifty more were killed, and right on the other side of that wall five hundred rebels were destroyed. We have buried them where they fell."

"I declare," said the President, "this is getting gloomy; let us drive away."

After driving a few rods the President said: "Jack," speaking to his companion, "can't you give us something to cheer us up? Give us a song, a lively one."

Whereupon, Jack struck up, as loud as he could bawl, a comic negro song, which he continued to sing while they were riding off from the battle ground, and until they approached a regiment drawn up, when the Commanding General said: "Would it not be well for your friend to cease his song till we pass this regiment? The poor fellows have lost more than half their number. They are feeling very badly, and I should be afraid of the effect it would have on them."

The President asked his friend to stop singing until they passed the regiment.

When this story was told to us we said, "It is incredible, it is impossible, that any man could act so over the fresh-made graves of the heroic dead." But the story is told on such authority we know it to be true. We tell the story now that the people may have some idea of the man elected to be President of the United States.

The *Statesman's* story is rather guarded. It does not give the name of the battlefield, of the Commanding General, or of the personal friend with Mr. Lincoln, who sang the comic song. Other papers made no reservation. Lamon was the friend who sang the song. General McClellan was the Commanding officer. Antietam the battlefield. Lamon wrote *The Life of Lincoln* in 1872, but makes no reference to this story. In Lamon's papers, published by his daughter, 1895, the story is told thus: "The story," said Lamon, "was blown about into a revolting and deplorable scandal on Mr. Lincoln, who was painted as the prime mover in a scene of fiendish levity more atrocious than the world has ever witnessed."

Lamon further states that he and Mr. Lincoln both smarted under the defamation; that he (Lamon) was anxious to silence it by denial, but Lincoln would not permit him to make a denial.
Lincoln said to Lamon: "Let the thing alone. In politics every man must skin his own skunk. These fellows are welcome to the hide of this one. Its body has already given out its unsavory odor."

General Piatt refers to the comic song story in his book, published in 1887, as if it were true, and believed to be true by the public. In 1895, after all the parties concerned were dead, Lamon's daughter, Dorothy, published a book she called *Lamon's Recollections of Lincoln*, in which is given the following account, taken from Mr. Lamon's papers:

> The newspapers and the stump speakers went on stuffing the ears of men with reports of what was known as the "Antietam Song-Singing" until the fall of 1864, when I showed to Mr. Lincoln a letter, of which the following is a copy. It is a fair example of hundreds of letters received about that time. The Antietam incident was then being discussed with increased virulence.
>
> The following is Mr. Perkins' letter to Mr. Lamon:
>
> Philadelphia, September 10.
>
> Ward H. Lamon:
>
> Dear Sir – Enclosed is an extract from the New York *World* of September 9th, 1864, entitled, *"One of Mr. Lincoln's Jokes."*
> "A few days after the battle of Antietam, while President Lincoln was driving over the field in an ambulance, accompanied by Marshal Lamon, General McClellan and another officer, heavy details of men were engaged in the task of burying the dead. The ambulance had just reached the neighborhood of the old stone bridge, where the dead were piled highest, when Mr. Lincoln, suddenly slapping Marshal Lamon on the knee, exclaimed: 'Come, Lamon! Give us that song about Picayune Butler; McClellan has never heard it' 'Not now, if you please,' said McClellan with a shudder. 'I would prefer hearing it at some other place and time.'
> "This story had been repeated in the New York *World* almost daily for the last three months. Until now it would have been useless to demand the authority. Now we have Marshal Lamon, General McClellan and another officer. The story is damaging to Mr. Lincoln, and is believed by many,

as is very evident from the doggerel verses accompanying the story, of which the following is a sample:

> "Abe may crack his jolly jokes
> Over bloody fields of battle,
> While yet the ebbing life tide smokes
> From men who die like butchered cattle,
> And even before the guns grow cold
> To pimps and pets Abe cracks his jokes."

I wish to ask you, sir, in behalf of others, as well as myself, whether any such occurrence took place? If it did not take place, please state who that other officer was, if there was any such in the ambulance in which President Lincoln was driving over the field of Antietam, while details of men were engaged in the task of burying the dead. You will confer a great favor by an immediate reply.

Most respectfully, your obedient servant,
A. J. Perkins.

Lamon states that he submitted the Perkins letter to Mr. Lincoln, and with it his own draft of a reply to Perkins. Lincoln read them both carefully, shook his head, and said: "No, Lamon; your reply won't do. Let me try my hand at it."

"Then," continues Lamon, "Mr. Lincoln sat down and wrote slowly, and with great deliberation and care, a letter, to be copied by me and sent to Mr. Perkins as my letter."

If the comic song story was false, why was it not tersely and shortly denied? Why did the Perkins letter require Mr. Lincoln to write that denial with "great deliberation, slowly and carefully?" Mr. Lamon's daughter gives the whole of Mr. Lincoln's letter to Mr. Perkins, which he wrote in the name of Lamon.

"The President," wrote Mr. Lincoln, "has known me intimately for nearly twenty years, and has often heard me singing little ditties."

Was this relevant? Was this even akin to denial? The letter then proceeds to give a minute account of their departure from Washington City, of meeting General McClellan coming from his headquarters near the battle ground, of reviewing the troops at Bolivar Heights, in company with McClellan, in the afternoon, of going with General Sumner next morning and reviewing the troops at Loudon Heights, of reviewing the troops at Maryland Heights, then at noon starting off to General McClellan's headquarters, of getting there only a little time before night, of next morning starting off to review Antietam battlefield. Was this minute detail of Lincoln and Lamon's movements during the two days previous to the comic song episode in the least necessary? Was it in the least pertinent to a denial?

If Mr. Lincoln had an honest denial to make, would he not have made it in a dozen or a half dozen words? "The story is false" (if it were false), would naturally have been the way to deny it. But even after arriving at Antietam, Lincoln made no direct denial. He continued to whip the devil around the stump.

> After getting through with General Burnsides' corps [wrote President Lincoln *for* Mr. Lamon] at the suggestion of General McClellan, he and the President left their horses to be led and went into an ambulance or ambulances to go to General Fitz Porter's corps. I am not certain whether the President and General McClellan were in the same ambulance or in different ones, but myself (Lamon) and some others were in the same with the President. On the way, in no part of the battle ground, and on whose suggestion I do not remember, the President asked me to sing the little sad song he had often heard me sing. After it was over some one of the party, I do not think it was the President, asked me to sing something else. I sang two or three little comic songs, of which "Picayune Butler" was one.

Is this a denial? Can any one believe that General McClellan or the officer with him in the Lincoln ambulance called for a comic song? Lamon had so long been in the habit of catering to the President's humor for comic songs, neither he nor Lincoln could realize how such songs would affect others, especially how they would harrow the feelings of army officers just through the awful ordeal of a bloody battle.

Even after this attempted denial Mr. Lincoln continued his minute descriptions of what he and Lamon did. "The battle ground was passed," wrote Lincoln, "the most noted parts examined." Then Mr. Lincoln gives a detailed account of what he, Lamon and General McClellan did the day after the comic song-singing incident. Was this to confuse the reader's mind, to divert attention from the main point, which was denial of comic song-singing? The conclusion of Mr. Lincoln's letter is peculiar: "Neither McClellan nor any one else made any objections to the singing. The place was not on the battlefield, the time was sixteen days after the battle. No dead bodies were seen, nor even a grave that had not been rained on since it had been made."

Was it likely that any army officer would run the risk of offending the President, who had the power of promoting or pulling down officers? Yet, though slowly and carefully as Mr. Lincoln had written the letter intended to be sent to Mr. Perkins, it was never sent. Why? Was it because Lincoln, shrewd lawyer that he was, saw his so-called denial would not hold water?

Lamon says Mr. Lincoln, not satisfied with his own attempt at denial, gave the letter to him to lay away for future use, but forbade any denial at that time. Was this because the two officers who were in the ambulance with Lincoln were still living and could have contradicted misstatements? No denial was made during the lifetime of any of the parties concerned. No denial was made until 1895, when Miss Dorothy Lamon published the story from her deceased father's papers. After having related the comic song story, Lamon's next page descants on Mr. Lincoln's extreme fondness for negro comic songs, "Picayune Butler" being his prime favorite. "The Blue-Tailed Fly" was a great favorite. "A comic song," says Mr. Lamon, "sung at a theater, always restored Mr. Lincoln to cheerful humor." To sing these songs seems to have been part of Lamon's duty to the President. Had Lincoln been a King, and had he and Lamon lived in ancient times, Lamon would have held the position of the King's Jester.

CHAPTER FOURTEEN

The True and the False. Apotheosizing Writers.
Miss Tarbell Takes the Lead. Why Thomas Lincoln Left Kentucky.
Apotheosizing Twaddle. Mr. Lincoln and Two Little Girls.

It is curious to compare some of what Lamon called the "pretended biographies" of Lincoln with the true story told by men who knew Lincoln and painted him just as he was in life, faults and all. In the smallest thing the "pretended biographies" misrepresent and misstate. Instance the following from Miss Tarbell's *Life of Lincoln*: "If Mr. Lincoln was not strictly orthodox, he was profoundly religious. He was a regular and reverent attendant at church." And this: "Lincoln never for a moment courted personal ambition before the cause of negro freedom."

Lincoln's own words convict him of utter indifference to the cause of negro freedom. This from Tarbell (Vol. I, p. 220):

> So great an evil did Thomas Lincoln and Nancy Hanks Lincoln (Lincoln's parents) hold slavery, to escape it they left their home in Kentucky and moved to a free state. Thus their boy Abe's first notion of slavery was that it was some dreadful thing to flee from, a thing so dreadful that it was one's duty to go to pain and hardship to escape it.

Holland and other apotheosizing biographers tell about the same story on this subject. The falsity of this is proved by Herndon, Lamon and Mr. Dennis Hanks, Lincoln's cousin. Lamon refutes the story thus:

It has pleased some of Mr. Lincoln's biographers to represent that Lincoln's father's move from Kentucky was a flight from the taint of slavery. Nothing could be farther from the truth. There was not at that time more than fifty negroes in all Harden County, which then composed a vast area of territory. It was practically a free community. There is not the slightest evidence that Lincoln's father ever disclosed any conscientious scruples concerning slavery. Abraham Lincoln's father got into trouble with a man named Enslow. They fought like savages. Lincoln bit off Enslow's nose. This affray and the talk it made was the cause of Thomas Lincoln's escape from Kentucky (See Lamon's *Life of Lincoln*, p. 916).

Lies are hard to kill. Notwithstanding the most positive evidence on this subject, the pretended biographers continue to tell falsehoods about Lincoln's hatred of slavery and his great piety.

Although General Piatt at first opposed the deification of President Lincoln, and disliked the "pious lies," still as the years went by and the "pious lies" continued with an ever-increasing "piety," they got in their work on Piatt's mind, despite his personal knowledge of how little they comported with the dead President's character. In 1887 Piatt wrote as follows: "It is strange now to know that during President Lincoln's life, and for years after his death, he was popularly regarded as a shrewd, cunning sort of man."

There was nothing strange in it. Lincoln was a shrewd, cunning sort of man, and the people knew it. During Lincoln's life, and for years after his death, Piatt well knew that Lincoln was a "shrewd, cunning sort of man." Every one who well knew Lincoln knew that Seward had judged correctly when he said Lincoln had a cunning which was genius. It was admitted by his friends that he was the shrewdest politician of his age. "But," continues Piatt, "the public mind will slowly come to dwell entranced on that grand central figure – Abraham Lincoln."

Entranced? Yes: not with the real Lincoln, but with the deified man the public is taught to think was the Lincoln of the '60s. Piatt himself had drawn Lincoln's pen portrait *before* the deified theory had entranced his faculties:

> I saw a man of coarse, rough fibre, without culture.

His views of human nature were low, but good-natured. This low estimate of humanity blinded him to the South. He could not believe that men would fight for an idea. Lincoln considered the Southern movement a game of political bluff. "The men of the South," he said, "won't give up the offices. Were it believed that vacant places could be had at the North Pole, the road there would be lined with dead Virginians."

Had this man been born of the blood and blackness of the Hottentot race, had he grown up in the jungles of Africa, he could not have known less of the nature of Virginia's sons. Did he ever come to see his mistake? Did he ever come to realize how men will fight for the idea of independence? When Robert E. Lee refused to accept high rank in the Union Army because he would not, could not, fight his own people, but was willing to fight and die in their defense, did Mr. Lincoln realize that at least one Virginian valued ideas and principles more than office? In Herndon's suppressed *Life of Lincoln* we are told that from early youth Lincoln's whole and sole ambition was to gain office. Politics was Lincoln's trade, office his aim. Did Lincoln look into his own soul and measure Virginians thereby?

On p. 237 of Lamon's *Life of Lincoln* is this:

> Mr. Lincoln was never agitated by any passion more intense than his wonderful thirst for distinction; distinction was the feverish dream of his youth. Thirst for distinction governed all his conduct up to the day the assassin ended his life. Mr. Lincoln struggled incessantly for place.

In Weik's *Story of a Great Life* he says: "Mr. Lincoln's restless ambition found its gratification only in the field of politics."

Piatt gives a pen portrait of Mr. Lincoln's face and form:

> Mr. Lincoln was the homeliest man I ever saw. His body seemed one huge skeleton in clothes. Tall as he was (six feet four inches), his hands and feet looked out of proportion, so long and clumsy were they. Every movement was awkward in the extreme. He had a face which defied the artist's skill to soften or idealize. It was capable of but few expressions. When in repose his face was dull and repellant. It brightened like a lit lantern when animated. I discovered that he was a skeptic.

Being a zealous abolitionist, Piatt sounded Mr. Lincoln on the question of slavery. Piatt says: "I soon discovered that Mr. Lincoln could no more feel sympathy for the wretched slaves than he could for the horse he worked or the hog he killed."

Trying to explain Mr. Lincoln's want of feeling for negroes, Piatt continued:

> Descended from the poor whites of the South, he inherited the contempt, if not the hatred, held by that class for the negro race. It is the popular belief that Mr. Lincoln was of so kind a nature his generous impulse often interfered with his duty. To prove this, attention is called to the fact that he never permitted a man to be shot for desertion or sleeping at his post. This belief is erroneous. I doubt whether Mr. Lincoln had at all a kind, forgiving nature. There was far more policy than kind feeling which made him refuse to sanction the death penalty for desertion. It pleased Mr. Lincoln to be the source of mercy as well as the fountain of honor.

Piatt's study of Lincoln's character led him to believe he was incapable of feeling pity for the suffering of others. Piatt also believed that God had created Lincoln callous of feeling to save him (Lincoln) from the pain of pity on witnessing the soldiers' sufferings. Lincoln told General Schenck that the sufferings he witnessed never interfered with his comfort. "I eat my rations three times a day," said Lincoln, "and sleep the sleep of the innocent." And this despite the horrors around him.

In her life of Lincoln, Miss Tarbell describes the sights of Washington City, which Mr. Lincoln could not avoid looking upon:

> After battles for days and days long, straggling trains of mutilated men poured into the city on flat cars, piled so close together that no attendant could pass between the wounded men. Occasionally these wretched men were protected from the cold by blankets, which had escaped with its owner, or from the sun by boughs put in their hands, to be held over their faces on reaching Washington. These suffering men were laid in long rows on the wharf or platform waiting until the ambulance carried them to hospitals. When one considers the wounded in the great Virginia battles he will realize

the length and awfulness of the streams of bleeding, suffering men which flowed into Washington City. At Fredericksburg they numbered 9,600, at Chancellorsville 9,762, in the Wilderness 12,070, at Spottsylvania 13,406. After the battle of Bull Run, churches, dwellings and government buildings were seized to put the wounded in. The hospitals could not begin to hold them.

By the end of 1862 Mr. Lincoln could hardly walk or drive in his carriage in any direction without passing a hospital full of the maimed, the dying. Even in going to his summer cottage he could not escape the sight of the wounded. The hillsides were dotted with tents during the entire war. Tents were close to the roadside, so as to get more fresh air. Mr. Lincoln frequently looked from his carriage window on the very beds of the wounded soldiers.

"The very beds." What does this mean, if not that Miss Tarbell's pity goes out not to the poor, mutilated, wounded, dying men in the tents, but to the high functionary who "could hardly walk or drive in his carriage in any direction without seeing suffering soldiers?"

"When Mr. Lincoln," continues Miss Tarbell, "visited these wretched sufferers, he freely shook hands with them, for which they were profoundly grateful." *"Freely?"* And why *"profoundly grateful?"* If gratitude was due from one side or the other, surely these maimed and bleeding men should have received it from the President who invited, or forced, them into the ranks to fight. They suffered while obeying *his* command.

Miss Tarbell puts on record other equally important acts of Mr. Lincoln. Instance the following:

> On one occasion two little girls, shabbily dressed, strayed into the White House. While gazing about, scared, President Lincoln happened to see them, and said: "Little girls, are you going to pass me without shaking hands?" Then he shook each child by the hand. Everybody was spellbound.

Can any man or woman in America see any good reason why "everybody" or anybody should be spellbound because an American President shook two little girls by the hand? Does Miss Tarbell look on all American Presidents as so high above common mortals that common mortals are "profoundly grateful" for a shake of their hands, whether "freely" made or otherwise? Does Miss Tarbell feel this way about every President, or is the above only the usual apotheosis twaddle Republican writers indulge in about Mr. Lincoln?

On the wall of one of the splendid art galleries in the palace of Versailles hangs a large painting representing a street scene in Paris. The central figure is a portrait of a Bourbon King. He stands amid a group of little beggar children, one royal hand on the top of a little beggar girl's head; the other is scattering coins among the children. In the background stands the King's attendants. If anybody was "spellbound" because a King patted the head of a little beggar girl on the street, no French historian has recorded the fact.

In the study of Mr. Lincoln's character I find traits which no biographer has seemed to see. When Lincoln was only one of the common people, only a plain, poor man, his speeches and letters indicate a liberty-loving nature. After he became what his worshipers fondly term a "great ruler," his every act and some of his writings betray the spirit of autocracy as strong as any Caesar ever felt. A few instances will illustrate. In 1854, 16th of October, in a speech delivered in Peoria. Illinois, Lincoln said: "No man is good enough to govern any other man without his consent." This is good Democratic doctrine. On hearing these words fall from Lincoln's lips in 1854, who would have thought it possible that within six short years from that time Lincoln would make himself the absolute master, not of one man alone, but of millions? In 1859 Lincoln still seemed to think and feel as a liberty-loving man. In that year a Boston committee invited Mr. Lincoln to speak at the celebration of Thomas Jefferson's birthday. Unable to accept, Lincoln wrote to the committee as follows:

> It is no child's play to save the principles of Jefferson from overthrow in this Nation. Some call these principles "dashing generalities," others "self-evident lies;" expressions which tend to the supplanting of the principles of freedom. All honor to Jefferson, to the man who, in the concrete pressure of a struggle for independence, had the courage to forecast and the capacity to introduce into a merely revolutionary document, an abstract truth applicable to all men all times, and so embalm it that in all coming days it shall be a stumbling block to the harbingers of a reappearing tyranny and

oppression.
                              Abraham Lincoln.

   This has the true ring of freedom. Alas! Alas! How soon did Lincoln lose sight of Jefferson's grand truths. How soon did he trample them out of sight deep down in the bloody mire of a hundred battlefields. I beg the reader to hold the above letter in mind, that he may compare it with one Mr. Lincoln wrote four years later (1863), after he had made himself the absolute master of all the millions in the Northern States, and was hard at work to subjugate the millions in the South. Had the one letter been written by Thomas Jefferson himself, and the other by the Czar of Russia or the Sultan of Turkey, the spirit, the tone, the words, the meaning of the two could be no more widely opposed. The one is as Democratic as the other is despotic. (*See Lincoln's letter in reply to committee requesting the liberation of Vallandingham, quoted in the second part of this volume.*)
   In a speech at Springfield, Illinois, June 26th, 1857, Lincoln quoted liberally from the Declaration of Independence, and laid great emphasis on the immortal words:

   "Governments derive their just powers from the consent of the governed." The author of the Declaration of Independence meant it to be as, thank God, it is now proving itself to be, a stumbling block to all those who in after times might seek to turn a free people back to the hateful paths of despotism. They know the proneness of prosperity to breed tyrants, and they meant, when such should appear in this fair land, for them at least to find one hard nut to crack.

   Lincoln never attempted to crack that nut; he simply ignored it until he was Commander-in-Chief of over 2,000,000 armed men and felt himself the absolute ruler of the unarmed millions of the North; then he boldly kicked that nut out of his way, and turned a free people back to the hateful paths of despotism. Those who believe in the possibilities of human foresight may easily fancy Mr. Lincoln at times possessed that occult power.
   In 1837, when Lincoln was 28 years old, he delivered a lecture in Springfield which seemed to foreshadow the part he himself was destined to play in the awful drama of the '60s. The title of this lecture was "The Perpetuation of Our Free Institutions." Lincoln began by

talking of the danger that was approaching the people of this country and the direction whence it would come:

> At what point shall we expect the approach of this danger? Shall we expect some trans-Atlantic military giant to step across the ocean and crush us at a blow? Never! All the armies of Europe, Asia and Africa, combined, with a Bonaparte for a commander, could not by force take a drink from the Ohio or make a track on the Blue Ridge in a thousand years. The danger will not come from abroad. If destruction be our lot, we ourselves must be its author and its finisher. As a nation of free men, we must live through all time, or die by suicide.

Lincoln then expressed the belief that the danger would come from the demoralization of the American people:

> That will be the time when the usurper will put down his heel on the neck of the people, and batter down the fair fabric of free institutions. Many great and good men may be found whose ambition aspires no higher than a seat in Congress, or a Presidential chair, but such belong not to the family of the Lion, or the tribe of the Eagle.
>
> What! Think you such places would satisfy an Alexander? a Caesar? or a Napoleon? Never! Towering ambition disdains a beaten path. It seeks regions unexplored. It sees no grandeur in adding story to story upon the monuments already erected to the memory of others. It scorns to tread in the footsteps of any predecessor, however illustrious. It thirsts, it *burns,* for distinction, and, if possible, it *will* have it, whether at the expense of *emancipating slaves or enslaving free men.*

When we remember Herndon's and Lamon's testimony that Lincoln's "thirst for distinction" was the master passion of his life, that his youth and manhood were spent in the restless and eager pursuit of office, of power, of place, the above words possess a strange, if not prophetic, significance. Did *Lincoln feel or fancy himself of the Lion family? Or of the Eagle tribe?* Did his "towering ambition" disdain to walk in the path trodden by the feet of preceding Presidents? Did he see no distinction in adding "story on story upon a monument already erected to others?" Did *he* "scorn to walk in the footsteps of any predecessor?" Was it "burning thirst for distinction above all other American Presidents" which made Lincoln "rush on carnage," enslave 5,000,000 of his own race, color and blood, and set free 4,000,000 of an alien race, a different color, blood and kin?

CHAPTER FIFTEEN

*A Brief Account of the Two Policies,
President Johnson's and That of the Republican Leaders.*

Soon after Johnson assumed the Presidency he sent General Grant, December 13, 1865, to make a trip over the Southern States to observe and report the state of the country, and especially the temper of the people. Were they disposed to keep the peace? Were there any signs of rebellion? Would they quietly return to the peaceful vocations of life? Grant made the following report to the President:

> My observations lead me to believe that the citizens of the Southern States are anxious to return to self-government within the Union as soon as possible. They are in earnest in wishing to do what is required of them by the Government, not humiliating as citizens, and will pursue such a course in good faith. There is such universal acquiescence in the authority of the general Government that the mere presence of a military force, without regard to number, is sufficient to maintain order. I am sorry to say that the freedman's mind (the negro) is not disabused of the idea (which has come from the agents of the Freedman's Bureau) that a freedman has a right to live without care or provision for the future. The effect of the belief in the division of the land is idleness and the accumulation of negroes in camps, towns and cities. Vice and disease will tend to the extermination or great reduction of the colored race. The necessity of governing any portion of our territories by martial law is to be deplored. If resorted to it should be limited in its authority, and should leave

all local authorities and civil tribunals free and unobstructed. If insurrection does come, the law provides the method of calling out the forces to suppress it.

These were the reasonably humane opinions Grant reported to President Johnson as a basis of action. These were Grant's views before the Republican leaders determined to impeach, depose, many said hang, Johnson. From this report Johnson formulated his policy, which was to permit the States of the South to re-enter the Union as equals and himself generously to exercise the pardoning power toward the conquered Confederates. The Chicago *Times*, January 26, 1868, tersely defined Johnson's policy as follows: "President Johnson is in favor of thirty-six States in the Union, instead of twenty-five. He advocates the extension of Federal rights to the whole country (including the Southern States). He prefers civil over military authority."

Republican leaders bitterly opposed this humane policy. In the March number of the *North American Review*, 1870, Wendell Phillips explains the Republican policy and why it was not carried out:

> We all see now that magnanimity went as far as it safely could when it granted the traitor his life. His land should have been taken from him and divided among the negroes, forty acres to each family. Before Andrew Johnson's treachery, every traitor would have been only too glad to have been let off with his life. Every rebel State should have been held as a territory under the direct rule of the Government, without troublesome questions. In his last years the late Vice-President, Henry Wilson, confessed to me that our party made a great mistake in not carrying out this policy. His only excuse was that the Republican party did not dare risk any other course in the face of the Democratic opposition.

In that same magazine, same year and month, James G. Blaine, of Maine, says that Republicans did not carry out that policy because it would have led to the overthrow of their party. No sense of justice or of mercy to the people of the South influenced them. While the two policies were struggling for dominance, many land owners in the South hurried off to Washington to obtain "pardons" for the crime of having done their best to defend themselves from an invading host. The elder brother of the writer of this, an officer in the Confederate army, was among the number of "pardon" seekers. Johnson received my brother in a friendly way – the two men before the war had been members of Congress and good friends. Neither man made any reference to the awful four years that lay between their parting and this meeting. My brother simply said: "Mr. President. I have come to you, an applicant for 'pardon.'" The last words must have stuck in my brother's throat, knowing as he did that of right pardons are due from the innocent to the guilty, not from the guilty to the innocent. But of this nothing was said. Without a moment's hesitation. President Johnson turned to his secretary and said: "Make out a pardon for Mr. —," and the conversation was resumed, as if no gulf of blood lay between them. With the fewest exceptions, Johnson granted every request of that nature. These pardons greatly angered Republican leaders. They had set their very souls on confiscating the land of the South, dividing it and giving forty acres to every family of negroes. A pardon was supposed to save its possessor's land from confiscation. The first attempt to impeach Johnson was based on the charge of making the "White House a den for pardon brokerage."

With one of these little pardon papers in his pocket, though his fields were laid waste, his peach-trees cut down, his cattle killed, his cotton gins, barns, stables, dwelling houses, all heaps of ashes, over which stood the chimneys "lone sentinels over the ruin;" despite all this devastation, the poor Confederate soldier returned to his despoiled home with a feeling of satisfaction in the thought that at least the ground under his feet would be a resting spot for wife and little ones to stand on, and work in, and look up from to the blue heavens above, and they thanked God for that much saved from the awful deluge of blood and the awful waves of flame that had swept over their country. My brother described the striking change he had observed in Mr. Johnson, the difference in the man since last they parted, the one to enter the camp of his people's deadliest foes, and the other to take up arms in defense of home, country, life, liberty; all that men hold dear. *Then* Mr. Johnson was a strong, vigorous man, fronting the world and fate, hopefully expecting high success in life. He was now in the highest office in the land, but his aspect, his eyes, showed no pleasure in that success. A deep depression seemed to weigh upon him; hope, happiness seemed to have fled. The whole man seemed to be weary, care-worn; yet in spite of all that might be seen the man's grim resolution to hold his own, to maintain at the risk of his life the policy he had determined to pursue. Though Johnson was on the conqueror's side and my brother on the conquered, the latter was more to be envied. He felt that satisfaction which comes from having performed a duty to the best of his ability. His soul was tortured by no remorse. He yielded to the inevitable without a murmur, realizing, as all the men of the South did that it is no new thing in the sad history of humanity for the wrong to triumph over the right. The writer of this believes that Andrew Johnson did not join hands with the Republican party for any purpose of despotic rule. He abandoned his people because he was deceived into the belief that Republicans were fighting to restore the Union of our fathers. Though a man of strong native abilities, Johnson's faculties and information were within limited boundaries. He knew but little of the Southern people beyond his own East Tennessee. In his own State. Johnson's political enemies had accused him of anarchistic tendencies, of intense hatred of the wealthy class. One orator had boldly, from the stump, said, "Andrew Johnson so hates rich men, he curses God in his heart because He had not made him a snake, that he might crawl in the grass and bite the heels of rich mens' children." One can imagine the horror that must have overwhelmed Johnson when he discovered that the party to serve which he had abandoned his own people and State, was monarchistic to its heart core, and had no intention of restoring the Union of our fathers; instead was determined to kill it, and erect on its ruins an Imperial Government. And to aid these men he had played traitor to his own State, to his own people! Who does not believe when Johnson came to know the truth, remorse, like a venomous serpent, lifted its head in his breast and fastened its fangs in his heart and gnawed and gnawed night and day. He had forever forfeited the affections of his own people, and now the men of the party he had served during the war hated him as fiercely as they hated the conquered "Rebel" lying with iron fetters on his feet in the dungeon cell of Fort Monroe. Though every day of his life a thousand curses were hurled on the name of that "Rebel" in Fortress Monroe, though iron chains and ball abraded and tortured him, though he was on the conquered side and Johnson among the conquerors, there is reason to believe that patient prisoner was a less miserable man than the man in the White House. The former felt no pangs of remorse; he well knew the more he was cursed and reviled, the tenderer and stronger would be the love of his own people. He was threatened with the death due to felons and assassins, but he knew no accusation of his enemies would abate one jot the reverence, the esteem his own people gave him. What recompense had Johnson? Where could he look for affection, for sympathy? Not one particle of pride or pleasure did Johnson derive from the high office he was in. The same Nemesis which had struck down his predecessor as he was about to take his seat for another four years on the throne of power, had upon Johnson her sleepless eyes, and, as he set his foot on the first step of Power's throne, that Nemesis touched it with her fatal finger, and lo! it became like unto red hot iron, scorching, shriveling, tormenting his very soul day and night during the whole period of his stormy term.

The portrayals of Abraham Lincoln's personal traits contained in preceding pages were made by his contemporaries, who knew him well; some of whom loved him well, all of whom now demand for him the highest honors, the deepest reverence mortal can receive. The question to be considered is, do the qualities of Mr. Lincoln, attested by men of his own party, indicate that greatness of soul, purity of heart, and unselfish devotion to principles which merit the esteem and reverence the Republican party now demands shall be awarded to him? Or do they betray a man of coarse nature, a self-seeking politician, who craved high office, more to satisfy his own burning desire for distinction than to use power for the betterment of his fellow mortals? If the first query is answered in the negative, the next question will be, on what rests the claim made for Mr. Lincoln, of greatness, grandeur, goodness? Does this claim rest on the solid rock of beneficent acts done in the days of his power, or on a foundation of sand, which the waters of Time will surely undermine and wash away?

The deeds done by Mr. Lincoln in the days of his great power will bear witness in posterity's court.

PART II

CHAPTER SIXTEEN

*Antagonistic Principles. The Great American Monarchist.
Federalists Fear and Hate Democracy. War on the South
Began 1796. The Olive Branch. The Pelham Papers.
New England Begins Work for Disunion and Secession in 1796.*

The underlying cause of every conflict between man and man, tribe and tribe, country and country, has been on the one side a craving for power, on the other side an effort to escape that power. The nascent spirit of one is Monarchy, of the other Democracy. These two principles are inherently and eternally antagonistic, and underlie nearly, if not every, war fought on earth. Stratas of superficial causes usually overlay and cover up the *real* causes of war, as they did in the war on the South.

The seven years' war which severed the seceded Colonies from British rule was an open, undisguised fight between Monarchy and Democracy. The four years' war between the Southern and Northern States was a fight between the same old enemies, Monarchy and Democracy, though the astute Republican party, while heart and soul Imperialistic, concealed and covered up that principle under loud declarations of Freedom and blatant professions of humanitarianism. Under these hypocritical cloaks, the Monarchic principles had full swing for four years, and committed every species of crime and outrage peculiar to enraged Monarchists. When the soldiers of Monarchy in 1783 took ships and sailed Eastward to their kingly country, the soldiers of Democracy fondly hoped they had driven their ancient enemy forever from this New Continent. The snake was scotched, but not killed. Nor was it banished. It remained here in our midst with veiled features and softened voice, biding its chance to up and regain its former power.

Alexander Hamilton was the head and front of American Monarchists. He wanted to make this Government a pure Monarchy. Hamilton advocated a "strong centralized Government," of imperial policy. Gouverneur Morris, a contemporary and friend of Hamilton, said: "Hamilton hated Republican Government, and never failed on every occasion to advocate the excellence of and avow his attachment to a Monarchic form of Government."

From the formation of the Union, the Federalists of New England hated and feared Democratic principles. Their great leader, Hamilton, made no secret of this feeling. In his speech at a New York banquet Hamilton, in high opposition to Jefferson's Democracy, cried out: "The People! Gentlemen, I tell you the people are a great Beast!"

In 1796 Gov. Walcott, of Connecticut, said: "I sincerely declare that I wish the Northern States would separate from the Southern the moment that event [the election of Jefferson] shall take place." Congressman Plumer, a Federalist and an ardent Secessionist, in 1804 declared that "All dissatisfied with the measures of the Government looked to a separation of the States as a remedy for grievances."

As early as 1796 men of Massachusetts began to talk of New England seceding from the Union. It was declared that if Jay's negotiation closing the Mississippi for twenty years could not be adopted, it was high time for the New England States to secede from the Union and form a Confederation by themselves. The Monarchic principles did not thrive under Hamilton's lead. Hamilton was too plain spoken. The Republican party became more astute. In 1861, while making loud professions of desiring the largest freedom for the people, that party was making ready to rob them of every liberty they possessed.

"At the formation of this Union," says E.P. Powell, "Hamilton laid before the Constitutional Convention of 1787 eleven propositions, which he wished to make the basis of the Union, but they were so Monarchistic in tone they received no support whatever."

The Republican war on the South stood solidly on Monarchic principles. The principles of 1776 were set aside in the '60s, but not for years after the South was conquered did Republicans openly admit they were inspired by the spirit of Monarchy. During McKinley's last campaign. Hamilton was loudly lauded and Jefferson decried as a visionary, a French anarchist. Hamilton Clubs were organized and Republican novelists set to writing romances with Hamilton as the hero. During

Garfield's campaign, a Republican paper, the Lemars, Iowa *Sentinel*, said:

> Garfield's rule will be the transitory period between State Sovereignty and National Sovereignty. The United States Senate will give way to a National Senate. State Constitutions and the United States Senate are relics of State Sovereignty and implements of treason. Garfield's Presidency will be the Regency of Stalwartism; after that – Rex.

Fate used the hand of an insane "Stalwart" to impede, if not estop, the Monarchic plans of that time. The New York *Sun*, July 3rd, 1881, quoted President Garfield as saying: "The influence of Jefferson's Democratic principles is rapidly waning, while the principles of Hamilton are rapidly increasing. Power has been gravitating toward the Central Government." Power did not gravitate, it was wrenched at one jerk to the Central Government by Lincoln's hand, as will be seen later on. Not until after Hamilton and Jefferson had passed away did the followers of Jefferson drop the name "Republican" which they had borne during his life, and assume the name "Democrat." Democracy – the rule of the people – is more expressive of Jefferson's doctrines. Not until 1854 did the men of the Federal and Whig persuasion unite and organize a party and take the name "Republican." The Republican party of the '60s was the legitimate offspring of the old New England Federalists, and inherited all its progenitor's faiths, hopes, hates and purposes, viz: passion for power, fear and hate of Democracy, hate of the Union, belief in States' Rights, in States' Sovereignty, in Secession, and the strong persistent determination to break the Union asunder and form of the Northeast section a Northeastern Confederacy. All these ideas belonged to the old Federalists of New England, and were handed down to the Republican party in 1854.

Wendell Phillips. New England's tongue of fire, speaking of the inherent purposes of his party, said: "The Republican party is in no sense a national party. It is a party of the North, organized against the South." The Republican party *was* organized against the South, organized to fight the South in every possible way; to fight as its progenitors, the Federalists, had fought from 1796 to 1854, with calumnies, vituperations, false charges, every word and phrase hate could use, until the time came to use guns, bayonets, bullets, cannon balls and shells;

and faithfully did that party carry out the ignoble and cruel purpose of its organization. The war on the South was begun by the Federalists of New England in 1796.

In 1814 a work of some four hundred and fifty pages, called *The Olive Branch,* was published in Boston, which throws electric light on certain almost forgotten events in New England's history. The *Olive Branch* contains extracts from a series of remarkable productions called the "Pelham Papers," which appeared in the Connecticut *Courant* in the year 1796. The *Courant* was published by Hudson and Goodwin, men of Revolutionary standing. The Pelham Papers were said to have been the joint production of men of the first talent and influence in the State. Commenting on these papers of 1796, the *Olive Branch* of 1814 says:

> A Northeastern Confederacy has been the object for a number of years. They [the politicians of New England] have repeatedly advocated in public print, separation of the States. The project of separation was formed shortly after the adoption of the Federal Constitution. The promulgation of the project first appeared in the year 1796, in these Pelham Papers. At that time there was none of that catalogue of grievances which since that period, have been fabricated to justify the recent attempt to dissolve the Union.

This refers to the efforts made in 1804 and 1814 to get the New England States to secede from the Union, so they might be separated from the Democratic Southern and Western States.

The *Olive Branch* continues:

> At that time there was no "Virginia Dynasty," no "Democratic Madness," no "war with Great Britain." The affairs of the country seemed to be precisely according to New England's fondest wishes. Yet at that favorable time (1796) New England was dissatisfied with the Union and begun to plot to get out of it. The common people, however, were not then ready to break up the Union. The common people at that time had no dislike of the Southern States.
>
> Then New England writers, preachers and politicians deliberately begun the wicked work of poisoning their minds against the Southern States. To sow hostility, discord and jealousy between the different sections of the Union was the

first step New England took to accomplish her favorite object, a separation of the States. Without this efficient instrument, all New England's efforts would have been utterly unavailing. Had the honest yeomanry of the Eastern States continued to respect and regard their Southern fellow-citizens as friends and brothers, having one common interest in the promotion of the general welfare, it would be impossible to have made them instruments in the unholy work of destroying the noble, the splendid Union.

But for the unholy work of having taught the common people of New England to hate the people of the South, the cruel war of the '60s would never have been fought. The *Olive Branch* continues:

For eighteen years [from 1796 to 1814], the most unceasing endeavors have been used to poison the minds of the people of the Eastern States toward, and to alienate them from, their fellow-citizens of the Southern States. The people of the South have been portrayed as "demons incarnate," as destitute of all the "good qualities which dignify and adorn human nature." Nothing can exceed the virulence of the pictures drawn of the South's people, their descriptions of whom would more have suited the ferocious inhabitants of New Zealand than a polished, civilized people.

The following extracts are from the Pelham Papers, published in the Hartford *Courant*, 1796:

Extract No. 1

The question must soon be decided whether we shall continue as one Nation. Many advantages were supposed to be secured and many evils avoided by a Union of States, but at that time those advantages and evils were magnified to far greater size than either would be if the question at this moment was to be settled. The Northern States can subsist as a Nation, a Republic, without any connection with the Southern. If the Southern people were possessed with the same political ideas, our Union would be more close than in separation.

Extract No. 2.

> It is a serious question whether we shall part with the States South of the Potomac. No man north of that river, whose heart is not thoroughly Democratic, can hesitate what decision to make. In a future paper I shall consider some of the great events which will lead to the separation of the United States. I will endeavor to prove the impossibility of a Union, lasting for any long period, in the future, both from the moral and political habits of the Southern States. I will carefully examine and see whether we have not already approached the era when the Union of States must be divided.

All through these extracts the reader will see it is the principle of Democracy which New England men wished to escape.

The *Olive Branch* of 1814 comments on the Pelham Papers as follows:

> It is impossible for a man of intelligence to read the Pelham Papers without feeling a decided conviction that the writers, and their friends, were determined to use all their endeavors to dissolve the Union, in order to promote their sectional views. These papers offer a complete clue to all the sectional proceedings that have occurred since that period.

From Carpenter's *Logic of History*, published in 1864, from the *Olive Branch*, published in 1814, and from the Pelham Papers, published in 1796, we learn:

1st. That the Federal leaders of New England, in 1796, advocated disunion, and were eager to get New England to secede from the Union, and to form a Northeastern Confederacy.

2nd. On finding that the common people of New England did not favor secession, did not want disunion, did not dislike the Southern States, and were proud of the Union, the Federal leaders resorted to measures to convert the masses to their views on secession and disunion.

3rd. These measures were of the meanest, the most contemptible character; were a direct and base violation of the Ninth Commandment, "Thou shalt not bear false witness." Politicians, newspapers, and preachers of New England engaged in the evil work of bearing false witness against the people of the Southern States, whom they painted as "savages." as "barbarians," as "demons incarnate," as unfit to live in the "same Union with the virtuous people of New England."

The following extracts from the *Olive Branch* throw light on this subject:

> The increasing effort to excite the public mind to that feverish state of discord, jealousy, and exasperation, which was necessary to prepare it for the consummation of their desire (the secession of the Eastern States), the unholy spirit which inspired the writers of these dissolution sentiments has been from that hour (1796 to the present [1814]) incessantly employed to excite hostility between the different sections of the Union. To such horrible length has this spirit been carried that many paragraphs have appeared in the Boston papers intended to excite the negroes of the South to rise and massacre the whites. This is a species of baseness of which the world has produced few examples.

The baseness was indeed extraordinary in face of the fact that these efforts to instigate negroes to rise and massacre the whites of the South were made while the people of New England were still enriching themselves by carrying on the slave traffic. The third extract, taken from the Pelham Papers of 1796, is astonishing.

Extract No. 3.

> If the negroes were good for food, the probability is that the power of destroying their lives would be enjoyed by their Southern owners as fully as it is over the lives of their cattle. Their laws do not prohibit their killing their slaves because those slaves are human beings, or because it is a moral evil to destroy them. Negroes are looked on only as brutes; they are fed or kept hungry, clothed or kept naked, beaten and turned out to the fury of the elements, with as little remorse as if they were beasts of the field.

The *Olive Branch* indignantly comments on these slanderous lies on the Southern people as follows:

Never were more infamous and false charges made on a people. Never more disgraceful to their authors. The turpitude of the writers is enhanced by the fact that at the period these charges were made, negro slavery existed in the New England and other Eastern States, and at that moment, and for long afterward, New England was actively engaged in the slave traffic.

The *Olive Branch* continues thus:

Some progress was made [toward teaching the common people of New England to hate the South], but the yeomanry of the Eastern States did not feel disposed to quarrel with the South for their supposed want of piety and morality. I do not assert that these contemptible charges were laid down in regular form as a thesis to argue upon, but I do aver that they form the basis of three-fourths of all the essays, paragraphs, and squibs that have appeared in the Boston papers against the Administration for many years. "The Road to Ruin," ascribed to John Lowell, is remarkable for its virulence, its acrimony, its intemperance, and the talent of the writer. But if you extract from his essays the assumption of these positions, all the rest is mere *caput mortuum*. The charges against the South are many, and in endless succession. These charges, however absurd, however extravagant they appear in their naked form, have, by dint of incessant repetition, made such an impression on the minds of a large portion of the people of the Northeastern States that they are thoroughly convinced of their truth. The Rev. Jedidiah Morse, in his geography, attempted to perpetuate these vile prejudices. Almost every page that represent his own section of the Union is highly encomiastic. Everything is covered with flattering tints. When he passes the Susquehanna, what a hideous reverse! Everything there is frightful caricature. Society is at a low ebb, the somber tints are used in order to elevate by contrast his own section, his Elysium, the New England States. He dipped his pen in gall when he portrayed the manners, habits and religion of Virginia, Maryland, the Carolinas, Georgia, or the Western country (*Logic of History*).

The children of New England who studied the old Morse geography, when grown, were ready to accept and credit the slander on the South conveyed by maps issued in New England in 1856, half white, half black; the white half intended to represent enlightened New England, the black half the barbarous States of the South.

From S.D. Carpenter's *Logic of History*, published 1864, I get the following:

> The Northeastern States early sought to create prejudice and disunion sentiment, not on account of any existing fact, but to array section against section, to stimulate hate and discord for the purpose of accelerating their darling object, the dissolution of the Union and the formation of a Northeastern Confederacy. Press, politicians and preachers were continually harping on causes which made disunion desirable. The motives which actuated New England disunionists was the desire to have what Hamilton called a strong government, understood to mean an autocracy similar to that of England, a large standing army, a heavy public debt, owned by the favored few, to whom the common masses should pay tribute, under the guise of interest. The main public offices were to be held by the rich and noble for long periods, or for life. It was argued that a national debt would be a national blessing, and prohibitive tariff, under the guise of protection, be a blessing. These were the motives which led the early Federalists to want disunion.

The reader's attention is particularly called to the fact that during all the years which the Federalists of New England were teaching the gospel of hate toward the people of the South, there was no anti-slavery sentiment mixed with that hate. On the contrary, the hate began while New England was enriching herself by the slave traffic, and while slaves were still held in New England. Not until some years after the end of the second war with Great Britain did New England mingle and mix anti-slavery sentiment with her animosity toward the people of the South. When the Democrat, Jefferson, succeeded the Federalist, Adams, and the Federalists of New England, as they put it, "saw power slipping from their grasp," their hope to effect disunion rose high. They set to work with great energy.

I charge that the gospel of hate inaugurated by New England Federalists in 1796 was the beginning of the war on the South. I charge that hate of Democracy was at the very bottom of that war; I charge that the South was hated because she was solidly Democratic. The Republican party, which, as Philips said, was organized against the South, had inherited all the Federalists' hate of Democracy, hate of the Union, hate of the South, and with great zeal and eloquence, from the hour of its organization in 1854, had preached the gospel of those three hates. Calumnies on the South were poured out in streams until all new England became infected as with a blood poison. The virulence of this hate never abated, never ceased, and finally culminated in that awful deluge of blood which overwhelmed the Southland in the '60s. Wars do not, like mushrooms, spring up in a single night. Nor do they, like rank weeds, grow strong and fully statured in a day or a week. They have their roots deep in the years of the past. The roots of the war on the South began to vitalize in the year 1796; those roots yet lie fathoms deep under New England soil; they yet live.

CHAPTER SEVENTEEN

Republicans Cover up the Real Cause of the War.
New England Secessionists. Early and Universal
Belief in the Right of Secession.

In J.C. Ridpath's history of the war between the States, he undertakes to give the cause which led to war. He says:

> The first and most general cause of the war was the different construction put upon the national Constitution by the people of the North and the South. This difference of opinion has always existed. The North held that the Union is indestructible under the Constitution; that the highest allegiance of citizens is due to the Union, not to their own State; that all attempts at disunion are treasonable. The South held that the Constitution is a compact between sovereign States, and that a State or States can withdraw from the compact they themselves made.

Although Mr. Ridpath has five letters, A.M., L.L.D., appended to his name to indicate his high standing in the world of letters, the most ignorant ploughman of the country could have made no greater mistake. At no period in the history of America before the war did any such distinct difference of opinion on this subject divide the people of the North from the people of the South. On the contrary, the student of New England's history knows that from the very formation of the Union, New England's foremost politicians were dissatisfied with it and begun to plan and plot to bring about disunion. Up to the very beginning of the war on the South, the Republican party advocated the principle of State sovereignty and the right of secession. The people of New England were the first to hate the Union, the first to desire secession, the first to strive to split the Union into two parts and to form of one part a Northeastern Confederacy composed of Northeastern States. The benefit that would result to New England from secession was openly discussed, as we have shown, as early as 1796. Colonel Timothy Pickering, an officer of the Revolutionary War, afterwards Postmaster-General and Secretary of War and Secretary of State in Washington's Cabinet, and after that a Senator for many years from Massachusetts, was a Federalist who believed strongly in the right of secession and in the advantages that would accrue to New England if she would separate herself from the Union, and thereby from legal contact with Democracy. In one of his letters Pickering talks of the "corrupt and corrupting influence of Southern Democracy," and adds: "But I will not despair: I will rather anticipate a new Confederacy, exempt from Democracy's influence. The principles of our Revolution point to the remedy – a separation; that this can be accomplished without spilling one drop of blood, I have little doubt."

Governor Walcott, of Connecticut, on this subject, said: "I sincerely declare that I wish the Northern States would separate from the Union the moment that event [the election of Jefferson] shall take place." In 1794 Fisher Ames said: "The spirit of insurrection has tainted a vast extent of country besides Pennsylvania." This referred to the spirit of disunion spreading in New England. The desire for disunion came from fear and hate of Democracy. It was declared in Massachusetts that if "Jay's negotiations closing up the Mississippi for twenty years could not be adopted it was high time for the New England States to secede from the Union."

Every few years something occurred which made New England declare it was high time for her to get out of the Union. When Louisiana Territory was purchased, and again when Louisiana was made a State, New England declared it was time for her to quit the Union. During the whole two years this country was waging its second war with Great Britain, New England preachers, newspapers, and politicians were anxious for secession, declaring it was high time New England was out of the Union, anxious for New England to make a separate treaty of peace with old England. Senator Henry Cabot Lodge, in his life of Webster, says:

It is safe to say there was no man in this country, from Washington and Hamilton on the one side to George Clinton and George Mason on the other, who regarded our system of Government, when first adopted, as anything but an experiment entered upon by the States, and from which each and every State had the right to peaceably withdraw, a right which was very likely to be exercised.

A convention in Ohio in 1859 declared the Constitution was a compact to which each State acceded as a State, and as an integral part, and that each State had the right to judge for itself of infractions and of the mode and measure of redress, and to this declaration Joshua Giddings, Wade, Chase and Dennison assented.

Later on extracts from speeches made by the foremost men in the Republican Party advocating secession, such men as Lincoln, Wade of Ohio, Philips of Massachusetts, will be given. First will be given extracts from a work by E.P. Powell, of New York, called *Nullification and Secession*, which throw light on New England's effort to secede from the Union in 1803 and 1804. Powell says:

> Of the Federal leaders in 1803, there remained in Washington, among others, Tracy, Griswald, Plumer and Pickering. These beheld with dismay and horror the dissolution of their party and their own loss of power. They found themselves out of the offices of the Nation, and Republicans [Democrats] pursuing them into their own States, depriving them of emoluments and honor. Angry, affrighted at their situations, they cried out: "The South has clearly invaded our rights. Thomas Jefferson is President."

Jeffersonian principles were the object of their fear and hate. Governor Walcott, years before, he declared that if Jefferson was elected to the Presidency he would want New England to leave the Union. Powell says:

> The people en masse were followers of Jefferson. Nothing was left of the Federal party in 1800-3-4 but a gang of hopeless, disappointed leaders. These men had been recreant to their trust. The history of the Federal party has been one of high taxation, high salaries, usurpation of power and

despotic legislation. Intrigue, corruption, tyranny, had been the triumvirate of its short rule under Adams. It rioted to its own destruction.

Will not every word of the above apply to the rule of the Republican party? Every word except those in the last line, *"It rioted to its own destruction."* Not yet has the Republican party rioted to its destruction. It still has its strong grip on the Government machinery, and still maintains itself in power and place, but the end of its rule is bound to come. It has made of this Government an imperial power. It has divided the people of America into two classes; on one side the office-holders are our rulers; millionaires are the nobility, which support the throne of power on which our rulers sit. On the other side are the laborers who toil and sweat to earn the wealth our rulers and nobility revel in. Meanwhile, monarchs of the Old World grin with delight over Democracy's downfall, and reach their hands across the ocean, jovially saying to our rulers, "Hail, brothers!"

Not only is the history of the Republican party one of high taxation, high salaries, usurpation of power, despotic legislation, but it is the history of more bloodshed, more misery, more anguish of soul than any other history of the same number of years in the Nineteenth Century. Every pen that writes that history is dipped in the blood of men slaughtered in the most unnecessary, remorseless, cruel war ever waged between two English-speaking peoples.

Finding themselves out of power and place, the Federals of 1804 set themselves actively to work on their old schemes to sever the Union in twain, for the purpose of forming a Northeastern Confederacy. Powell says: "These Federalists undertook to pull down what Washington and Jefferson had builded, that they might rule in the corner of its ruins!" The man who fancies that the secession of New England or of any State from the Union would leave it in ruins is not only ignorant of the logic of history, but is a foolish believer in the divine right of governments as against the inherent rights of the people. Whether Mr. Powell ranks himself a Democrat or an Imperialist, I know not, but I do know that when any man talks of this great American people being ruined by the withdrawal of one or of a dozen States, he talks from the imperialistic standpoint, the kingly standpoint, which made George the Stupid in 1776 fancy his empire would be ruined if the thirteen jewels from his crown were not restored. Thinkers of this sort entirely lose sight of the fact that the *"people,"* the great body of the people, is the *country*, not the mere machinery of the Government and the few men who run that machinery. The Roman Empire broke asunder, but were the *people* of Europe any the worse?

Had the New England secessionists succeeded in 1796, or in 1804, or in 1814, to get New England out of the Union, and had they formed of her States a Northeastern Confederacy, in all human probability no gulf would have been dug between the Southern and Northern States, no gulf filled with the blood and bones of slaughtered men. No Democratic President would have resorted to bloody coercion. President Madison, in 1814, was not ignorant of the secession work going on in New England during the time this country was in the throes of war with a powerful foe, but Madison took no step to punish or estop New England's secession. As a true Democrat, he knew if the people of New England chose to secede they had the right. Secession failed in 1796, because, as the secessionists themselves put it, "the common people did not feel power slipping from their grasp, as the leaders did."

Mr. Powell gives extracts, showing how the politicians and newspapers of New England worked for the secession of New England in 1803 and 1804. From *Nullification and Secession* we take the following:

Mr. Rive, of Connecticut, wrote Tracy in Congress: "I have seen many of our friends, and all I have seen, and many I have heard from, believe we must separate, and that this is the most favorable moment."

Timothy Pickering wrote: "The people of the East cannot reconcile their habits and views and interests to those of the South and West."

Ex-Governor Griswald wrote Oliver Walcott: "The project we had formed was to induce the Legislatures of the New England States which remain Federal to commence measures which would call for a reunion of the Northern States." The three States Mr. Griswald relied on were Massachusetts (then including Maine), Connecticut and New Hampshire.

Pickering wrote:

> I believe the proposition to secede will be welcomed in Connecticut, and can we doubt in New Hampshire? New York must be associated; how is her concurrence to be ob-

tained? New York must be made the center of the New Confederacy. Vermont and New Jersey will follow, of course, and Rhode Island of necessity.

George Cabot was cautious. He wrote:

> While a separation at some remote period may take place, I think separation now is impracticable. The multitude do not feel as the leaders, who saw power sliding from their grip. We shall go the way of all governments wholly popular, from bad to worse, until the evils, no longer tolerable, shall generate their own remedies.

After consulting Chief Justice Parsons, Fisher Ames, and Atkins, Cabot wrote from Boston:

> While some of the same opinion as Pickering think the time not quite ready, for myself I cannot believe essential good will come from separation while we retain the maxims and principles [Democratic] which all experience and reason pronounce to be impracticable and absurd. Even in New England, where there is more wisdom and virtue than in any other part of the United States, we are too Democratic altogether, and I hold Democracy to be the government of the worst.

"More virtue and wisdom." This is a sample of New England's self-righteousness. Griswald was in despair. He wrote Walcott that, "While we are waiting for the time to arrive in New England, it is certain that Democracy is making daily inroads on us, and our means of resistance are lessening every day. Yet it appears impossible to induce our friends to make any decisive exertions."

Democracy was always the object of New England's hate. "A Democracy," wrote Dennis' *Portfolio*, "is scarcely tolerable at any period. It is on trial here and the issue will be civil war." The war came in the '60s; Democracy on one side, and Imperialists on the other.

Fisher Ames said: "Our country is too big for Union, too sordid for patriotism, too Democratic for liberty." Cabot is credibly reported to have openly advocated a President for life, and a hereditary Senate.

February 18, 1804, Burr was nominated for the Governor's office in New York. Pickering wrote:

The Federalists anxiously desire Burr's election. If a separation of States is deemed proper for the New England States, New York and New Jersey will naturally be united. If Colonel Burr becomes Governor of New York by Federal votes, will he not be considered the head?

Griswald replied: "Such is the jealousy of Massachusetts, it will be necessary to allow her to take the lead. Her magnitude and jealousy will render it necessary that the operation begin there. The first active measures must come from Massachusetts' Legislature next summer." Hamilton wrote: "Dismemberment of our Union will give no relief to our real disease, which is Democracy, the poison of which by subdivision will only be more concentrated in each part, and the poison become more virulent."

Always Democracy.

Pickering wrote: "By supporting Mr. Burr we gain some support, though of a doubtful nature. We think Burr alone can break the Democratic phalanx." George Cabot wrote: "If delay is tolerated. Democracy will have its work of ruin accomplished."

Still harping on Democracy.

Congressman Plumer announced that a convention (in the interest of secession) would be held in the fall and that Hamilton would attend. Burr was not elected Governor of New York, and soon after, in a duel, he killed Hamilton. The planned convention fell through, the Federals lost hope of the immediate success of secession, but their work in that direction did not cease. Cabot wrote: "We must wait, If the United States can be involved in another war with Great Britain, our chance will come."

They waited for that chance, but never slackened in preaching the gospel of hate; on the contrary, the virulence of that hate, augmented as the years went by, hate of Democracy, hate of the Union, because its highest officers were Democrats, hate of the South because her people were a unit in voting for Democratic officials.

Mr. Powell says: "In all these efforts to sever the Union there was no anti-slavery sentiment." Nor was any anti-slavery sentiment mixed with all their hate of the South. Federal hate of the Union and desire to secede was based on fear and hate of Democracy. Powell says:

It must be borne in mind that not once in all this plotting of 1803 and 1804 was the right of a State, or of a group of States, to secede questioned. The only argument any one made against secession was the unripeness of the common people. Not one flash of loyalty to the Central Government. Their intent was to create an oligarchy.

Why should there have been a flash of loyalty to the Central Government? No party in America at that time thought that more loyalty was due to the Union Government than to the State Governments. This doctrine was never declared until Lincoln inaugurated war on the South, on the pretext that she was disloyal to the Union. Up to the very hour of that war Lincoln's own party held that the South had the right to secede, the right to independence. Lincoln, Seward, Wade of Ohio, Philips of Massachusetts, and hosts of other high Republican speakers had publicly declared the South's right to secede, as will be shown later on.

CHAPTER EIGHTEEN

New England's Effort to Secede in 1812 and 1814 and 1815.

The extracts given in the preceding pages show how anxious were New England politicians, preachers and newspapers to get New England to secede from the Union in 1796, and again in 1803 and 1804. We will now show New England's still greater anxiety to get out of the Union in 1812, 1814 and 1815. New England selected this time to secede because the Union was in the throes of war with a powerful foe. Was this from a desire to do the Union as much harm as possible? In 1799, when the Federalist, John Adams, was President, Federalists counseled obedience, honor and respect to "rulers." When Democrats were in office their tune was changed. We will first give extracts from the sermons of that time to show the spirit of the people. The Rev. Dr. Parish, of Boston, a divine of high standing and influence, in 1799 instructed his congregation to hold their magistrates in "reverence, honor and obedience," even to the extent of using for them the sword. "Cursed," said this divine, "is he that keepeth back his sword from blood, and he that hath none, let him sell his coat and buy one." In a sermon delivered April 7, 1814 at Ryefield, Mass., the Reverend Parish felt and talked in a very different strain. The Government was then at war with Great Britain, and New England, through newspapers, politicians and from pulpits denounced Government officials as a band of ruffians, and held up Old England as the most beneficent country that ever was.

The Reverend Parish said in a sermon: "No peace will be made until the people say there shall be no war. War will continue till the mountains are melted in blood, till every field in America is white with the bones of her people." In another sermon at Ryefield he discoursed as follows:

> The Israelites became weary of yielding the fruit of their labor to pamper their splendid tyrants. Where is our Moses? Where is the rod of his miracles? Where is our Aaron? Alas! No voice comes from the burning bush. Such is the temper of American Republicans [Democrats at that time were called Republicans]. A new language must be invented before we can attempt to express the baseness of their conduct or describe the rottenness of their hearts. Do you not owe it to your children, owe it to your God, to make peace for yourselves? You may as well expect the cataract of Niagara to turn its current to the head of Superior as a wicked Congress to make pause in the work of destroying this country. Tyrants are the same on the banks of the Nile and the Potomac, at Memphis and at Washington, in a Monarchy or in a Republic; like the worshipers of Moloch, the supporters of this vile administration sacrifice their children on the altar of Democracy. The full vials of despotism are poured out on your heads, and yet you may challenge the plodding Israelite, the stupid African, the feeble Chinese, the drowsy Turk, or the frozen exiles of Siberia to equal you in tame submission to the powers that be.

The reader's attention is especially called to two words in the above extract; words of the deepest significance. *"Stupid Africans."* These words are something to ponder over. *"Stupid Africans."* Up to that time, 1814, and for years after, the Federal party had no respect and no love for negroes. New England men had imported negroes from Africa, and consequently knew something of negro nature. At that time they had no more idea of setting the African on a pinnacle high above the Caucasian than of putting the "feeble Chinese" thereon. All through the years from 1796 up to the year the Rev. Parish preached his sermon (1814) calling negroes "stupid Africans," the Federal party held negroes as inferior to the white race. In one of his sermons this eager secession preacher said:

> *Here* we must trample on the mandates of despotism, or *here* we must remain slaves forever. Has not New England

as much to apprehend as the sons of Jacob had? Let every man who sanctions this war remember he is covering himself and his country with blood; the blood of the slain will cry out from the ground against him. This war not only tolerates crimes, but calls for crimes – crimes are the food of its life, the arms of its strength. This war is a monster which every hour gormandizes a thousand crimes, and yet cries give! give! The first moment the Dragon moved, piracy and murder were legalized. Those Western States which have been violent for this abominable war of murder, God has given them blood to drink. Their men have fallen; their lamentations are deep and loud.

These extracts from sermons are taken from Carpenter's *Logic of History*, pages 37, 38, 39.

A sermon delivered in Trinity Church, Boston, by the Rev. F.F. Gardiner, rector, April 9, 1812, contains this:

> England is willing to sacrifice everything to conciliate us, except her honor and independence. The British, after all, save us by their convoys infinitely more property than they deprive us of where they take one ship they protect twenty. Where they commit one outrage, they do many acts of kindness.

A discourse delivered by this same secessionist divine on July 23, 1813, contained these passages:

> This is a war unexampled in the history of the world, wantonly proclaimed on the most frivolous pretenses against a nation from whose friendship we might derive the most signal advantages.
>
> Let no consideration, my brethren, deter you at all times, and in all places, from execrating the present war. It is unjust, foolish, ruinous.
>
> As Mr. Madison had declared war, let Mr. Madison carry it on. This Union has long since been virtually dissolved. It is full time that this part of the United States should take care of itself.

The Reverend Dr. Osgood, pastor of the Medford Church, Massachusetts, in a discourse delivered April 8th, 1810, has this:

> The strong prepossession of so great a proportion of my fellow-citizens in favor of a race of demons [the people of the South] and against a nation [the British] of more religion, virtue, good faith, generosity, beneficence, than any that now is or ever has been upon the face of the earth, wrings my soul with anguish, and fills my soul with apprehensions and terror of the judgments of heaven upon this sinful people.

Think of it, gentle reader, this good Christian preacher, this follower of the Merciful Nazarene, tells his audience that his soul is wrung with anguish and apprehension and terror of God's judgments upon them, because they had not all accepted the gospel of hate, and come to believe that the people of the South were a "race of demons," and the British the purest and best nation on the earth. In another discourse the Reverend David Osgood said:

> Each man who volunteers his services in such a cause [the war with Great Britain] or loans his money for its support, or by his conversation, his writings, or in any other mode of influence, encourages its prosecution, that man is an accomplice in the wickedness, and loads his conscience with the blackest crimes, and brings the guilt of blood upon his soul, and in the sight of God and his law, he is a murderer.

On May 9, 1809, the Reverend Osgood discoursed before the Lieutenant Governor and the Legislature of Massachusetts, and preached resistance to the Union Government, as follows: "If we would preserve the liberties of that struggle [1776] so dearly purchased, the call for resistance now is as urgent as it was formerly against the mother country."

The same Reverend Osgood, June 26, 1812, in a sermon, predicted war on the South. He said: "If at the present moment no symptoms of civil war appear, there certainly shall soon, unless the courage of the war party fail them. A civil war is as certain as the events that happen to the known laws and established course of nature."

In a sermon delivered in Ryefield, 1814, Rev. D. Parish had this: "How will the supporters of this anti-Christian war endure the sentence, endure their own reflection, endure the fire that forever burns, the worm which never dies, the Hosannas of Heaven, while the smoke of their torment ascends forever and ever?"

The following extracts from the New England Press may be found in Carpenter's *Logic of History*, pages 40, 41 and 42.

The Boston *Centinel*, December 10, 1814, had this:

> Those who startle at the danger of the separation tell us the soil of New England is hard and sterile, that deprived of the productions of the South, we would soon become a wretched race of cowherds and fishermen. Do these people forget what energy can do for a people? Have they read of Holland? Holland threw off its yoke of Spain (our Virginia) and its chapels became churches, its poor men's cottages princes' palaces.

Was it not the very insanity of hate to liken the Presidency of Virginia's men – Washington, Jefferson, Monroe and Madison – to the despotism Philip II. of Spain wielded over Holland? Federalists called these four men's election to office the "Virginia Dynasty," and ramped and raged over their Presidency as the crudest despotism. "It is said that to make a treaty of commerce with the enemy is to violate the Constitution and to sever the Union. Are these not already virtually destroyed?" (Boston *Centinel*, Dec. 14, 1814).

On December 15, 1814, the *Centinel* had this:

> By a commercial treaty with England, which shall provide for the admission of such States as may wish to come into it, and which shall prohibit England from making a treaty with the South or West, our commerce will be secured to us, our standing in the Nation raised to its proper level, and New England's feelings will no longer be sported with or her interests violated.

And this while the Union Government was at war with Old England. This while the men of the South were bravely doing all they could by their valor in the army and their money to aid the Government in its struggle with a powerful foe.

Though prohibited by acts of Congress, all during this country's war with Old England, New England carried on with the enemy illicit intercourse. The moment our government gunboats were out of Boston harbor, British merchantmen, continually hovering about the coast, would come in, deliver their contraband cargo, receive specie and British bills of exchange, and return for another cargo. If States could blush, New England's face, even to this day, would burn with shame at the false, the treacherous part, she played during the second war with Great Britain.

The Boston *Centinel*, December 7, 1814, had this:

> If we oppose them [the administration] with a high-minded and steady conduct, who shall say we shall not beat them all? Why this delay? [Delay of making a separate peace with Old England and seceding from the Union.] Why leave that to chance which our firmness should command? Let no difficulties stay our course, no danger draw us back. We are convinced the time has come when Massachusetts must make a resolute stand. The sentiment is hourly extending, and in the Northern States will soon be universal, that with respect to the South we are in the condition of a conquered people.

New England had been conquered at the polls. Democracy had won by ballots the victory over Federalism. This was the conquest New England men rankled and raged over. On January 10, 1814, Deerfield, Massachusetts sent a petition, numerously signed, to the State authorities, from which we take the following extract:

> Should the present administration, with the aid and adherence of the Southern States, still persist in the prosecution of this wicked war, and in unconstitutionally creating new States in the mud of Louisiana, the inhabitants of which country are as ignorant as the alligators of its swamps, in opposition to the rights and privileges of New England, much as we deprecate a separation of this Union, we deem it an evil much less to be dreaded than co-operation with them in their nefarious projects.

What rights and privileges had New England over and above the rights and privileges of other States? The word privilege is out of place under a free and equal government. The Federalists of New England fancied themselves more fit to govern than Democrats. They fancied the privilege of rule was theirs by right divine. The love of power and high place was the very passion of the Federal soul.

In Crisis No. 3 we find this: "The public welfare will be better promoted in a separate than in one Federal Constitution. The attempt to unite this vast territory under one head is absurd" (*Logic of History*).

The *Federal Republican*, 1814, asked this question: "Is there now the least foundation to build a hope on that this Union will last twelve months? A peaceable separation will be for the happiness of all sections."

In an Ipswich, Massachusetts memorial, September 18, 1813, we find this:

> The Government of these States has almost completed their ruin. The time has arrived when Massachusetts must make a resolute stand. What shall we do to be saved? Only one thing. The people must rise in their majesty and compel their unworthy servants to obey their will. The Union is already practically dissolved.

The Boston *Centinel*, September 10, 1814, had this:

> The Union of the Northern and Southern States is very much opposed to the interests of both sections. The extent of territory is too large to be governed by the same representative body. Each section will be better satisfied to govern itself. Each is large and populous enough for its own protection. The Western States will govern themselves better than the Atlantic can govern them. It is certain that the Atlantic States do not want the aid or counsel of the Western States. The public welfare would be more promoted in a separate than in a Federal Constitution.

This was true then and is true now.

> The sufferings so thick about us have aroused New England. She will now meet every danger until her rights are returned to the full. She will say to the men of New England, if they hope to lead in the cause of New England's independence, they must do it in the spirit of New England men (Boston *Centinel*, December 7, 1814).

The Boston *Advertiser*, 1814, said: "Our plan is to withhold our money and make a separate peace with Great Britain."

The Federal *Republican*, 1814, had this:

> The Eastern States are marching steadily and straight forward up to revolution. In times past there was much talk and loud menace, but little acting, among the friends of reform [secession from the Union]. Now little is said and much done. The new constitution of the Hartford convention is to go into operation as soon as two or three States shall have adopted it.

On January 5, 1815, at a meeting held at Reading, Massachusetts, a string of resolutions was passed, one of which is as follows: "*Resolved*, That we place the fullest confidence in the Government and Legislature of Massachusetts, and in the State authorities of New England, and to them, under God, we look for aid and direction." These Federalists, as was their offspring, the Republican party, were strong States' rights advocates up to the hour the war began at Fort Sumter. Then they made a sudden summersault, and declared States' rights and secession unpardonable crimes resulting from leprosy of the mind as foul as leprosy of the body.

The Boston *Repertory*, 1814, was so eager for New England to leave the Union, and so full of the idea that there would be a war with the South, it addressed the people of New England with an air of command: "Americans!" cried out the *Repertory*, "prepare your arms! You will soon be called to use them!"

The New York *Commercial Advertiser* had this:

> Old Massachusetts is as terrible to the Americans now as she was to the British Cabinet in 1775. America has her Butes and her Norths. Let the commercial States breast themselves to the shock. Then, and not till then, shall they humble the pride of Virginia and chastise the insolence of the madmen of Kentucky and Tennessee, who aspire to the Government of these States.

January 31, 1814, the citizens of Newburyport, Massachusetts, sent a memorial to the Legislature of Massachusetts, from which we get this extract:

CONCERNING THE WAR ON THE SOUTH 149

> Our unquestionable rights are invaded. We call upon our State Legislature to protect us in our privileges, to defend which we are ready to resist unto blood. We are ready to aid you to our utmost power in securing our privileges, peacefully if we can, forcibly if we must; and we pledge ourselves in support of every measure the dignity and liberties of this free, sovereign and independent State may seem to your wisdom to demand.

The only complaint these men had against the Government was, it was waging war with Great Britain.

The *Federal Republican* of November 7, 1814 put forth this terrible threat: "On or before the 4th of July, if James Madison is not out of office, a new form of government will be in operation in the Eastern section of the Union; the contest then will be whether to adhere to the old or join the new government."

From an open letter to James Madison, published and largely circulated through New York and New England, in May, 1814, titled "Northern Grievances," we give the following:

> If the impending negotiations with Great Britain are defeated; if the friendly and conciliatory proposals of the enemy should be met so as not to terminate this infamous war, it is necessary to apprise you [President Madison] that such conduct will be no longer borne. The injured States of New England will be compelled by duty and honor to dash into atoms the bonds of tyranny. It will then be too late to retreat; the die will be cast; freedom purchased. A separation of the States will be inevitable. Motives numerous and urgent will demand this measure. The oppressors will be responsible for the momentous events arising from the dissolution of the Union. It will be their work. Posterity will admire the independent spirit of the Eastern section of our country, and will enjoy the fruits of our firmness and our wisdom. The descendants of the South and West will have reason to curse the folly of your counsels. Bold and resolute in the sacred object, no force can withstand our powerful arms. The most numerous army will melt before our manly strength. History will instruct you that the feeble debility of the South could never

face the vigorous activity of the North. A single spark of Northern liberty will explode the whole atmosphere of sultry Southern despotism. Do you imagine the energy of the Northern freemen is to be smothered?

No human was trying to smother their energies. On the contrary, Mr. Madison would have been delighted had those Northern freemen put some of their energy into the war against Great Britain, instead of doing all they could to give aid and comfort to the enemy.

"Do you think," continued this curious letter, "that we will allow ourselves to be trampled on? and by whom? The Southern and Western States?" History does not show the slightest sign of any effort or wish of the Southern and Western States to trample on New England. The letter continues:

The aggregate strength of the South and West, if brought against the North and East, would be driven into the ocean or back to their own wilds, and they might think themselves fortunate to escape other punishment We would fight for freedom, they to enslave. Beware! Pause! before you take the fatal plunge. You, sir, have carried your oppression to the utmost stretch. We will no longer submit. Name an immediate peace. Protect our seamen. Unless you comply with these just demands without delay, *we will withdraw from the Union.*

Oh, would to God New England then and there had withdrawn from the Union! It would have been a bloodless withdrawal. Madison and Monroe had both expressed the opinion that to coerce a seceding State would be suicidal to freedom. Legal divorce from the States New England had so long hated might have abated somewhat the insanity of that hate. Juster, kinder feelings might have softened her heart toward a people who certainly had not given New England cause to hate. Had separation *then* taken place the Northern people might not have aided and abetted the Republican party in committing the awful crime of drenching American soil with brothers' blood. Had New England States *then* seceded, no blood would have been shed to force them back into a Union she detested. Every Democrat in America knew and knows that the Union Government had and has no moral or legal right to coerce seceding States. Such was then the opinion, both North and South. In the convention of 1787 the question of secession and coercion was up for discussion. Madison said: "A Union of States with such an ingredient as coercion would seem to provide for its own destruction." It certainly would provide for the destruction of the principles of liberty itself.

Looked at by the lurid light of the '60s, one expression in the above letter to President Madison will make the reader pause and reflect a moment. The *"feeble debility of the South could never face the vigorous activity of the North."* The Republican party had inherited from its progenitor, the Federal, the above idea of the South's feeble debility. Members of that party invited United States Senators and Congressmen to take their wives and daughters out to see the first fight of the war, especially to "see the rebels run at sight of Union soldiers." Everybody knows how the rebels ran at Bull Run. Republican officers of the Union army have expressed their opinion of the South's "feeble debility." General Donn Piatt, a Union officer, on this subject wrote this in 1887:

> The true story of the late war has not yet been told. It probably never will be told. It is not flattering to our people; unpalatable truths seldom find their way into history. How rebels fought the world will never know; for two years they kept an army in the field that girt their borders with a fire that shriveled our forces as they marched in, like tissue paper in a flame. Southern people were animated by a feeling that the word fanaticism feebly expresses. [Love of liberty expresses it.] For two years this feeling held those rebels to a conflict in which they were invincible. The North poured out its noble soldiery by the thousands, and they fought well, but their broken columns and thinned lines drifted back upon our capital, with nothing but shameful disasters to tell of the dead, the dying, the lost colors and the captured artillery. Grant's road from the Rapidan to Richmond was marked by a highway of human bones. The Northern army had more killed than the Confederate Generals had in command.

"We can lose five men to their one and win," said Grant. The men of the South, half starved, unsheltered, in rags, shoeless, yet Grant's marches from the Rapidan to Richmond left dead behind him more men than the Confederates had in the field!

General Piatt speaks as follows of the "feeble debility" of a Virginian General: "It is strange," says Piatt, "what magic lingers about the mouldering remains of Virginia's rebel leaders. Lee's very name confers renown on his enemies. The shadow of Lee's surrendered sword gives renown to an otherwise unknown grave" (Grant's). The Reverend H. W. Beecher preached a sermon in his church on the "Price of Liberty," which he said was not only eternal vigilance, but eternal self-sacrifice. Beecher astonished his congregation by illustrations from the South. The preacher exclaimed:

> Where shall we find such heroic self-denial, such upbearing under every physical discomfort, such patience in poverty, in distress, in absolute want, as we find in the Southern army? They fight better in a bad cause than you do in a good one; they fight better for a passion than you do for a sentiment. They fight well and bear up under trouble nobly, they suffer and never complain, they go in rags and never rebel, they are in earnest for their liberty, they believe in it, and if they can they mean to get it.
>
> What words can express the baseness, the devilish wickedness of a party which waged a bloody war to rob such people of the liberty which was theirs by right? Theirs by inheritance from their forefathers of '76?

The Republican leaders of the '60s were as ignorant of the nature of Southern men as were their progenitors who talked of the "South's feeble debility." Piatt relates an interview he had with Lincoln before the outbreak of the war. "Lincoln's low estimate of humanity," says Piatt, "blinded him to the South. He could not understand that men would fight for an idea. He thought the South's movement a sort of political game of bluff."

"The South can't fight," said one; "she has no resources."

Hannibal Hamlin said: "The South will have to come to us for arms, and come without money to pay for them."

"And for coffins," said John P. Hale, with a laugh.

"To put a regiment in the field," said Mr. Speaker Banks, "costs more than the entire income of an entire Southern State." It was not long before the men of the North found that the South's soldiers supplied themselves with arms and clothing captured from Union soldiers.

CONCERNING THE WAR ON THE SOUTH

Extracts from an address to the Hartford convention:

The once venerable Constitution has expired by dissolution in the hands of the wicked men [Democrats] who were sworn to protect it. Its spirit, with the precious souls of its first founders, has fled forever. Its remains will now rest in the silent tomb. At your hands, therefore, we demand deliverance. New England is unanimous, and we announce our irrevocable decree that the tyrannical oppression of those who at present usurp the power of the Constitution is beyond endurance, and we will resist it (Boston *Centinel*, December 28, 1814).

New England will look with an eye of doubt on those who oppose us. She will meet every danger and go through every difficulty, until her rights are restored. Throwing off all connection with this wasteful war and making peace with the enemy would be a wise and manly course (Boston *Centinel*, December 17, 1814).

Extracts from a memorial of the citizens of Newburyport to the Legislature of Massachusetts, January 31, 1814:

Is there a Federalist patriot in America who thinks it is his duty to shed his blood for Madison, for Jefferson, and the host of ruffians in Congress who have set their faces against us for years, and spirited up the brutal part of the populace to destroy us? Mr. Madison cannot complete his term of service if this war continues; it is not possible. Mr. Madison may rest assured there is in the hearts of many thousands in this abused, ruined country a sentiment and energy to resist unto destruction when his mad men shall call it into action.

The following extract from an address to the Hartford convention, December 24, 1814, will show the feeling of the Federal disunionists toward white people of the South, as well as toward the negroes:

Long enough have we paid taxes and fought the battles for the Southern States; long enough have we been scouted and abused by men who claim a right to rule us; long enough have we been slaves to the senseless representatives of the South, the equally senseless natives of Africa, and the barbarous huntsmen of the Western wilderness. Realities alone can work our deliverance, and deliverance we solemnly and irrevocably decree to be our right and we will obtain it (Boston *Centinel*, December 24, 1814).

The reader will note the significant phrase, *"equally senseless natives of Africa."* A few years from that time New England placed negroes on a tall pinnacle and put saintly aureoles around their heads, and all good Republicans did them homage.

On the 8th of October, 1814, a committee of the Massachusetts Legislature submitted a report by Mr. Otis, chairman, in favor of calling a convention for all the New England States with the object of forming a Northeastern Confederacy. The result was the Hartford convention, which met December 15, 1814. This convention, as we have shown by extracts, took the strongest possible stand for States' rights. In a report this convention enunciated its opinion of States' rights in these words: "It is not only the *right*, but the *duty*, of each State to interpose its authority in the manner best calculated to secure its own protection. States must be their own judges and execute their own decisions."

New England, during the second war with Great Britain, acted boldly and openly on States' rights principles. She refused to aid and support the Union. Her preachers, press and politicians praised the English and in every way manifested a friendly feeling toward Old England, all the while abusing their own Government as managed by a "gang of ruffians." On February 14, 1814, the two Houses of the Massachusetts Legislature put forth a report in which is this solemn declaration: "The question of New England's withdrawal from the Union is not a question of power or of right to separate, but only a question of time and expediency." A few years later Massachusetts called such doctrines blackest treason, and sent armies on the Southern people to kill, conquer or annihilate them for having acted on those doctrines.

The doctrine of States' rights was taught by politicians, press and preachers of New England up to the very hour the South seceded. This fact is indisputable. Not until Lincoln began war on the South were secession and States' rights called a political crime. The *Olive*

Branch (1814) said: "Massachusetts has dared the national Government to conflict. She has seized it by the throat, determined to strangle it if she can."

A committee of the New York Legislature (1814) made the following statement: "It is the opinion of this committee that the New England Federalists mean to make peace with the enemy and to forcibly separate New England from the Union." So universal was this opinion, on the 11th of October, 1814, thirteen Democratic Senators and thirty-five Congressmen issued a strong but kindly worded protest against New England's disunion movements, to which one of New England's Federal leaders angrily replied: "Do you imagine that we will allow ourselves to be trampled on by the South and West?"

The only shadow of being trampled on was the fact that the Democrats of the South and West had elected Democrats to the national offices, and the South and West approved of the war then going on with Great Britain, and gave the administration all the moral and financial support they could, opposed to the wishes of New England.

A speaker in the Massachusetts Legislature in 1814 made the following solemn declaration: "The Constitution has expired by dissolution. The Union Government is beyond endurance; we will resist. New England will bear no half way measures. She wants men who will lead the cause of New England independence."

An address delivered in the Hartford convention rehearses the wrongs it was claimed that New England suffered which necessitated secession from the Union: "They," the said wrongs, "may be traced to implacable combinations of individuals and States to monopolize power and office, and to trample without remorse on the rights and interests of the commercial section of the Union."

Because of these fancied wrongs New England hated Democrats, hated the South, hated the Union, was eager to leave it, and fiercely wanted to war on the Southern people. Up to that hour not one particle of anti-slavery sentiment was mingled with New England's animosity, or with her desire to secede from the Union. Up to the year 1815, with New England's insane hatred of the Southern whites, she had not yet mixed an insane love for Southern blacks. Up to that year New England's political speakers, press and preachers, when referring to negroes, called them "stupid Africans," "senseless blacks," or other names conveying contempt and belief in negro inferiority.

In his work, *Nullification and Secession*, E.P. Powell says:

It is very partial partisan reading of American history not to see that from the acceptance of the Constitution in 1790 there has been a tendency to assert the rights of States, and the rights of States to sever relation to the Union. New England, in 1803-04, tried to get five States to secede, New York, New Jersey and the New England States. In 1812-14 New England practically withdrew from co-operation with the Union.

Mr. E.P. Powell, of New York, wrote *Nullification and Secession* in 1897, thirty-two years after the war of conquest on the South. A conquest which, as Mr. Powell knows, was made by the Republican party on pretense that that party looked on secession as the most damnable crime a people can commit. Was Mr. Powell *afraid* to tell the whole truth about the secession principles held and taught by the Republican party and its progenitors, the Federals? Mr. Powell timidly says: "From 1790 there has been a *tendency* to assert States' rights, and the right of the States to sever relation to the Union." The word *tendency* means an inclination, a leaning, a drift in one or another direction. Did not Mr. Powell know that the Federal party, almost from the formation of the Union, had been dissatisfied with it? He certainly knew, as he shows in his work, *Nullification and Secession*, that this party not only had a *"tendency"* toward States' rights and secession in 1804 and on to the end of the second war with Great Britain, but a decided intention and determination to get the Northeastern States to secede and to form a Northeastern Confederacy. Mr. Powell knows how hard the men of New England worked for secession, and how boldly they avowed and maintained the doctrine of States' rights. Is it possible that he does not also know that the Republican party continued the work of the Federals in that direction up to the very hour of the South's secession? Does he not further know that after the Republican party conquered the South on the pretext that it (the Republican party) so loved the Union it waged a bloody war to save it, this same Republican party now tries to bury out of sight its former advocacy of secession and States' rights, and frowns severely on any writer who dares to bring to the front that part of its history? Was it *fear* of Republican frowns that made Mr. Powell use the gentle word *tendency* instead of the plain English word *advocacy*, and the strongest sort of advocacy at that?

S.D. Carpenter, a close and critical student of political events,

CONCERNING THE WAR ON THE SOUTH

in his invaluable work, *The Logic of History*, published in 1864, says:

> The Northeastern States early sought to create prejudice and disunion, not on account of any existing facts, but to array section against section, to stimulate hatred and discord for the purpose of accelerating their darling object, dissolution of the Union and the establishment of a Northeastern Confederacy. For years the disunionists of the North have manifested the boldness of a Cromwell, the assiduity of beavers, the cunning of a fox and the malignity of Iscariot.

Do not the extracts I have laid before the reader show determination to arouse hatred of the Southern people? The reader must never lose sight of the fact that Federal and Republican hatred sprung from hatred of Democracy. The Union was hated because the majority of men in the Union elected too many Democratic Presidents. These Presidents – Washington, Jefferson, Monroe and Madison – were hated and called the "Virginia dynasty." A New Englander was the first man in the American Congress to threaten disunion. January 11, 1811, Josiah Quincy, of Massachusetts, from the floor of Congress declared:

> The purchase of Louisiana and the admission of that State into the Union would be a virtual dissolution of the Union, rendering it the right of all, as it becomes the duty of some men to prepare definitely for the separation of the States, amicably if they might, forcibly if they must.

Mr. Quincy reduced the above to writing and sent it to the Clerk of the House. Mr. Poindexter of Virginia, sprang to his feet: "That," he cried, " is the first threat on the floor of Congress to break up the Union" (Hildreth's *History of United States*, Vol. IV, page 226). In 1813 Mr. Quincy, this same zealous secessionist and disunionist, was chairman of a committee in the Massachusetts Legislature, still pushing on secession plans. Mr. Quincy offered the following resolution, which was adopted:

> Resolved, That the act passed the 8th day of April, 1812, entitled, "An Act for the admission of the State of Louisiana into the Union and to extend the laws of the United States to said State," is a violation of the United States Con-

stitution, and that the Senators of the State of Massachusetts be instructed, and the Representatives thereof be requested to use their endeavor to obtain the repeal of the same.

Governor Strong, of Massachusetts, wanted New England to secede from the Union, and after secession schemes were stopped by the glorious ending of the second war with Great Britain, won by Southern soldiers under the immortal Jackson, Governor Strong, to console himself and his friends, said: "Even though New England has failed to break the Union, the Western States ere long of themselves will get out of the Union. We then will be happy neighbors, whereas in a Union will always be friction."

The reader may have observed in some of the foregoing extracts references made to Massachusetts' jealousy. Bancroft, the historian, himself a son of Massachusetts, said of his mother State: "An ineradical dread of the coming power of the South and West lurked in New England, especially in Massachusetts." Jealousy owes its life to selfishness; it is a mean quality of which every large mind is ashamed; when its origin is generally known, even those affected with jealousy will strive to suppress or at least hide it. A sample of New England's jealousy in this way may be found in Mr. Rives' *Life of Madison*. Rives states that in the convention which framed the Constitution, Mr. Gouverneur Morris, delegate from Pennsylvania, was made spokesman for the Eastern States. Mr. Morris said:

> I look forward to that range of States which will soon be formed in the West. These new States will know less of the public interests than the old, will have interests in many respects different. It must be apparent they will not be able to furnish men equally as enlightened as the Eastern men to share in the administration of the common interest. If the Western States get power in their hands they will ruin the Atlantic States' interests. I think the rule of representation ought to be so fixed as to secure to the Atlantic States the prevalence in the national council. This will provide a defense to the Northeast.

Mr. Gouverneur Morris never thought of providing a defense of the Western States against Eastern greed of power and money. Mr. King and Mr. Gerry, of Massachusetts, took up the subject, repeating the alarm sounded by Mr. Morris. Mr. Gerry said: "If the Western States acquire power they will abuse it; they will draw our wealth into the Western country and oppose commerce."

One of the charges New England repeatedly made against the South was that she opposed commerce. This supposed opposition was used to excuse their desire to secede from the Union and form a Northeastern Confederacy. These jealous and selfish men submitted to the convention the following proposal: "Whatever may be the future population of the new States in the West, the total number of their representatives shall not exceed the total number of representatives of the old States."

The men from Virginia firmly opposed this proposition. "The new States of the West," argued Colonel Mason, of Virginia, "must be treated as equals and subjected to no degrading discrimination. They will have the same pride and other passions we have, and will probably revolt from the Union if they are not in all respects placed on an equal footing with the Eastern States." Mr. Madison said: "I am clear and firm in the opinion that no unfavorable distinction should be made between the Atlantic and the Western States, either in policy or justice."

The proposition of the Eastern men was put to a vote: *Yeas* – Massachusetts, Connecticut, Maryland, Delaware. *Nays* – Virginia, North and South Carolina and Georgia. Pennsylvania was divided.

Judge, oh, you men of the West! which section – New England or the South – displayed the higher sense of justice? Less selfish greed for power? But for the resistance of Virginia's freedom-loving men, Mason and Madison, the limbs of the infant Hercules of the West would have been so bound by the men of the East, the West would have been crippled and cramped for life, or would have broken its bonds asunder and by its sword won equality.

CHAPTER NINETEEN

Contains Further Evidence Proving New England's Secession and Disunion Sentiments – Her Eagerness to Sever the Union in Twain.

The extracts given in Chapter Twenty-Eight. are mostly from S. D. Carpenter's *Logic of History*; a few are from the *Democratic Speaker's Handbook*. As the case of the South versus the Republican party will ere long be taken into posterity's court for final judgment, I trust the reader will find the evidence bearing on this case of sufficient interest to read the following extracts, taken from Mr. E. P. Powell's work, *Nullification and Secession*:

Extracts.

When the United States declared war in 1812 against Great Britain the Federalists in Congress issued an address to the people of New England declaring the war needless and unwise. The Massachusetts House of Representatives promptly voted an address denouncing the war as a wanton sacrifice of New England's interests, and calling for town meetings to denounce the war. The address to the people:

"Let the sound of your disapprobation of this war be loud and deep; let there be no volunteers except for defensive war."

This [remarks Mr. Powell] at the very outset was practical secession from the Union.

Every possible hindrance was thrown in the way of securing enlistments for the army. Those who did enlist were arrested on real or fictitious charges of debt, and the courts cheerfully insisted that *"while a man was debtor he was the property of the creditor and could not be allowed to leave the State."*

Governor Griswald of Connecticut declared he did not believe the militia of that State could be ordered to obey a Continental officer. The Legislature of Connecticut resolved that the conduct of His Excellency the Governor in refusing to order the militia of this State into the service of the United States on the requisition of the Secretary of War, met with the entire approbation of the Assembly.

The South and West were overwhelmingly loyal to the Union; the Southern people were devoted to the Union. The Federalists declared it was capable of proof "that Madison and Jefferson were in league with Napoleon." The clergy preached and the politicians orated in the same strain. As 1812 drew toward a close the condition of affairs was pitiful. Madison in his message spoke warmly of the course taken by New England, as practically destroying the Union; instead of one nation we were acting as two in the face of the enemy. He defined the war as an expression of our determination to compel England to formally renounce the right of impressment of sailors on American ships. Along the ocean coast the British had adopted a war of incursion, plunder and the torch. They had burned several towns in Connecticut and elsewhere, had occupied Washington, driven out the Government and burned the capitol. Everywhere a determined front of the people was seen except in the East. No son of New England can remember without pain and shame the record of that section.

With how much more pain and shame ought New England to remember her course toward the South in the years of the '60s? The South only acted on the principles of secession New England had openly taught from the hour she entered the Union, yet, more savage than any enraged tiger, New England turned on the South, shouting rebel! traitor! traitor! rebel! and when Lincoln let slip the dogs of war, as they bounded southward. New England sicced them on to greater fury, crying, "On, Lion! On, Tiger! On, Wolf! Tear! Rend! Devour!"

Unlike New England, the South did not choose a time to secede when it could hurt the Union. New England deliberately and of set purpose deferred secession until the Union was in the throes of war with a powerful enemy. It was stated at that time that –

> Two-thirds of the army in Canada are at this moment eating beef provided by American [New England] contractors. The road to St. Reges is covered with droves of cattle and the river with rafts, destined for the English. "Were it not for these supplies," wrote General Isard to the Secretary of War, "the British forces would soon suffer a famine." In return Old England exempted Massachusetts, Connecticut and New Hampshire from blockade.
>
> The Federalists now discussed the plan of withdrawing all New England troops to their own soil. Governor Crittenden of Vermont issued orders to Vermont regiments in New York to return home. The officers read the proclamation to the troops; all of them united in sending back word to Crittenden that they would not obey him. "We are," said they, "in the service of the United States, and your power over us is suspended until we are discharged. We regard your proclamations with mingled emotions of pity and contempt."

After Lawrence's splendid sea fight the whole nation held a holiday, but the Massachusetts Legislature passed a resolution that, "It does not become a religious people to express any approbation of military or naval exploits not immediately defensive."

"This was twaddle," remarks Powell. It was worse than twaddle. It was an effort to throw a religious cloak over a mean, contemptible act.

> The proposition was discussed of forming a separate treaty of peace with Great Britain.
>
> The Governor of Connecticut in August withdrew all the State militia from the command of national officers. New England was practically in rebellion. It had seceded from united national action, and had set up a new Confederacy. Governor Strong called the Legislature and said to them: "The national Government has failed to protect Massachusetts from invasion or attack; we must henceforth look to God and ourselves." He more than hinted that the time had come for separate New England alliances.

The Boston *Centinel* declared the Union was as good as dissolved.

The very day that dispatches from Ghent announced the peace proposals of England, the Massachusetts Legislature issued a call for a conference of New England States to be held at Hartford. Connecticut and Rhode Island promptly *responded*. The Boston *Centinel* spoke of Massachusetts, Connecticut and Rhode Island as the first three pillars in a new Federal edifice. It was proposed to make a special and separate treaty of peace with England. In the conference at Hartford there were thirty-six delegates, representing not only the three States named, but parts of Vermont and New Hampshire. Governor Morris wrote: "If not too tame and timid, you will be hailed hereafter as the patriots and sages of your generation."

It was proposed in the Hartford convention that New England should create State armies for self-defense. The Massachusetts Legislature, in session at Boston, passed a resolution to send a delegation to demand the taxes, as proposed by the Hartford convention. Governor Strong undertook at once to raise a State army and in every way to create an independent commonwealth. It was proposed to seize the national taxes. At the same time Massachusetts refused to cooperate with the Union Government in driving the British from Maine.

Jackson reached New Orleans in time. He swept hindrances out of the way with a high hand, and then nearly annihilated the British. The victory was complete. Meanwhile at Ghent had been signed the most extraordinary treaty England ever executed. Beginning with high and lofty demands, her commissioners had been crowded by the Americans to yield at one point and another until we had won a triumph of diplomacy greater than our triumphs at arms.

The points first demanded by England were that America must yield all the Northwest, including Michigan, Wisconsin, Illinois, a large part of Indiana, and one-third of Ohio, as a perpetual Indian Territory, a barrier between Canada and the United States; that we must renounce our right to keep armed vessels on the lakes or military posts on the shores, and thirdly, we must relinquish a considerable portion of Maine to be British property. These terms the members of the Hartford convention and the foremost men of New England declared were just and liberal. The rest of the States indignantly spurned the proposals. Adams wrote to Madison to continue the war forever rather than yield one acre of territory or the fisheries or *impressments*.

New England, by election, resolutions and conventions, had declared all the British demands were just, and to grant them would be political wisdom.

Peace was declared, but not one single British demand had been yielded. The war had been fought under terrible disadvantages [fought by Democrats drawn from the South and West], but it had accomplished more permanent advantages to civilization than any other two years' war in history. It made the oceans a vast republic. It established the freedom of the seas. It established the great doctrine of individual rights (Powell's *Nullification and Secession*).

Of Massachusetts' treacherous course Jefferson wrote to General Dearborn:

> Oh Massachusetts! how have I lamented the degradation of your apostasy – Massachusetts, with whom I worked with pride in 1776! If her humiliation can just give her modesty enough to suppose that her Southern brethren are somewhat on a par with her in wisdom, in information, in patriotism, in bravery, even in honesty, she will more justly estimate her relative momentum in the Union.

For Massachusetts, modesty was not possible. Too long she had been teaching herself that she was the most virtuous and intellectual State in the Union, if not in the world. Even in her youth she had conceitedly drawn close about her a robe of self-righteousness and said to the South and West, "Stand back! I am holier than thou."

New England had so long calumniated Southern people, calumniation had become a sort of craze with her. It is quite possible that she had come to believe her own falsehoods. While using slavery as a weapon to beat down the Union, the people of the South, the Democratic party she hated, now and then she managed to get possession of some negro, who may or may not have been cruelly abused by his master, and she made use of that negro to charge every man and woman in the South with cruelty.

It never occurred to her to remember that as good a charge of cruelty could be brought against every husband in America because now and then some husband cruelly abused his wife, beat or choked her to death. Even in 1796, while still engaged in the slave traffic, while still bringing cargoes of negroes from Africa and sending them South to be sold to rice and cotton planters, this self-righteous New England had the gall to proclaim the lying charge that the people of the South were barbarians, were a "race of demons," and would "enjoy killing and eating negroes if they liked the taste of black flesh" – eating negroes *they*, the pious Puritans of New England, had stolen from Africa and brought to this Western continent!

CHAPTER TWENTY

New England's Three Hates Still Active. The Republican Party is Organised, 1854. Republican Historians not Trustworthy. Ambassador Choate bears False Witness. Senator Sumner's Curious Lapse. A Few Facts Uncovered.

Notwithstanding all the evidence we have given, and as much more staring the seeker of historic truth in the face, it now suits Republican writers to assert that the people of the Northern States always had held that secession is a political crime, always had abhorred disunion, always had felt that a higher allegiance was due to the Union Government than to that of their own States. Republicans persist in the assertion that South Carolina was "the breeding place of secession and that secession was and is a leprosy of the mind more loathsome than leprosy of the body." In *Nullification and Secession,* the author makes the statement that "from the day of our great victory over Great Britain, in 1815, New England became among the faithful most faithful to the Union." On what evidence Mr. Powell based this statement does not appear; it certainly is far from fact. New England continued to hold her three hates, each one as strong, black and bitter, as before the war of 1812. Her hate of the Union had not for a moment ceased or softened; her hate of Democracy and of the people of the South because they were Democrats was as unrelenting as ever; her desire to sever the Union was as strong as ever.

New England experienced no change of heart, as will be seen from the extracts I shall now lay before the reader. Ample proof exists that New England was as eager as ever for disunion. On the 24th of February, 1842, John Quincy Adams presented a petition in the House of Representatives, signed by a large number of citizens of Haverhill, Mass., for a peaceable dissolution of the Union, assigning as one of the reasons the inequality of benefits conferred upon the different sections. See Blake's *History of Slavery*, page 524, and Carpenter's *Logic of History*, page 26.

On the 28th of February, 1842, Mr. Joshua R. Giddings, member of Congress from Ohio, presented a petition from a large number of citizens of Austinburg in his district, praying for a dissolution of the Union. Mr. Triplett of Kentucky, who considered the petition disrespectful to both Houses, moved that it be not received. Ayes 24 for reception. Noes 116 (See Blake's *History of Slavery*, page 529).

The following extract, page 145, from one of a series of pamphlets issued for circulation in Massachusetts in 1852, shows New England's unabated animosity to the Union: "Fidelity to the cause of human freedom and allegiance to God require that the existing national compact should be instantly dissolved; that secession from the Government is a religious and a political duty."

In another paragraph of this same paper is the following emphatic declaration: "To continue this disastrous alliance longer is madness." In 1854 the dismembered Federals of New England and the disorganized Whigs united and formed the Republican party. These old disunionists under their new name took up the fight on the three objects of New England's hate – Democracy, the Union and the South – exactly where the Federals had ceased their open fight in 1815. So far from New England's sentiments having softened since that time, her three hates, under the lead of Republicans, assumed the force and fury of insanity, as may be seen in reports of speeches, sermons and lectures. Men of New England who emigrated West carried with them all three hates, and when the Republican party was organized they made haste to enter its ranks and take up the work of disunion and secession. These men of the new party possessed more zeal, more audacity, more duplicity and less candor than their progenitors, the Federals. These latter had always fought Democracy in the open; the more astute Republicans saw that they could never win the suffrages of the common people if they exposed their imperialistic features; therefore from the day of their organization they fought behind a mask. The Republican party never at any period took the people into their confidence. But they affected high moral ideas and benevolent principles, which won many to their ranks. The old Federals had always spoken of negroes in contemptuous terms. Republicans saw what an engine of power they could make of slavery to batter, beat down and cover with false charges and malignant calumnies the three objects of their hatred, and effective use they made of that engine. They either forgot or ignored the fact that their own New England States were chiefly responsible for the existence of that black curse on this Western continent. Men of Massachusetts scrupled at no subterfuge, no deception, no falsehood, in efforts to make the world believe their own States were and ever had been free from the sin of slavery. They pushed back out of sight the hideous fact that Massachusetts men had built ships and sent them to Africa to bring back cargoes of negroes, which they sold either in the West Indies, the Bermudas or to Southern planters. The dreadful word, *"Middle Passage,"* with all its horrors, was seldom or never uttered or written by a Massachusetts man. Men of New England affected to believe only the Southern States were guilty of the sin of slavery. Lecturers, historians and senators joined in this deceptive work, and to this day falsehoods are told on this subject. Instance the address delivered by Ambassador to England Choate a few months ago to the Philosophic Society of Edinburg, Scotland. Branching off from the main line of his address, Ambassador Choate seized the occasion to enlighten the members of that philosophical society on the subject of slavery in America. The Ambassador said:

> Negro slavery was firmly established in the Southern States at an early period of their history. In 1619 a Dutch ship discharged a cargo of African slaves at Jamestown, Virginia. All through the colonial period their importation continued. A few negroes found their way up into the Northern States.

This is the way New England men "make and take their history." *"A few negroes found their way up into the Northern States,"* and this from a descendant of Puritans who carried on the slave traffic, importing negroes from Africa for over a hundred years. The careful way Ambassador Choate phrases his sentences to make them bear false witness is something to wonder at, and the dishonesty involved is something to blush for. What are the plain facts of history?

A Dutch ship *did* stop at Jamestown in 1619 and leave, *not* a cargo, but eleven slaves, not one of which remained on Virginia soil. Those eleven negro slaves had been brought from the Earl of Warwick's plantation, on the Isle of Summers, one of the Bermudas. Their owner, the Earl of Warwick, had them carried back as soon as possible to his plantation on the Isle of Summers.

If the importation of negroes continued all during the colonial period, New England ships carried on that importation, and New England State kept up that importation until the year 1808. Massachusetts went into the slave traffic as early as 1637. Chief Justice Parsons declared from the bench that "slavery was introduced into Massachusetts soon after its first settlement." Is it possible that Ambassador Choate is ignorant of these facts?

George H. Moore, L.L.D., librarian of the New York Historical Society, afterwards superintendent of the Lenox Library, in *Notes on the History of Slavery in Massachusetts*, says: "I charge nearly all the orators, historians, lawyers, clergymen and statesmen of Massachusetts with either ignorance of the facts of history or evading and falsifying them." Mr. George W. Williams, Judge Advocate of the Grand Army of the Republic of Ohio, in his *History of the Negro Race in America*, calls attention to the above charges of Mr. Moore and comments thus:

> Despite the indisputable evidence of the legalized existence of slavery in Massachusetts, the historians, lawyers, clergymen, orators and statesmen of New England continue to assert that slavery, though it did creep into the colony of Massachusetts and did exist, it was not by force of any law, as none such is known to have existed.

Moore says: "Massachusetts' first code of laws established slavery in that colony, and, at the very birth of the foreign commerce of New England, the African slave trade became a regular business." Yet in spite of indisputable evidence, showing that New England from 1637 to 1808 was actively engaged in the slave traffic, and that New England ships brought over cargoes of negroes from Africa, discharged those left alive from the horrors of the "Middle Passage" at New England ports, there to recuperate before sending them South to be sold to the cotton and rice planters, in spite of all this evidence. Ambassador Choate had the hardihood to represent to his Scotch audience that the Northern States were guiltless of the sin of slavery, and only a *"few negroes found their way up to Northern States."*

On June 28, 1854, Charles Sumner, a son of Massachusetts, from the Senate floor, made the false assertion that "in all her annals no person was ever born a slave on the soil of Massachusetts." I charge that men making such assertions were and are either disgracefully ignorant of the facts of history or disgracefully dishonest. In Elliott's *Debates in the Convention of 1787*, Vol. I, pages 264-5, may be found the following story illustrative of Massachusetts character: "The original committee of thirteen in 1787 recommended that the constitutional license to the slave traffic should cease at the period of 1800." This not suiting some of New England's States at that time engaged in the slave traffic, it was moved and seconded to amend the report of the committee of eleven, entered on the journal of August 21, 1787, as follows:

> To strike out the words *eighteen hundred* and insert the words *eighteen hundred and eight*.
> This motion was seconded; the vote stood as follows:
> *Yeas* – New Hampshire, Connecticut, Massachusetts, Maryland, North and South Carolina, Georgia.
> *Nays* – New Jersey, Delaware, Pennsylvania and Virginia (See Carpenter's *Logic of History*).

By this it is seen that Massachusetts and two other New England States, by their votes, procured the continuance of the damnable slave traffic eight years longer than Virginia wanted it to continue.

Dr. Dabney of Virginia states that it is estimated that in the years from 1787 to 1808 New England's slave ships brought from Africa and sold either to the South's planters or in the West Indies one million slaves. Yet from that year, 1787, from the very hour New England's three States voted to continue the slave traffic, Massachusetts has held close about her the robe of self-righteousness, scornfully saying to Virginia, "Stand back! I am holier than thou!"

CHAPTER TWENTY-ONE
☆ ☆ ☆ ☆

Save the Union, Free Slaves the Pretext, Not the Purpose, of the War on the South. Real Cause, Hatred of Democracy.

Mr. A.K. Fisk, a distinguished Republican, throws some light on the relationship of the two parties, Hamilton's and Jefferson's; in other words, the party favoring Monarchy and the party favoring Democracy, the rule of the people.

In the *North American Review* of April, 1879, page 410, Fisk says:

> Hamilton and Jefferson represent the two opposing ideas which prevailed at the time our Government was formed, and which, with some variations, have been the basis of our political divisions into parties ever since, and have been involved in all the contests and controversies in our constitutional career. Hamilton embodied the tendency to a centralization of power in the national Government. There is no doubt that he would have preferred a monarchy. Jefferson, on the other hand, represented the demand for a complete diffusion of sovereignty among the people, and its exercise locally and in the States, and the confining of national functions as closely as possible under the most restrictive interpretation of the Constitution.

Mr. Fisk admits that Hamilton, the monarchist, represented the party which opposed the sovereignty of the people. A writer in the St. Louis *Globe-Democrat*, a staunch advocate of Hamilton's strong government doctrines, in that paper, March 6, 1898, made this significant comment:

> The resemblance between Hamilton and Lincoln is so close no one can resist it. Hamilton is dwarfed by no man. A just parallel of Hamilton and Lincoln will show them alike in many ways. They were alike almost to the point of identity. Hamilton's work made Lincoln's possible.

Hamilton's monarchic principles certainly made Lincoln's work possible. Lincoln put in practice what Hamilton had advocated. Hamilton made no concealment of his monarchic principles; he preferred a monarchy such as England has, but failing that he wanted a President for life and the Governors of States appointed by the President. Until seated in the White House, Lincoln *talked* Democracy and affected great esteem for Jefferson's Democratic principles. As soon as he held in his grip the machinery of government, he schemed for absolute power, and as soon as he was commander in chief of nearly 3,000,000 armed men, no imperial despot in pagan time ever wielded more autocratic power than did Abraham Lincoln, and Republican writers of today are so imbued with imperialism they laud and glorify Lincoln for his usurpation of power.

Although well informed Republicans know that the war on the South was waged neither to save the Union nor to free slaves, it does not suit that party to be candid on this subject. Now and then, however, some Republican forgets the party's policy of secrecy and tells the truth. That boldly imperialistic Republican journal, the *Globe-Democrat*, of St. Louis, in its issue of April 9, 1900, had an article which uncovers facts, even to the foundation stones, on which rested the war of the '60s. Consider the following:

> Lincoln, Grant and the Union armies gave a victory to Hamiltonism [Monarchy] when it subjugated the Confederates (Democrats) in the South. [This is strictly true; it was a victory over Democracy by Monarchy.] The cardinal doctrines of Democracy are the enlargement of the power of the States. All the prodigious energies of the war could not extinguish these. The lesson of the war was extreme and extraordinary, and yet in a sense ineffective.
>
> Ineffective, because it did not crush out the very life of Democ-

racy. Monarchists always appear to be ignorant of the fact that there is a streak of divinity in Democracy which can not be killed. Monarchy a thousand and ten thousand times has fancied it has forever put an end to Democracy, but sooner or later it rises up, fronts and fights for the rights of humanity with all its power. "The Democrats," continues the *Globe-Democrat*, "have been since the war more strenuous than before in insisting on the preservation of the power of the States."

The cardinal doctrine of the Democratic party has not been, since the formation of the Union, the *enlargement* of State power, but has been the *preservation* of the power reserved to the States by the Constitution. The cardinal power of the Republican party, since the day Mr. Lincoln assumed the Presidency, has been the enlargement of executive power. No well-informed man can deny this. "If there was no absurd sentiment," says the *Globe-Democrat*, "about the privileges of the States there would be no campaign on imperialism." Had there been no absurd "sentiment" about human freedom in 1776 there would have been no campaign against the English King.

"Back of all opposition," continues the *Globe-Democrat*, "to imperialism, whatever form it takes, is the old doctrine that the rights reserved by the Constitution to the States are being invaded." This is strictly true. What shadow of right had or have imperialists to encroach on the rights reserved by the Constitution to the States? Such encroachment is an audacious usurpation of power and a dishonest violation of the original contract between the States and the Federal Union.

"The old Federals," says the *Globe-Democrat*, "fought it [Democracy] valiantly, but it was reserved for the Republican party to conquer it." Had the Republican party fought in the open, as did the old Federals, it never would have defeated Democracy. Had it fought in the open, exposing its monarchic principles, the people of the Northern States never would have aided it to crush and conquer Democracy. From its birth in 1854, the Republican party has fought behind a mask. Its imperial features have never been uncovered and exposed to the people's gaze. It has ever posed before the people as the champion of the people's rights.

The following extracts, mostly taken from S. D. Carpenter's *Logic of History*, show New England's continued hate of the Union. In Massachusetts' State convention, 1851, it was – "*Resolved*, That the one issue before the country is dissolution of the Union, in comparison with which all other issues are as dust in the balance; therefore, we have given ourselves to the work of annulling this covenant with death."

In 1856 Lloyd Garrison in a speech loudly declared: "I have said, and I say again, that in proportion to the growth of disunion will be the growth of the Republican cause. This Union is a lie!"

James S. Pike, appointed Minister to the Netherlands, said: "This Union is not worth supporting in connection with the South."

Frederick Douglas, half negro, half white, a great man in the Republican party, in a speech said: "From this time forth I consecrate the labor of my life to the dissolution of the Union, and I care not whether the bolt that rends it shall come from heaven or from hell!" *Loud and long applause.*

These were the sentiments, so far as I can learn, of every man in the Republican party. The Rev. Andrew T. Foss, at a meeting in New York, May 15th, 1857, said: "There never has been an hour when this infamous Union should have been made, and now the hour has to be prayed for when it shall be dashed to pieces forever! I hate the Union!"

In 1850 William Lloyd Garrison, in a speech, shouted out with great vehemence: "A thousand times accursed be this Union!"

Eli Thayer, in *Kansas Crusade*, says: "These men of New England were the original secessionists. They had advocated secession and dissolution of the Union for twenty years before Jefferson Davis put those doctrines in practice." Mr. Thayer makes a mistake by fully forty years. The men of New England first, as Federalists, had preached disunion and secession from 1796 up to the very hour the Republican party took up the work in 1854. The reader must not lose sight of the fact that the Republican party is the legitimate offspring of the Federals, and had inherited all its progenitor's faiths, ambitions and hates.

The genesis is straight, as follows:

Federals in 1796–1804–1814.

Federal-Republican in 1824.

Republican in 1854. Union-Republican from the beginning of the war to its close.

In 1855 Senator Wade of Ohio, at a mass meeting in Maine, in a grand passion of scorn and hate of the Union, threw his arms out wide and shouted: "Let us sweep away this remnant which we call a Union." In another speech Wade cried out: "After all this talk of a Union you have no Union worthy the name."

After the first State had seceded, Wendell Phillips cried out rapturously:

Disunion is the sweetest music! What if a State has no right to secede? Of what consequence is that? A Union is made up of willing States, not of conquerors and conquered. Confederacies invariably tend to dismemberment. The Union was a wall built up hastily; its cement has crumbled hastily. Why should we seek to stop seceded States? Merely to show we can? Let the South go in peace.

Alas! Alas! This just spirit did not remain with Phillips. Did the smell of blood from battlefields gangrene his mind and heart? As the war went on there came times when Mr. Phillips' hate of the South seemed to hurt him so, he cried out in spasms of pain, as when in a speech in Beecher's church his hate became so acute and frenzied he demanded the exile or hanging at one fell swoop of 347,000 men of the South. Before Phillips became poisoned by the smell of blood he had boldly declared the South's right to independence, right to secede, and as boldly had warned President Lincoln that he had no right to send one armed man on the South.

In another speech, full of insane hate of the South, Phillips said: "Washington was a sinner! It becomes an American to cover his face when he places Washington's bust among the great men of the world."

Redman, a friend and follower of Phillips, had the hate insanity as badly as Phillips. "And I," shouted Redman, "would like to spit on that scoundrel, Washington."

It is quite possible that both these men had come to believe so strongly in their own self-righteousness as to think they hated Washington because he had been a slave-holder. It never occurred to them to remember the sins of their own Massachusetts ancestors, their long continued traffic in slaves.

The True American, a Republican paper of Erie, Penn., said: "All this twaddle about preserving the Union is too silly and sickening for anything."

August 23d, 1851, the New Hampton, Massachusetts, *Gazette* announced that a petition was circulating in that region for the dissolution of the Union, and that more than one hundred and fifty names of legal voters had signed it. In 1854 New England sent to Congress a petition, numerously signed, praying for the dissolution of the Union, using these words: "We earnestly request Congress to take measures for the speedy, peaceful and equitable dissolution of the Union."

In 1854 John P. Hale, Chase and Seward voted to receive and consider a petition demanding the dissolution of the Union. These three men had long been anxious to break the Union to pieces. In 1848 Seward voted to receive a petition to dissolve the Union, yet Seward was the man who urged Lincoln to begin war, on the pretext of saving the Union.

In 1857 a meeting was held in Massachusetts, during which the question of war on the South was discussed. Gerritt Smith, an ardent disunion Republican, said: "The time has not yet come to use physical force on the South."

Mr. Langdon of Ohio in a speech said: "Why preserve the Union? It is not worth preserving. I hate the Union as I hate hell!"

Carpenter's *Logic of History* says in 1852 a series of pamphlets were issued advocating disunion, from which is taken the following: "To longer continue this disastrous alliance [the Union] is madness. Allegiance to God and fidelity to the cause of freedom requires that the national compact shall be instantly dissolved. Secession from the Government is a religious and political duty."

Joshua R. Giddings, one of the Republican great men, in 1848 introduced a petition for the dissolution of the Union. Mr. Lincoln appointed Mr. Giddings Consul to the Canadas. Anson Burlingame so hated the Union and the Constitution he declared publicly that "we needed disunion, we needed a new Constitution, a new Bible, and a new God." Mr. Lincoln was so pleased with Mr. Burlingame he sent him Minister to China, at the same time pretending to look on disunion as the most monstrous crime a people can commit, and to punish which he was devastating the South with an army of over 2,000,000 men.

At a Republican convention, held at Monroe, Green county, Wisconsin, in 1856, the following resolution was passed: *"Resolved, That it is the duty of the North, in case we fail in electing a President and Congress that will restore freedom to Kansas, to revolutionize the Government."* The Boston *Liberator* had an article headed in large type: "But one issue! The dissolution of the Union," and urges the people to get up monster petitions to Congress for dissolution of the Union" (See Carpenter's *Logic of History*).

In his debate, 1858, with Parson Pryne, Parson Brownlow, a red hot Republican, said: "A dissolution of the Union is what a large portion of the Republicans are driving at."

In 1855, only one year after the Republican party was organized, Senator Wade, of Ohio, in a speech made in Portland, Maine, said: "There is really no Union now between the North and the South. I believe no two nations on earth entertain feelings of more bitter rancor toward each other than these two peoples." William Lloyd Garrison said: "The Republican party is moulding public sentiment in the right direction for the dissolution of the Union." Charles Sumner was heart and soul a disunionist. In 1854, September 7th. at Worcester, Massachusetts, in a speech Sumner said: "The whole dogma of passive obedience to law must be rejected, in whatever guise it may assume and under whatever alias it may skulk, whether in the tyranny and usurpation of king, parliament or judicial tribunal."

On November 2d, 1859, in a speech made in Brooklyn, Wendell Phillips made the following remarkable assertion: Virginia is not a State! Mr. Wise is not a Governor! The Union is not a nation! All these so-called Governments are organized piracies" (*Logic of History*, page 68). The New York *Herald* of December, 1859 gives an account of a Republican meeting in Tremont Temple, Boston. The Hon. John Andrews, afterwards Governor of Massachusetts, said: "The logic of bayonets and rifles and pikes will be henceforth used against the South." Emerson, the so-called New England philosopher, was at that meeting and said: "We must go back to the original form; in other words, go back to the original right of resistance and revolution, and nullify the Constitution and the laws."

General Jamison, on January 22, 1862, made a speech to his soldiers, which was published in the Leavenworth *Conservative*, in which he said: "This is a war which dates way back of Fort Sumter; ever since 1854 we have been making the long campaign." The Republican party was organized in 1854. General Jamison's knowledge of New England's history did not go back of that date; he knew, as Wendell Phillips had proclaimed, that the Republican party was organized to work against the South, but apparently did not know that party merely took up the warfare its progenitors, the Federals, had been waging against the South since the year 1796.

On December 25, 1860, in the United States Senate, Stephen Douglas said:

> The fact can no longer be disguised that many Republican Senators desire war and disunion under pretense of saving the Union. For partisan reasons they are anxious to de-

stroy the Union. They want this done without holding them responsible before the people.

The Boston *Commonwealth*, Senator Sumner's organ, said: "How dare any one pray for the preservation of that sin and shame, the Union?" In another issue that organ said: "Unity of the States is a crime! May the tongue wither that prays for the preservation of that festering shame, the Union."

In a convention held in Massachusetts in 1856, a series of resolutions were passed, of which the following are samples: *"Resolved,* 1st. That the necessity of disunion is written in the whole existing character and condition of the two sections of the country. No government on earth is strong enough to hold together such opposing forces." The Roman Empire's government was strong enough to hold together for years, yet in time it broke to pieces. This imperial republican government sooner or later will do the same. The second resolution of that convention is as follows:

> *Resolved,* 2d, That this movement does not merely seek disunion, but the expulsion by the Northern States from the Union of the Southern States. The one great issue before the country is the dissolution of the Union, in comparison with which all other issues are as dust in the balance; therefore we devote ourselves to the work of annulling this covenant with death.

So long had the gospel of hate been preached, those New Englanders had come to hate the South so venomously they wanted to force her out of the Union she loved. Yet, when a few years later the Southern people left the Union, driven to secede by the unrelenting persecution of New England, these very people of New England called her secession a crime and waged upon her bloody war for doing what they had invited her to do, as will be seen from this item.

In 1859, at a Republican convention in New York, the following resolution was unanimously passed: *"Resolved,* That we invite a free correspondence with the disunionists of the South, in order that we may decide upon the most suitable measures to bring about so desirable a result."

The New York *Tribune*, a Republican paper, edited by Horace Greeley, native of New England, said: "Who wants a Union which is nothing but a sentiment to lacquer Fourth of July orations withal? We have no wish for its preservation." At a meeting in Faneuil Hall, Boston, January 2, 3, 4, 1854, it was *"Resolved*, That we seek the dissolution of this Union, and that we hereby declare ourselves the friends of a new Confederacy of States, and for a dissolution of the Union."

William Lloyd Garrison, a son of New England, a great man in the Republican party, in a speech to a large audience cried aloud: "If the church is against disunion, I pronounce the church of the devil. Up with the flag of disunion!" In a speech made May, 1858, in New York city, Wendell Phillips declared that for the last nineteen years he had labored to get sixteen States out of the Union. When in 1856, February 25th, a friend said to Senator Hale, he was certain there would ere long be war with the South, Hale, eager for war, rubbed his hands and gleefully said: "Good! Good! War can't come to soon."

The reader will observe that these Republicans were as anxious for a war on the South as their progenitors, the Federals, had been. In 1856, Banks of Massachusetts, in a speech at Portland, Maine, said: "I am not one who cries for the perpetuation of the Union, I am willing to let it slide." Yet while Banks' party was drenching the Southland with blood and filling all the country, North and South, with mourning, under pretense of saving a Union it long had despised, this same Banks, with a general's epaulets on his shoulders, marched at the head of armed legions on the South to assist in the murderous work.

In 1857, in the fair month of May, the Rev. Andrew Forbes shouted out. "There never was an hour when this blasphemous and infamous Union should have been made; now the hour must be prayed for when it will be dashed to pieces." Does this evidence manifest any change of heart in New England? Had she come to hate Democracy less? Had she come to hate the Union less? The South less? Was she any better satisfied to remain in the Union? Any less anxious to break it to pieces? Had she ceased to believe in State's sovereignty? In the right of States to secede?

Yet, in the face of the above evidence, Mr. E.P. Powell calmly announces that after "New England's shameless conduct during the second war with Great Britain she became of the faithful the most faithful to the Union." Was Mr. Powell *afraid* to tell the plain truth?

A few extracts from the utterances of distinguished Republicans will show how they hated and detested the United States Constitution. In a speech to a large audience, Wendell Phillips cried out: "The Constitution is a mistake! Tear it to pieces! Our aim is disunion!" Hincle, a Republican speaker, cried out in high scorn: "The United States Constitution! I would blow it away as a child blows a feather!" At a meeting in Faneuil Hall, January 23d, 1850, it was –

> *Resolved*, That we seek a dissolution of the Union; and
>
> *Resolved*, That we do hereby declare ourselves the enemies of the Constitution, of the Union, and of the Government of the United States; and
>
> *Resolved*, That we proclaim it as our unalterable purpose and determination to live and labor for the dissolution of the present Union.

The Boston *Daily Mail*, the New York *Independent*, the New York *Herald*, the Boston *Times*, and other papers, reported these meetings and the speeches; some papers condemned, some gibed, some called the speakers foolish fanatics, and dismissed the whole proceeding as absurd, but, so far as I can discover, not a paper called these men rebels, traitors, or their teachings treason.

At a meeting in Boston, May, 1849, Wendell Phillips blazed out in these words: "We confess that we intend to trample on the Constitution of this country. We of New England are not a law-abiding community. God be thanked for it! We are disunionists; we want to get rid of this Union" (*Democratic Speaker's Handbook*, page 72). At South Farmington, on July 5th, 1854, the United States Constitution was publicly burned. Mr. Seward despised the Constitution and called it a paper kite. Beecher jeeringly called the Constitution a sheep-skin Government. May 16, 1863, resolutions passed by the Essex County mass meeting contained this: "Resolved, That the war prosecuted to preserve a Union and a Constitution which should never have existed and which should be at once overthrown, is but a wanton waste of property and a dreadful sacrifice of human life." Horace Greeley said: "All nations have their superstitions; that of our people is the Constitution." Henry Ward Beecher said: "A great many people raise a cry about the Union and the Constitution. The truth is, it is the Constitution that is the trouble; the Constitution has been the foundation of our trouble." The Boston *Liberator*, April 24, 1863, said: "No act of ours do we regard with higher satisfaction than when several years ago, on the 4th of July, in the presence of a great assembly, we committed to the flames the Constitution of the United States and burned it to ashes."

During Garfield's campaign, that outspoken Republican paper, the Lemars (Ia.) Sentinel, voiced Republican principles as follows:

> The Stalwarts do not care a fig for the Constitution, and will trample it under foot today as did Lincoln and the Union hosts from '61 to '65.
>
> The Constitution of the United States has been little beside a curse and a hindrance. It is so today as much as it has been at any time since it was framed. It is the barrier now to the pathway of the nation.

The Wakefield (Kansas) *Semi-Weekly*, a Republican paper, in August, 1880, wanted to destroy the Constitution:

> Let us tear up the present Constitution by the roots, wipe out the same and the laws and so-called Constitutions of every State in this Union. Let the Stalwarts now make their grand attack on the United States Senate, which is the bulwark of State sovereignty.

Seward despised the Constitution, but was careful not to proclaim it to the people. Seward said to General Piatt: "We are all bound by tradition to the tail end of a paper kite called the Constitution. It is held up by a string."

"Why, Mr. Senator," said Piatt, in some heat, "you don't believe that of our Constitution?"

"I certainly do," replied Seward, "but I generally keep it to myself. Our Constitution is to us of the North a great danger. The Southerners are using it as a shield."

The Constitution *was* a shield on which the South relied, but the Republican party overwhelmed the people who held that shield before their breasts; seized that shield, dashed it on the ground and trampled it down in the bloody mire of battlefields. Lincoln, like all Republicans had no respect for the Constitution, but Lincoln was always too shrewd a lawyer to make public his real opinions. General Piatt relates the following story, which illustrates Lincoln's want of reverence for the Constitution. When Amasa Walker, a distinguished New England financier, thought of a scheme by which could be filled the Government treasury, Mr. Davis Tailor went to Secretary Chase and laid before him Amasa Walker's scheme. Chase heard him to the end and then said: "That is all very well, Mr. Tailor, but there is one little obstacle in the way which makes the plan impracticable, and that is the United States Constitution."

Mr. Tailor then went to President Lincoln and laid the matter before him. "Tailor," said Lincoln, "go back to Chase and tell him not to bother himself about the United States Constitution. Say that I have that sacred instrument here at the White House, and I am guarding it with great care."

Chase, Tailor and Lincoln then held a conference. Chase explained how the scheme to raise money was a violation of the Constitution. Lincoln, after his usual habit, swept away Chase's statement of facts by a story:

> Chase, down in Ilinois I was held to be a pretty good lawyer; now this thing reminds me of a story. An Italian captain run his vessel on a rock and knocked a hole in her bottom. He set his men to pumping and went to prayers before a figure of the Virgin Mary in the bow of the ship. The leak gained on them until it looked as if the vessel would go down with all on board. Then the captain, in a fit of rage at not having his prayers answered, seized the figure of the Virgin Mary and threw it overboard. Suddenly the leak stopped, the water was pumped out and the vessel got safely into port. When docked for repairs the statue of the Virgin Mary was found stuck head foremost in the hole.

Chase, who never liked Lincoln's stories, told the President he did not see the application of the story. "Why, Chase," returned Lincoln, "I didn't intend precisely to throw the Virgin Mary overboard – by that I mean the Constitution – But I will stick it into the hole if I can." And he did stick it in the hole. The Iowa editor told the tale more tersely, when he admiringly said: "Abraham Lincoln kicked the Constitution into the Capitol cellar, and there it remained innocuous until the war ended."

When the bill for dismembering Virginia was up for consideration Thaddeus Stevens gave vent to his respect for the Constitution as follows:

I will not stultify myself by supposing that we have any warrant in the Constitution for this proceeding. This talk of restoring the Union as it was under the Constitution is one of the absurdities repeated until I have become sick of it. This Union shall never be restored, with my consent, under the Constitution as it is.

As its progenitors, the Federals of 1796, had believed in the right of secession, so did their legitimate offspring, the Republican party, born in 1854, believe in secession from the day of its birth. The highest orators of that party publicly declared such belief. Even before the organization of the Republican party, Mr. Lincoln proclaimed his faith in the right of secession. On the 13th day of January, 1848, from the floor of Congress, Mr. Lincoln declared for the right of States to secede from the Union:

Any people anywhere, being inclined and having the power, have the right to rise up and shake off the existing government and to form one that suits them better. Nor is this right confined to cases in which the people of an existing government may choose to exercise it. Any portion of such people that can, may make their own of such territory as they inhabit. More than this, a majority of any portion of such people may revolutionize, putting down a minority intermingling with or near them who oppose their movements (Appendix to *Congressional Globe*, 1st Session, 30th Congress, page 94).

These words ring with the spirit of 1776. The South's secession fulfilled every requirement laid down by Lincoln. The South *had* the right and she exercised it with decency and dignity. She did not rise up and shake off the Union Government in a turbulent manner; she quietly withdrew. She did not, as New England did in 1814, select a time to withdraw when it might endanger the Union. She bade her old political associates a sorrowful farewell. She assured them of her desire to remain at peace, and respectfully asked them to make a just settlement of their partnership affairs. Buchanan received those overtures in a friendly spirit; so did the great body of the North's people. How did Lincoln receive them? For six weeks Lincoln and Seward pursued an ambiguous, deceitful course; they did not take the people of the North into their confidence; they strove to deceive; they made speeches now looking toward war, now toward peace. Lincoln afterward said the hardest work he ever did was making these speeches intended to deceive. Not until Lincoln was ready to strike the first blow of war did he cry out to the South, "Rebel! Traitor!" When he called for 75,000 armed men on the pretense of defending his Capitol, he falsely asserted and deceived the people of the North into the belief that the South was eager for war, and intended to invade the North. Lincoln's war on the South began with falsehoods and was run on falsehoods to the bitter end. In the court of posterity how will this dissimulation be judged?

In *Recollections of Lincoln*, Lamon says of his journey from Springfield to Washington:

> Mr. Lincoln's speeches were the absorbing topic of the hour. The people everywhere were eager to hear a forecast of his policy, and he was eager to keep silence. After having been en route a day or two he told me he had done much hard work in his life, but to make speeches day after day with the object of speaking and saying nothing, was the hardest work he had ever done (page 34).

At no period of Mr. Lincoln's presidency was he candid and sincere to the people. It was his nature to trick and deceive. Imperial Republicans of to-day laud and admire this trait in his character. They praise his ability to use the fox's skin when the lion's was too short.

Senator Wade of Ohio was one of the highest lights in the Republican party. Wade, as emphatically as Lincoln had done, declared the right of secession on December 4th, 1856, from the Senate floor Senator Wade of Ohio proclaimed the South's right to secede as follows:

> I am not one to ask the South to continue in such a Union as this. It would be doing violence to the platform of the party to which I belong. We have adopted the old Declaration of Independence as the basis of our political movement, which declares that any people, when their government ceases to protect their rights, have the right to recur to original principles, and if need be to destroy the government under which they live, and to erect on its ruins another conducive to their welfare. I hold that the people of the South have this right. I

will not blame any people for exercising this right whenever they think the contingency has come. You can not forcibly hold men in the Union, for the attempt to do so would subvert the first principles of the Government under which we live (*Congressional Globe*, 3d Session, 34th Congress, page 25).

In all the long and woeful story of man's treachery to man is there an instance of treachery blacker than this of which the Republican party was guilty in the '60s? For more than 60 years that party, first as Federals then as Republicans, had preached and prayed for secession, had urged the South to secede, had invited the South to aid it to break the Union asunder, had hated and denounced the Union as a covenant with hell, yet, when at last the Southern people, to escape the hate so long poured upon them, peacefully, quietly withdrew from the Union, that same Republican party turned on them with a fury, a vindictive ferocity, a hellish animosity, which not even savage and enraged tigers could surpass.

CHAPTER TWENTY-TWO

Republicans Ascend to Power. Lincoln and Seward Make Ambiguous Speeches. Webster Davis on the Awful Carnage of the War. Seward's Remarkable Letter to Lincoln. Nicolay and Hay Comment on Seward's Letter. A Moral Pervert.

The reader must bear in mind that in 1860 there were three Presidential candidates in the field. Lincoln was a sectional candidate and a minority President. Of the 4,700,000 votes cast the Republican party only got 1,850,000. Of these 1,850,000, the greater number did not want Lincoln. Seward or Chase was their real choice. Lincoln had only been affiliated with the party two years. Eastern Republicans knew little if anything of Lincoln. What little they did know they did not like or admire. It was said at the time, and is still said by the knowing, that a blunder of Thurlow Weed's lost the prize to Seward and threw it at the feet of Lincoln. Hence during Lincoln's life Republicans called him "His Accidency," not His Excellency. Holland's *Life of Lincoln*, published 1865, seems to have been written to serve two purposes: 1st, to bolster up the apotheosis theory of Lincoln's divinity; 2nd, to laud and glorify the Republican party. Holland never permits a fact to stand in the way of any pretty or pleasing falsehood he may wish to use, yet he sometimes records facts worth remembering. Instance the following:

During the first month of Lincoln's presidency he was thronged with office seekers, and was holding protracted Cabinet meetings. All these labors were performed with consciousness that his nominal friends (men of his own party), as well as the great majority of the people throughout the Union, had not the slightest sympathy with him. There was distraction even in his councils.

From this is seen that not only the great majority of the people throughout the Union, but the men in Lincoln's own party, even in his Cabinet, were opposed to Lincoln's war schemes. McClure, Greeley, Nicolay and Hay, and many other Republican writers bear testimony to the almost universal opposition to war in the Northern States. Lincoln and Seward for a time were the only members of the Cabinet eager to begin war. During the first month of Lincoln's presidency, after the Cabinet members discovered that Lincoln was fixed in his determination to begin war. the question was discussed at what point should it begin. Seward opposed beginning at Fort Sumter; he wanted to strike the first blow on the gulf at Pensacola.

Hapgood says the New York *Tribune*, New York *Herald*, and many other papers representing different parties in the Northern States, as well as in the middle, in Massachusetts and Boston itself, at first opposed war on the South, and boldly declared that the South had acted on her rights. Hapgood seems to be ignorant of the fact that the Republican party itself was a secession party, and for over twenty years had zealously worked for disunion.

Chase said: "Dissolution of the Union is better than a conflict. I will oppose any attempt to reinforce Sumter if it means war." Seward said in the Cabinet: "Even preparation to reinforce will precipitate war." Gideon Wells, Secretary of the Navy, was weak on this question. Of all his Cabinet, Lincoln only found Blair in favor of reinforcing Sumter. There was not a man in the Cabinet that did not know that the attempt to reinforce Sumter would be the first blow of war.

A few blood-thirsty leaders of the Republican party had entered into a conspiracy to force war on the country at any and every cost, despite the opposition of the great majority of people in the Northern States, and despite the South's pleas for peace.

February 2d, 1861, Mr. Stephen Douglas, in a letter published in the Memphis *Appeal*, wrote of the Republican leaders as follows:

> They are bold, determined men. They are striving to break up the Union under the pretense of preserving it. They are struggling to overthrow the Constitution while professing undying attachment to it, and a willingness to make any sacrifice to maintain it. They are trying to plunge the country into

a cruel war as the surest means of destroying the Union upon the plea of enforcing the laws and protecting public property.

Shortly after Douglas wrote the above letter. Senator Zack Chandler of Michigan wrote a letter to Governor Austin Blair, which proves the guilty conspiracy of the men determined on war. Virginia had solicited a conference of States to see if some plan could not be devised and agreed on to prevent war and save the Union. Chandler wrote Governor Blair that he opposed the conference, and no Republican State should send a delegate. He implored Governor Blair to send stiff-backed delegates or none, as the whole thing was against his judgment. Chandler added to his letter these sinister words: "Some of the manufacturing States think that a war would be awful; without a little blood-letting this Union will not be worth a curse" (Carpenter's *Logic of History*, page 138).

Assistant Secretary of the Interior Webster Davis, in an oration on Decoration Day at Arlington, said: "Counting the men who fell in battles and received wounds not mortal at the moment, but who died afterward from these wounds, 700,000 soldiers who wore the blue died of that awful war." These 700,000 men in blue were sacrificed on the pretext of defending the flag and saving the Union. Both pretexts were impudent falsehoods. Not a man in the Republican party respected the flag. Both Union and flag were scorned and hated by Republicans. The New York *Tribune* was in the habit of adorning its columns with doggerel deriding the flag. For example:

> Tear down the flaunting lie;
> Half mast the starry flag:
> Insult no sunny sky
> With Hate's polluted rag.

Is there a flag on earth worth the sacrifice of 700,000 lives, to say nothing of the anguish of hearts left behind to mourn over the sacrifice?

No man acquainted with the history of the Republican party can for one moment doubt that, from the day of its organization in 1854 to the hour Fort Sumter was fired on, Republicans had striven might and main to dissolve the Union. In view of this indisputable fact, what will Posterity think of the trickery, the cunning, the mean and base deception of Republican officials, who inaugurated and for four years waged the most cruel war ever fought between English-speaking people on the flimsy pretext of saving the Union?

During the first month of Lincoln's presidency he was busy looking after office-seekers. Not a step did he take toward war. Seward, the man utterly callous to human suffering, became impatient to begin war, not only with the South, but with two European kingdoms as well. Tremendous war schemes brooded in Seward's brain. Exulting in the possession of power, Seward was eager to use it for the destruction and misery of his fellow-mortals. At the end of the first month, unable longer to bear the quiet of peace, Seward longed to plunge this country, as well as two European countries, into a sea of human blood. To hurry up Lincoln, Seward wrote a carefully prepared paper intended for Lincoln's eye only. We give this singular document verbatim. It was headed – "Some Thoughts for the President's Consideration."

> First. We are at the end of a month's administration and yet without a policy.
>
> Second. This, however, is not culpable, it has been unavoidable. The presence of the Senate with the need to meet applications for patronage have prevented attention to other and more grave matters.
>
> Third. But further delay to adopt and prosecute our policy for both domestic and foreign affairs, would not only bring scandal on the administration, but danger on the country.
>
> Fourth. To do this we must dismiss the applicants for office, but, how? I suggest that we make the local appointments forthwith, leaving foreign or general ones for ulterior and occasional action.
>
> Fifth. The policy at home. My system is built on this idea as a ruling one, viz: That we must change the question before the public from one upon slavery or about slavery, to a question of Union or Disunion. In other words, from what would be regarded as a party question, to one of Patriotism or Union. The occupation and evacuation of Fort Sumter although not in fact a slavery or party question is so regarded. Witness the temper manifested by the Republicans of the Northern States, and by the Union men in the South. For the rest I would simultaneously defend and reinforce all the

Forts in the gulf, and have the Navy recalled from foreign stations to be prepared for a blockade. Put the Island of Key West under martial law. This will raise distinctly the question of Union or Disunion. I would maintain every fort and Federal possession in the South. I would at once demand explanations from France and Spain categorically. I would demand explanations from Great Britain and Russia, and send agents into Canada, Mexico, and Central America, to rouse a vigorous Continental spirit of Independence on this continent against European intervention. And if satisfactory explanations are not received from Spain and France, I would convene Congress and declare war against them. For this reason it must be somebody's business to pursue and direct it incessantly. Either the President must do it and be all the while actively in it, or devolve it on some member of his cabinet. Once adopted debates must end and all agree and abide. It is not my especial province, but I neither seek to evade or assume responsibility.

Wm. H. Seward.

It does not appear that this letter of Seward's was ever laid before the Cabinet. It does not appear that his proposal to pick a quarrel with France and Spain, and make war on those two countries as well as on the South, was ever discussed in the Cabinet. The evidence goes to show that Seward gave the letter to Lincoln for his private consideration only, and that Lincoln said nothing about it, but accepted the advice to drop their party's issue, *slavery*, and in its place put the issue, *"Save the Union."* He rejected the advice to seek a quarrel with and make war on France and Spain. No act of Lincoln's and Seward's lives shows a more autocratic spirit than the way they turned down their party's issue and set up an issue their party hated. Both Lincoln and Seward were creatures of the Republican party, put in office by Republican votes, yet in the very outset of their official career they offered the grossest possible insult to that party by spurning its most cherished issue, *slavery*, and putting in its place the *Union*, a thing their party had ever despised, hated, and denounced from a thousand rostrums.

In Nicolay and Hay's *Life of Lincoln*, Vol. 3, page 440, we find this comment on Seward's letter:

On April 1st, 1861, Seward made Lincoln a proposition to turn his back on the party which had put him into office, and by certain arbitrary acts he would plunge the country into foreign wars, and asked Lincoln to invite him [Seward] to manage all this, to bring on the wars and carry them on.

Nicolay and Hay seemed to perceive something of the stupendous crime and the egregious folly involved in Seward's proposition to plunge the country into war with two unoffending kingdoms of Europe, but neither of these two men seemed, even dimly to perceive the equally stupendous crime of forcing a conflict between the people of the Northern and the people of the Southern States, both peoples at that time feeling kindly toward each other, both anxious to avoid war, both loving peace, believing there was no just cause for war. Nicolay and Hay were ready enough to condemn Seward for *inviting* Lincoln to turn his back on his party's issue, *slavery*, and to take up an issue, *the Union*, which his party had hated from the day of its organization, but not one word of blame have these two apotheosizing men for Lincoln, who so readily accepted Seward's advice on the issue question and his advice to begin war on the South, but rejected the advice to pick a quarrel with and declare war on France and Spain. Nicolay and Hay were two young men of Springfield, Illinois, who, when Lincoln went to Washington city, accompanied him thither, and were Lincoln's private secretaries until his death. In 1890, twenty-five years after Lincoln's death, these two men jointly concocted ten large volumes, which they labeled *The Life of Lincoln*, and dedicated to Robert Lincoln, the dead President's son. As the whole work seems to have been gotten up under the influence of the apotheosis ceremony, more for the purpose of glorifying the deified dead President than to show him to the public as he was in life, a more appropriate title would be *A Ten Volume Monument to the Deified Lincoln*.

The reader should here pause and carefully consider Seward's letter to Lincoln. Look at its items one by one, consider the fact that Seward had long been an honored and trusted member of the Republican party, whose votes had put him and Lincoln into power; consider the fact that the darling desire of his party had ever been to sever the Union in twain, that to free slaves was its war cry, its hobby. Consider the insult to his party, the treachery to party principles, the outrage to party feelings, involved in Seward's proposal to cast aside as a useless rag his party's banner blazoned with the mottoes they loved, "Free Slaves! Down with the Union!" and in their place put the motto, "Save the Union!" A thing which stunk in their nostrils. *Save* a thing they had ever hated? *Save* the thing whose destruction they had prayed for, labored for, since their party's birth? What induced Seward and Lincoln to take this ungrateful, this insulting course toward their own party? The reasons are not hard to find; they lie on the surface, to be seen by all with eyes to set and judgments to understand. Lincoln and Seward were of the nature to revel in the use of power. To be commanders and dictators of a great war would greatly enhance their power. Determined to make war, yet finding that the great body of the Northern people had set their faces as flints against a war based on the slavery issue, these two men, the one keenly astute, the other with a "cunning that was genius," both destitute of moral scruples, both with hearts of stone, for one month pondered over the situation. The people would not support a war based on slavery; the problem they had to solve was by what means could they rouse the peace-loving people of the North to the fury of war? They saw but one way, and that was to turn their backs on their own party, cast that party's issue to the dogs, set up the word "Union" as a god to fight and die for, and make the Northern people believe the South intended a war of invasion on their States, on their Union Government. Imperialists always look on the people as sheep, to be deceived and driven. Alas! in this case the people were indeed deceived and driven into war, and 700,000 men who wore the blue were sacrificed on the altar of that false god, the Union. The scheme was successfully carried out, the people of the North were tricked, the people of the South forced into war. In all the black history of man's treachery to man, I know of nothing more damnable than this.

    The arguments Seward used in his letter to Lincoln are as foolish as they are false. "Delay," wrote Seward, "to prosecute our policy [the policy of war] will not only bring scandal on the administration, but danger to the country." As war is the greatest evil that can befall a people, except dishonor, how could delay in bringing that evil bring scandal and danger? The scandal and danger was in bringing the war, not in the delay of bringing it. Seward and Lincoln had not been elected to bring war on the people; the people did not want war. From what source, then, could the danger come? Certainly not from the South. The South was pleading for peace. Secession had been an accomplished fact for months before Lincoln took his seat in the Presidential chair. There was not the faintest shadow of danger in that direction. Would the reader like to understand the mental and moral traits of the man who wrote that remarkable letter to Lincoln? General Piatt, a personal friend and great admirer of Seward, in 1887 sketched his character thus:

> Seward begun life as a school teacher in the South. He had been treated with condescending indifference by the unenlightened masters, which treatment he never forgot. [Was it spite that made Seward so vindictive toward the Southern people?]
>
> Seward looked down on the white men of the South in the same cynical way that he did upon the slaves. He had no pity for the slaves, and no dislike for the master. He was a great favorite with the last named. He had contempt for them, which he concealed as carefully as he did his contempt for the United States Constitution. Seward had trained himself to believe that worldly wickedness indicated ability. He thought to be bad was to be clever. He thought that devotion to wine, women and infidelity gave proof of superior intelligence. He affected a wickedness he did not feel, because such wickedness, in his estimation, was good form.

In presenting to the public this picture of his friend, General Piatt seems to have had no suspicion that he was writing down that friend as a moral degenerate, a mental pervert. No mentally and morally sound man can possibly believe that *"wickedness indicates mental ability,"* or that *"devotion to wine, women and infidelity gives proof of a superior intelligence."* Everyone knows when men talk of devotion to wine and women they mean devotion to drink and prostitutes, not to the honest wives, mothers and daughters in the land. Yet to this moral degenerate, this mental pervert, Lincoln delegated power as despotic as any Bourbon King of old exercised over his subjects. Lincoln was as eager for war on the South as Seward. He made haste to drop the slavery issue and put in its place the Union. The old leaders of the party were angry enough at this outrage to their party's feelings and principles, and when Lincoln called for 75,000 men to fight for the Union, some of those leaders took the stump and tried to prevent enlistments. Parker Pillsbury, in a speech, said to young men:

> Recognize your own manhood; your own divine rights and destiny, and believe yourselves too sacred to be shot down like dogs by Jeff Davis and his myrmidons; die rather at home in the arms of a loving mother and sisters. Be shot down, if you must, *at home*; die like Christians, and have a decent burial, rather than go down and die in the cause of a Union blistered all over with the curses of God.

Wendell Phillips, speaking of Lincoln, cried out in high scorn: "Who is this huckster in politics? Who is this county court lawyer?" In another speech Phillips denounced the war and denounced "that slave-hound from Illinois!" In another speech Phillips denounced the war and denounced Lincoln roundly:

> Here are a series of States girding the gulf which think they should have an independent government; they have a right to decide that question without appealing to you or to me. Standing with the principles of '76 behind us, who can deny them that right? Abraham Lincoln has no right to a soldier in Fort Sumter. You cannot go through Massachusetts and enlist men to bombard Charleston and New Orleans.

But not only did Lincoln go through Massachusetts and enlist men to bombard the cities of the South, he soon brought Wendell Phillips to embrace despotism as ardently as lover ever embraced his bride. He made Phillips repudiate and spit on the principles of '76, made him shout loudest of all to the South, "Rebel! Traitor! Rebel! Traitor!"

On another occasion Phillips told his audience that he "had labored for nineteen years to dissolve the Union, and now success has come at last." Before utterly subjected to despotism, in a speech Phillips said: "Let the South go! Let her go with flags flying and trumpets blowing! Give her her forts, her arsenals, and her sub-treasuries. Speed the parting guest! All hail disunion! Beautiful on the mountains are the feet of them who bring the glad tidings of disunion!" Not only did Wendell Phillips voice the opinion of the majority of his own party, but on the subject of war on the South he voiced the feelings and opinions of all classes of men in the Northern States. Yet, in spite of this immense opposition to war, Seward and Lincoln, as Greeley said, "clearly put themselves in the wrong and rushed on carnage," and not only did these men turn their backs on their own party, but they turned their backs on their own opinions, privately and publicly declared, as will be shown in the next chapter.

CHAPTER TWENTY-THREE
☆ ☆ ☆ ☆

Seward's Falsehoods. Treachery Blacker than Benedict Arnold's. Lincoln Confesses that He, at Medill's Demand, Made War on the South.

On April 4th, 1861, Seward said to Russell, the London *Times* correspondent: "It would be contrary to the spirit of the American Government to use armed force to subjugate the South. If the people of the South want to stay out of the Union, if they desire independence, let them have it." On April l0th, 1861, Seward officially wrote C.F. Adams, then Minister to England: "Only a despotic and imperial government can subjugate seceding States."

With a treachery blacker than Benedict Arnold's, knowingly, deliberately, these two men, Seward and Lincoln, determined to change the American Government from a free Republic to an imperial despotism. During the first month of Lincoln's Presidency the question of war or peace was freely discussed in the Cabinet. Few members were in favor of war. Chase strongly opposed war. Chase always had been a disunionist; he welcomed disunion and wanted to let the South possess the peace and independence that was hers by right. Not one single member of the Cabinet was ignorant of the fact that an attempt to reinforce Fort Sumter would be the first blow of war. In a discussion of this question in the Cabinet, Seward said:

> The attempt to reinforce Sumter will provoke an attack and involve war. The very preparation for such an expedition will precipitate war at that point. I oppose beginning war at that point. I would advise against the expedition to Charleston. I would at once, at every cost, prepare for war at

Pensacola and Texas. I would instruct Major Anderson to retire from Sumter.

Lincoln preferred to open the war at Sumter. If there is a man in America so ignorant as to believe the falsehood put forth by these unscrupulous men that the South began the war, that Lincoln was averse to war, that he called for 75,000 armed men to protect Washington City, let him consider the story found in Miss Tarbell's *Life of Lincoln*, page 144, Vol. II. Medill, of the Chicago *Tribune*, tells the story, and Miss Tarbell puts it in her book. It is a very valuable item of history, for it kills the old, old lie so often told that the South began the war of the '60s:

> In 1864 [relates Medill] when the call for extra troops came, Chicago revolted. Chicago had sent 22,000 and was drained. There were no young men to go, no aliens except what was already bought. The citizens held a mass meeting and appointed three men, of whom I [Medill] was one, to go to Washington and ask Stanton [the War Secretary] to give Cook County a new enrollment. On reaching Washington we went to Stanton with our statement. He refused. Then we went to President Lincoln. "I can not do it," said Lincoln, "but I will go with you to Stanton and hear the arguments of both sides."
>
> So we all went over to the War Department together. Stanton and General Frye were there, and they both contended that the quota should not be changed. The argument went on for some time, and was finally referred to Lincoln, who had been silently listening. When appealed to, Lincoln turned to us with a black and frowning face: "Gentlemen," he said, with a voice full of bitterness, "after Boston, Chicago has been the chief instrument in bringing this war on the country. The Northwest opposed the South, as New England opposed the South. It is *you*, Medill, who is largely responsible for making blood flow as it has. *You* called for war until you had it. I have given it to you. What you have asked for you have had. Now you come here begging to be let off from the call for more men, which I have made to carry on the war you demanded. You ought to be ashamed of yourselves. Go

home and raise your 6,000 men. And you, Medill, you and your *Tribune* have had more influence than any other paper in the Northwest in making this war. Go home and send me those men I want."

Medill says that he and his companions, feeling guilty, left without further argument. They returned to Chicago, and 6,000 more men from the working classes were dragged from their homes, their families, forced into the ranks to risk limbs and lives in a war they had no part in making, while the men that *forced* that war on an unwilling people remained at home in comfort and safety, and made enormous fortunes by the war. Is it any wonder educated workingmen often become anarchists and hate all governments?

Reflect, oh, reader, on Lincoln's words: "*You*, Medill called for war. I have given you war. What you asked for you have. You demanded war. I [Lincoln] have given you what you demanded, and you, Medill, are largely responsible for all the blood that has flowed." In the court of posterity Lincoln will not be able to throw all of that responsibility on Medill. Had Lincoln been true to his trust, true to the principles of '76, true to the United States Constitution he had sworn to obey, true to the party whose vote had put him in office, true to the great body of the Northern people, who opposed war, true to his own declaration of the right of secession, no number of Medills and no number of Chandlers could have made him begin that awful war of the '60s. These three men – Lincoln, Seward and Medill – were the chief conspirators against American liberty. They lived to see the triumph of their evil work. They lived to see the principles of Democracy trampled down into the bloody mire on a hundred battlefields. They lived to see the desolation of the States they had hated for their adherence to Jefferson's principles. They lived to see the once free people of the States on the South Atlantic coast robbed of every liberty they had won by their swords from England's King. They lived to see the South's fair and fruitful fields desolate deserts, her homes heaps of ashes, her fertile land a wide waste; and if, during all that devilish work, one word of sympathy for the suffering people of the South, one word of pity for the anguish and agonies endured, ever passed the lips of either of these three men I have failed to find any record thereof. On the contrary, the more cruel officers and soldiers were in the field, the more highly they were commended.

It is related that the last utterance that fell from Lincoln's lips was a gibe at the crushed and conquered South. "Shall the orchestra play Dixie?" he was asked as he sat in his box in Ford's theatre that fatal night. "We have conquered the South," returned Lincoln gleefully, "we may as well take her music." Even as he spoke the unseen Nemesis was standing near, her eyes upon him. In her hidden hand the missile of death. To the sound of the South's spirit-stirring air the soul of the man who had rushed on carnage fled from its house of clay to stand before the bar of the Great Judge and receive sentence for the deeds he had done on earth.

CHAPTER TWENTY-FOUR

Greeley Opposes War on the South. He Speaks To and For the Republican Party. He Declares the Right of Secession. Why Lincoln did not Sooner Begin the War. Why Buchanan Did Not Begin It.

Before giving Mr. Greeley's testimony, it is well to show the people of this age how he stood with his own party. Greeley was a life-long abolitionist. All abolitionists believed in the right of secession. All hated the Union and wanted to break it to pieces. No man stood higher in the Republican party than Greeley. In *Our Presidents, and How We Make Them*, McClure says: "Greeley was one of the noblest, purest and ablest of the great men of the land. Greeley was in closer touch with the active sense of the people than even President Lincoln himself."

After Lincoln's death, and the apotheosis ceremony had been performed, it became the custom of Republican writers and speakers to talk of "Lincoln's being in touch with the people." This is nothing but apotheosis twaddle. Lincoln was no more in touch with the common people than he was with the distinguished leaders of his own party. It is almost the unanimous testimony of Republicans who knew the living Lincoln that he was neither trusted or beloved by the people of any class. Stanton, when on his death-bed, told General Piatt that the common soldiers in the army had to be warned by their officers not to manifest their dislike to Lincoln when he came to review them.

McClure says: "Greeley's *Tribune* was the most widely read Republican paper in the country, and was more potent in moulding Republican sentiment." In a letter to Robert J. Walker, Lincoln said: "Greeley is a great power: to have him firmly behind me would be equal to an army of 100,000 men." At no time did Lincoln have Greeley behind him. It is said Greeley was always a thorn in Lincoln's side. He was a very large thorn in opposing the war, and after the war was on Greeley was a severe critic of Lincoln's methods of management. Any Democrat as outspoken as Greeley would promptly have been sent to prison. Before it was certain that Lincoln meant coercion, day in and day out Greeley opposed coercion. In one issue of his *Tribune*, Greeley said: "If the cotton States decide that they can do better out of the Union than in it, we insist on letting them go in peace." In another issue he said: "If eight States, having 5,000,000 people, choose to separate from us, they cannot be permanently prevented by cannon." Greeley did not then dream it was the purpose of Lincoln and Seward to change the form of the Union Government from the principles of '76 to the monarchic strong central Government advocated by Hamilton, which would enable them forcibly to hold the South in the Union.

On December 17, 1860, three days before South Carolina seceded from the Union, the *Tribune* had this: "The South has as good a right to secede from the Union as the colonies had to secede from Great Britain. I will never stand for coercion, for subjugation. It would not be just." This was good Democratic doctrine, but not yet was Lincoln ready to arrest and imprison men for such utterances.

Again: "If the Declaration of Independence justified the secession from the British Empire of 3,000,000 of colonists in 1776, we do not see why it would not justify the secession of 5,000,000 of Southerners from the Federal Union in 1860." Democracy of this sort was hard to bear, but still Lincoln and Seward were silent.

In the *Tribune* of February 23. 1861, five days after Jefferson Davis was inaugurated President of the Southern Confederacy, Greeley's *Tribune* had this: "If the cotton States or the gulf States choose to form an independent nation, they have a clear moral right to do so. If the great body of the Southern people have become alienated from the Union and wish to escape from it, we will do our best to forward their views."

When Greeley wrote these articles, in his heart was a strong sense of Democratic justice. Greeley knew that for over twenty years his own party had done and said everything the bitterness of hate could devise to alienate the Southern States and drive them out of the Union. He knew that his party, day in and day out, for years had been hurling on Southern men and women every species of calumny and insult the

English language could convey. He knew his party was extremely anxious to have the South secede. He knew that the foremost men of his party had publicly invited the men of the South to join them in measures to break up the Union. Democratic doctrines of this nature daily appearing in the Republican party's most influential paper greatly annoyed and alarmed Lincoln and Seward, but not yet had the time arrived to apply the thumb screws of force. The *Tribune* continued to give forth what war Republicans called Democratic screeches.

On November 5, 1860, in his *Tribune*, Greeley said:

> Whenever a considerable section of our Union is resolved to go out of the Union, we shall resist all coercive measures to keep them in. We hope never to live in a Republic when one section is pinned to another by bayonets. Those who would rush on carnage to defeat the separation demanded by the popular vote of the Southern people would clearly place themselves in the wrong.

On March 2, 1861, in the *Tribune*, Greeley had this:

> We have repeatedly said, and we once more say, the great principles embodied in the Declaration of Independence, that Governments derive their just powers from the consent of the governed, is sound and just. If the Southern people choose to secede and found an independent government of their own, they have the moral right to do so.

This was the last trumpet-toned blast from Greeley. Lincoln and Seward were now ready to act. "This must be stopped or it will stop us," muttered the man whose foot was on the step of the first American throne. "Give me a little bell," returned his high chief counselor, "and I'll ring for the arrest of every Democratic screecher." What measures were used to silence Greeley, or rather to make him sing an entirely different tune, may never be known, but they were effective. The change was made in a single night. On the morning following his strongest Democratic utterance, Greeley completely reversed his position, and thenceforth the pages of the *Tribune* were freely besprinkled with words grown obsolete under Democracy's rule – words native to kingly climes – rebel, traitor, treason, loyal, disloyal, truly loyal, etc. Under cover of darkness Greeley cut loose forever from the principles of 1776, and fled to the camp of the men who represented the dogmas of George III. of England. He became not only the advocate of those dogmas, but the ally and servitor of the men who rushed on carnage. He not only upheld the wrong he had so eloquently denounced, but viciously turned on the victims of that wrong, traduced and maligned them to excuse his own ignoble and cowardly abandonment of sacred principles. After the war ended Greeley wrote a book called the *American Conflict*, and as if to justify his change from the principles of '76 to the doctrine of imperialism, he affected to believe that the South had fought for slavery and the Republican party to destroy slavery. No man in America better than Greeley knew that the South fought for precisely the same principles for which the colonies of '76 had fought – independence. No man better than Greeley knew that Lincoln inaugurated war from precisely the same motives which made George III. of England wage war on the colonies – conquest. To sustain the falsehood that the South fought for slavery, Greeley plentifully besprinkled the pages of his book with words intended to convey the idea that slavery was the animus, the germ of the war. The words "rebels, traitors, slave-holders' rebellion, slave-holders' war, slave-holders' treason," stare out from every page of Greeley's book. No man better than Greeley knew it was no more the slave-holders' war than was the war of '76. Greeley knew that the great body of the South's people almost to a unit wanted independence, and fought to gain it. He knew that the great body of the South's people were not slave-holders. Blair, of Maryland, a close friend of Lincoln, on this subject said: "It is absurd to say this is the slave-holders' war. In all the South are only about 250,000 slave holders. These rich men are not too eager for war. It is the Southern *people's* war. The *people* want independence and mean to get it if they can."

The cotton, rice and sugar planters were mostly the slave holders of the South. These were not the men most eager to risk life and property in battling for independence. As a general rule, the rich are conservative, are afraid of untried conditions. The thousand and one insults, the slanders, the intense hatred New England, first led by Federalists, then by the Republican party, for sixty years had hurled on the South's people, had driven them to secession. Who would not wish to leave a house of hate?

Greeley said that the *Tribune* had plenty of company in its antiwar sentiments. It is stated that over two hundred of the foremost journals in the East coincided with Greeley in opposition to war. The New York *Herald*, November 9, 1860, said:

> For far less provocation than the South has had, our fathers seceded from Great Britain. Coercion is out of the question; each State possesses the right to break the tie of the Union, as a nation has to break a treaty. A State has the right to repel coercion as a nation has to repel invasion.

Morse, in *Lincoln, One of the American Statesmen Series*, published in 1892, says: "It was appalling to read the columns of Greeley's *Tribune*." It was appalling only to the few men of that time who, with Seward, Lincoln, Chandler and Medill, were eager to begin war, and impatient at the people's opposition. In his *Life of Lincoln*, published in 1865, Holland gives the reason why Lincoln did not call for armed men to "suppress rebels" before the fall of Sumter:

> Up to the fall of Sumter, Mr. Lincoln had no basis for action in the public feeling. If he had raised an army, that would have been an act of hostility, that would have been coercion. A thousand Northern presses would have pounced down on him as a provoker of war. After the fall of Sumter was the time to act.

This shows how almost unanimous was the public feeling against war until after the Northern people had been worked up by the lie that the South intended to invade the North. Republican writers of today call the opposition of that time treason, and the opposers "traitors." If they were traitors, then more than two-thirds of the American people in the North were traitors. John T. Morse, in *Lincoln, American Statesman Series,* 1892, excuses President Buchanan on the same ground that Holland excuses Lincoln. He says:

> While Buchanan's message to Congress [announcing that he had no constitutional warrant to coerce seceding States] had been bitterly denounced a palliating consideration ought to be noted, viz: The fact that Buchanan knew that he had no reason to believe that if he had asserted the right and duty of war, he would be supported by either the moral or the physical force of the people. The almost universal feeling of

the people in the North was strongly opposed to any act of war. Their spirit was conciliatory.

McClure, author of *Lincoln and Men of the War Time*, page 292, says: "A very large proportion of the Republican party, including its most trusted leaders, believed that peaceable secession would result in reconstruction."

CHAPTER TWENTY-FIVE

Almost Universal Opposition to War on the South. Indiana Longs for Peace. Governor Morton's Desperate Fidelity. "I am the State." Congressman Cameron's Bosh on the "Life of the Nation." Nicolay and Hay's Bosh on "Treason."

Morse, p. 250, says: "Most of Lincoln's ministers were against the re-enforcement of Fort Sumter." They opposed a re-enforcement because they knew a re-enforcement meant war. Mass meetings were held in Northern States denouncing war, and messages sent to Lincoln, warning him that if he sent an army South he would find a fire in his rear.

Is it not marvelous that men of today seem to believe it quite a credit to Lincoln that he alone begun the war in opposition to the great body of the people? Morse and other Republican writers seem to believe it redounds to Lincoln's glory, that *he* made war on the South in opposition to the people's wishes. They seem to forget that the basic principle of this Government is that the will of the people shall rule, not the will of one man.

In *American Conflict*, page 356, Greeley says: "The Southern States had the active sympathy of a large majority of the American people." It is now the Republican's custom to say that this sympathy was caused by "demoralization." By what right did the small minority force war on the large majority? Morse says: "Greeley, Wendell Philips, Seward and Chase, representative men of the Republican party, were little better than secessionists." Is it possible that Mr. Morse is so ignorant of the history of the Republican party as not to know that from its organization, in 1854, up to the first blow of war struck by Lincoln at

Sumter, the whole Republican party were secessionists, and that party had labored for disunion, labored for secession? Is it possible that Mr. Morse knows nothing of the efforts the Federal forefathers of Republicans made in 1804 and 1814 to get New England to secede from the Union and to form a Northeastern Confederacy? Is it possible he is ignorant of the fact that such men as Senator Wade of Ohio, Abraham Lincoln, and other high lights in the Republican party long before the South seceded, made speeches declaring the right of the South to secede? The right to form an independent government? What right has Morse, or any man, to attempt to write history when he is ignorant of the most important facts of said history?

Boutwell, member of Congress from Massachusetts, says: "With varying degrees of intensity the whole Democratic party sympathized with the South and arraigned Lincoln and the Republican party for all the country endured." No man worthy of the name Democrat can refuse to sympathize with a brave people fighting at desperate odds for their homes, their lives, their liberties. Was there one Democrat in all America who did not sympathize with the brave Boers of South Africa? Only imperialists and monarchists can fail to feel for brave men fighting for freedom.

Boutwell says: "During the entire period of the war New York and Illinois were doubtful States. Indiana was only kept in line by the desperate fidelity of Governor Morton." "Desperate fidelity" here means Morton's desperate determination to make himself absolute master of Indiana. This he did, by Lincoln's aid, and for two years Morton was able to say, *"I am the State."* In Foulk's *Life of Governor Morton*, published 1899, Chapter Twenty-Two is headed by the words, *"I am the State,"* and Republicans of today glory in the fact that a man elected Governor of a free State in the Union was able to rob the people of that State of every liberty they possessed, and make himself their master for two years. The facts were these: The people of Indiana were weary of the war. Lincoln had refused to permit two commissioners from the South to enter Washington City. The people believed the art of diplomacy might end the war, and believed that Lincoln made no effort that way. All over Indiana, as, indeed, all over every State on the West and the South, went up the anguished wail, "Oh, the cruel war! Oh, the cruel war!" The people of Indiana elected to the Legislature men pledged to use every effort to promote peace and stop bloodshed. Morton and Lincoln resolved that these peace-loving men should never act as legislators. By Lincoln's aid Morton's "desperate fidelity" made him master of the State for two years. Not a man elected to the Legislature was allowed to perform his duties. Nicolay and Hay, as all other modern Republican writers, justify Morton's usurpation of State power on the ground that "disloyalty was widespread throughout the West." Disloyalty means anything opposed to Lincoln's policy of conquering the South by bloody battles. Disloyalty is always the ready excuse for despotism.

Holland, in his *Life of Lincoln*, says: "In proportion as people were treasonable they opposed the suspension of the habeas corpus and denounced arbitrary arrests." To condemn despotism is always treasonable in the opinion of despots and despot worshipers. In the *Life of Vice-President Hannibal Hamlin*, p. 459, is this: "If we [the Republican war party] had had a common union in the North, and a common loyalty to the Lincoln Government, we could have ended the war months ago." This means that the people of the North so hated the war it impeded the wicked work of conquest.

In Andrews' *History of the United States*, p. 95, the author says: "An absurd prejudice against coercion largely possessed the loyal masses throughout the whole North: the feeling was strong against all efforts at coercion." It is gratifying to humane hearts, even at this late day, thirty-eight years after the end of that woeful war, to know that the great masses of the North's people had such kindly feelings toward the South's people as to oppose the bloody war of conquest which Lincoln and Seward waged upon them. This knowledge will do much toward restoring friendly feelings in the South. On February 20, 1901, in the House of Representatives, referring to the opposition of the '60s to Mr. Lincoln's war, Mr. Cameron, of Illinois, said: "When the life of the Nation was at stake, men all over the North stood behind the firing line and encouraged desertion from the army. I thought if 8,000 or 10,000 Copperheads had been shot the result would have been less desertion." The reader must bear in mind that Copperhead was the pet name Republicans in the '60s gave to Northern Democrats, and further bear in mind that any man who dared to doubt the justice of Lincoln's war on the South was a Copperhead, a secessionist, a traitor, all in one. I, for one, thank Mr. Cameron for his little item of information; I rejoice that numbers of men, large or small, under the dark despotism of Lincoln's rule, had the courage to stand behind the firing line and advise soldiers to escape from the danger, the wickedness, of fighting a war of conquest on a free people. When Mr. Cameron talks of the *"life of the Nation at stake,"* he talks without judgment and without truth. Never for a moment was the life of the Nation or of the North's Union Government at stake. The South never threatened the life of the Nation or of the North's Union Government.

In Rope's *Story of the Civil War* (war of conquest) he says: "During the winter of 1860 Congress took no action whatever looking toward the preparation for the conquest of the outgoing States." That Congress well knew it had no constitutional or moral right to conquer the South. It had no inclination; that Congress, as well as the people of that time all over the North, were in a peaceful mood and hated the very idea of coercing the South.

Morse says: "Most of Lincoln's ministers were against the re-enforcement of Fort Sumter." They knew the attempt to re-enforce meant war. They did not want war. On January 21, 1861, before an immense gathering in New York, an orator said: "If a revolution is to begin, it shall be inaugurated at home." This was roundly cheered. Before Lincoln let slip the dogs of war, the distinguished Chancellor Walworth said: "It will be as brutal to send men to butcher our brothers in the South as it would be to massacre them in the North." It certainly was as brutal and as unjust. This brutality the Republican party committed.

A large meeting in Faneuil Hall, Boston, was emphatic against war. Horace Greeley says in *American Conflict*:

> The symptoms were that vast numbers were infected with such sentiments. It was feared at the North that blood would flow in Northern cities as soon and as freely as in Southern, if forcible coercion should be attempted. Matters looked even worse for the Union in Congress than in the country. The prevalent desire was for peace, while some adopted secession doctrines. Daniel Sickles, in the House, threatened that the secession of the South should be followed by that of New York City.

On page 441, Vol. I, Nicolay and Hay, in their *Life of Lincoln*, give the following picture of the Northern people's state of mind at that time:

It will hardly be possible for readers in our day [1890] to understand the state of public sentiment in the United States during the month of March, 1861. The desire for peace, the hope for compromise, strangest of all, a national lethargy utterly impossible to account for, seemed to mark a decadence of patriotic feeling. This phenomenon is attested in the records of many public men, and shown in the words and example of military officers, in their consenting to shut their eyes to the truth that it is the right of a Government to repel menaces as well as blows.

Were logic of this nature only used by the few it would not merit a moment's attention, but stuff of this flimsy and false texture is used every day by Republican writers and politicians. The *"desire for peace, the hope for compromise"* felt by the great majority of the North's people, Nicolay and Hay have the stupidity to say *"marked a decadence of patriotic feeling."* Patriotism does not mean eagerness for wars of conquest. War is the worst calamity that can befall a people, except subjection to despots. The great body of the Northern people knew there was no danger threatening from the South. The South at that time had commissioners in Washington pleading for peace, and because the North's people preferred giving them peace to giving them bloody war, Nicolay and Hay talk of "patriotic decadence." The future psychologist will decide that men afflicted with the madness of war, men like Chandler, Medill, Seward and Lincoln, eager to plunge two peaceful peoples into cruel war, were the decadents, the degenerates of our race. How fearfully distorted must be that man's judgment who calls the lovers of peace "decadents." How crooked must be that man's channels of thought, who thinks it patriotism to uphold the government of bloody-minded despots. *Patriotism!* These men did not know the meaning of the word.

When Nicolay and Hay talk of the "right of a government to repel menaces as well as blows," do they mean to assert that the South menaced the Government, or the people of the North? There is not the shadow of foundation for such an assertion. In the most respectful manner, with the dignity of free born men, the South's commissioners prayed the Union Government for amicable adjustment of their partnership affairs, and expressed the desire to live in peace and friendship with their Northern neighbors, and offered to pay the South's just proportion of the national debt. With their usual trickery and falsehood, Republicans made every effort to inflame the minds of Northern people by representing that one consequence of the separation of the States would be to lose the free navigation of the Mississippi River. The fact is, as early as the 25th of February, 1861, an act was passed by the Confederate Congress and approved by President Davis to declare and establish the free navigation of the Mississippi River. If any man thinks these approaches a menace deserving to be repelled by bloody war, his judgment is distorted beyond the hope of remedy.

"Treason," continues Nicolay and Hay, "was everywhere." The reader must bear in mind the fact that Republican writers never hesitate to misuse words. To justify their own misdeeds, they call everything opposing those deeds *treason*. Opposition to their war policy was treason. As the principles of '76 opposed their war of conquest, faithfulness to those principles was treason. The large majority of the people in the Northern States opposed the policy of war. According to modern Republican writers, these people were traitors. The majority of members in Lincoln's Cabinet at first opposed war. Nicolay and Hay excuse this on the ground that at that time the Cabinet members did not recognize Lincoln's greatness. Not until after Lincoln's death did those Cabinet members, or any other distinguished Republican, "see Lincoln's greatness."

"The men in Lincoln's Cabinet," says Nicolay and Hay, "at that time looked on him as a simple frontier lawyer, to whom chance had given the Presidency." It is true that chance *had* given Lincoln the Presidency. It is true that he was neither the choice of the American people at large nor of the majority of his own party. The great majority of his own party preferred Chase or Seward. Accident gave the office to Lincoln. But if any man in his Cabinet looked on him as a *simple* backwoods lawyer, he could have made no greater mistake. Lincoln was the least *simple* man of the age. Simple means plain, open, not given to trickery or duplicity, undesigning, sincere, not complex. In his suppressed *Life of Lincoln*, Herndon says, "Lincoln made candor and simplicity a mask." Lamon says Lincoln was the shrewdest politician of the age. Lamon, who knew and loved Lincoln like a brother, says of him:

> Mr. Lincoln was never agitated by any passion more intense than his wonderful thirst for distinction. This passion governed all his conduct up to the hour the assassin struck

him down. He was ever ready to be honored; he struggled incessantly for place. Whatsoever he did in politics, at the bar, in private life, had more or less reference to the great object of his life.

Nature had bestowed on Mr. Lincoln two gifts which he used to gain power and place. The one, as Seward described it, "a cunning that was genius." The other was the gift of eloquence of a peculiar order, inasmuch as its power and beauty seemed to be little appreciated by *hearers*, but readers were struck with admiration. Probably this was owing to Mr. Lincoln's shrill, piping voice, ungainly person and extremely awkward movements. Instance the Gettysburg address, now thought to be the finest specimen of American oratory. Lamon, who heard it, describes its effect on Lincoln's audience as follows: "Mr. Lincoln," says Lamon in his *Recollections of Lincoln*, said to me, 'I tell you, Lamon, that speech was like a wet blanket on the audience. I am distressed about it.'"

On the platform, the moment after Mr. Lincoln's speech was concluded, Mr. Seward asked Mr. Everett, the orator of the day, what he thought of the President's speech. Mr. Everett replied: "It is not what I expected. I am disappointed. What do you think of it, Mr. Seward?" The response was, "He has made a failure." In the face of these facts it has been repeatedly published that this speech was received by the audience with loud demonstrations of approval, that –

> Amid the tears, sobs and cheers it produced in the excited throng, the orator of the day [Mr. Everett] turned to Mr. Lincoln, grasped his hand and exclaimed, "I congratulate you on your success," adding in a transport of heated enthusiasm, "Mr. President, how gladly would I give my hundred pages to be the author of your twenty lines!" Nothing of the kind ever occurred. The silence during the delivery of the speech, the lack of hearty demonstrations of approval after its close, were taken by Mr. Lincoln as certain proof that it was not well received. In that opinion we all shared. I state it as a fact and without fear of contradiction, that this famous Gettysburg speech was not regarded by the audience to whom it was addressed, or by the press and people of the United States, as a production of extraordinary merit, nor was it com-

cmented on as such until after the death of Mr. Lincoln (Lamon's *Recollections of Lincoln*, p. 173).

It is now said that Lamon's *Life of Lincoln* is fast disappearing from the face of the earth; that the same agency which swept out of existence Herndon's *Life of Lincoln* is fast pursuing the same course with Lamon's book. Is this because Republicans do not want their apotheosizing romances about Mr. Lincoln exposed and corrected, as Lamon exposed and corrected the twaddle about the Gettysburg speech?

Before the South seceded, the foremost men in the Republican party openly maintained the right of secession. William Lloyd Garrison, Wendell Phillips, Sumner, Wade of Ohio, Henry Ward Beecher, Chase, Lincoln and hosts of others were among the number. In fact, the whole Republican party taught that the principle of secession was right and labored for disunion. Some of these men after South Carolina and other States had seceded, continued to assert the right of secession. Phillips, in a speech joyously announcing secession, said: "Twenty years ago the men of the North resolved to dissolve the Union. Who dreamed success would come so soon?"

In a speech in Faneuil Hall, Boston, February 2, 1861, Edward Everett said: "To expect to hold fifteen States in the Union by force is preposterous. If our sister States must leave us, in the name of Heaven let them go in peace." The New York *Herald*, independent in politics, November 11, 1860, said:

> The South has an undeniable right to secede from the Union. In the event of secession, the City of New York, the State of New Jersey, and very likely Connecticut, will separate from New England, where the black man is put on a pinnacle above the white. New York City is for the Union first, and for the gallant and chivalrous South afterwards.

Holland, in his *Life of Lincoln*, says: "For months after South Carolina had seceded, while State after State was passing secession ordinances and were seizing forts and arsenals in their boundaries, neither President or Cabinet or Supreme Court at Washington took one step toward coercion." Why should these high powers take a step toward coercion? The highest legal authority in the land had advised President Buchanan that neither he nor Congress had any right to coerce seceding States. Not only this, the great majority of the North's people had accepted that advice as right and just, and opposed coercion. In his *American Conflict*, Greeley says: "The active and earnest sympathy of a large majority of the American people was with the South." The Legislatures of Illinois and New Jersey were nearly unanimous in that direction. On page 513, Greeley says: "There was not a moment when a large portion of the Northern Democracy were not hostile to any form or shade of coercion. Many openly condemned and stigmatized a war on the South as atrocious, unjustifiable and aggressive." No Democrat that ever lived could think a war of conquest on free States right. This belief is left for men of the imperialistic Republican party.

On page 270, Morse says:

> By the end of May, 1861, Mr. Lincoln looked forth on a spectacle as depressing as ever greeted the eye of a great ruler. Eleven States, with an area and a population and resources for constituting a powerful nation, their people in entire unity of feeling, and two-thirds of the North's people in sympathy with their secession.

Reader, mark the two last lines of the above. The Southern people *in entire unity of feeling (in wanting independence) and two-thirds of the North's people in sympathy with secession.* Yet, ten thousand times have Republicans tried to blacken the South's cause by the infamous lie that they were fighting the slave-holder's war to maintain slavery. The reader should also notice the title, "great ruler," which Mr. Morse gives to Lincoln. When the principles of Democracy pervaded this country, men elected to office were called the servants of the people, not the rulers. Never yet have the people of America elected any man to rule them, but to serve. Lincoln was the first President who usurped the power to rule the American people.

McClure, page 56, says: "When Lincoln turned to the military arm of the Government he was appalled by the treachery of the men whom the Nation should look to for protection. Nearly one-third of the officers in the regular army resigned." It is appalling in this age to see the judgments of men like McClure so distorted as to call opposition to war and love of peace treachery. Treachery to what? To whom? Certainly not to the principles of freedom. Certainly not to the United States Constitution. These demanded that the South should be free; not conquered, not subjugated. Certainly not to the North's people; these Mc-

Clure and other historians state were of the same opinion as the military men who resigned from the regular army rather than fight a war of conquest on a free people. McClure makes the serious mistake of calling the small number of men determined on war "the Nation." He and others tell us that the great majority of the Northern people opposed war. This majority is entitled to be called "the Nation." The small minority which held in its grip the machinery of Government had no more right to call itself *"the Nation"* than the Bourbon King had the moral right to say "I am the State."

General Keifer says, about March, 1861: "Disloyalty among the prominent officers was for a time the rule." Disloyalty here means loyalty to the principles of '76. Hapgood says of the officers who resigned from the army rather than fight a war of conquest on the free people at the South: "These men who had been favored with offices proved false to the hand that pampered them." Had these officers received commissions as favors or because they were expected to render good service to the country therefor? The word *pamper* means *fed to the full*. Does Hapgood mean to say that the President, who commissioned officers for the regular army, bestowed those commissions as *favors* and then *pampered* (*fed to the full*) those favored officers? Only a moral or mental pervert will condemn an officer for resigning rather than fight his own people. These Southern officers were educated at West Point, as much at the expense of the South as of the North, and were under far more obligation to the South than to the North.

Woodrow Wilson, in *Disunion and Reunion*, has this: "President Buchanan agreed with his Attorney-General that there was no constitutional measure or warrant for coercing a State; *such for the time seemed to be the general opinion of the country."* Seemed? Did not Professor Woodrow Wilson *know* it was no *seeming*, but long had been the *actual* opinion of the country? Yet Republican writers of today have the hardihood to charge a whole country with "disloyalty," with "appalling treachery."

Morse says: "None of the distinguished men of his own party whom Lincoln found about him in Washington were in a frame of mind to assist him efficiently." The most distinguished men of his own party were unwilling to assist Mr. Lincoln in his wicked policy of waging on the South a war of conquest. These men well knew their party from its birth had labored for disunion, had advocated secession, had held conventions and sent invitations to men of the South, urging them to help them break the Union asunder.

Everyone knows the character of Charles Sumner, Senator from Massachusetts, one of the most honored and trusted members of the Republican party. No man, not even Greeley, more strongly opposed war on the South than Senator Sumner. Sumner said: "Nothing can possibly be so horrible, so wicked or so foolish as a war on the South" (*North American Review*, October, 1879, p. 378). Yet Lincoln, aided by Seward, contrary to the wishes and will of the great majority of Northern people, did this horrible, wicked and foolish thing.

McClure says: "Even in Philadelphia, nearly the whole of the commercial and financial interests were at first arrayed against Lincoln." In *American Conflict* (page 387), Greeley describes a tremendous demonstration against the war made in New York, February, 1861. He records expressions of the purpose not only not to coerce the South, but to aid her in case of war. Such expressions were received with warm applause. In a speech of James S. Thayer it was alleged that these views had been asserted by 333,000 voters in New York in the last election (C. L. Minor's *Real Lincoln*). As evidence of the widespread opposition to Lincoln's war Greeley relates the following:

> On the eve of the battle of Bull Run the Fourth Pennsylvania Regiment of Volunteers and the battery of artillery of the Eighth New York militia, whose term of enlistment had expired, insisted on their discharge, though the General and Secretary of War, both on the spot, tried hard to make them stay five days more. The next morning when the Union army moved into battle these troops moved to the rear to the sound of the enemy's guns.

Greeley concludes the story thus:

> It should be added that a member of the New York battery aforesaid, who was most earnest and active in opposing General McDowell's request to remain five days longer, and insisting on an immediate discharge, was, in full view of all these facts, *at the next election chosen sheriff of New York, the most lucrative office filled by popular election in the country.*

No man more strongly opposed war than Greeley himself, but

the despotism of the Lincoln Government forced Greeley to acquiesce in that war.

Ex-Governor Reynolds, of Illinois, in a speech made December 28, 1860, said: "I am heart and soul for the South. She is right in principle, and from the Constitution." This was warmly applauded. Such was then the opinion of the great body of the people in the Northern States. Three days after South Carolina seceded, Governor Reynolds said: "The Government itself, the army and the navy, ought to remain with the South."

On December 9, 1860, the New York *Herald*, in a dispatch from Washington, had this: "The current of opinion seems to set strongly in favor of reconstruction, and leaving out the New England States. These latter are thought to be so fanatical it would be impossible there would be any peace under a Government to which they were parties." All this Republicans of this day call "treason." No Republican of that day ventured to call the opinions of the great body of the North's people treason.

In *American Conflict*, page 436, Greeley says:

> Throughout the Northern States eminent and eager advocates of adhesion to the new Confederacy were well and widely heeded. It was understood that Governor Seymour, of New York, Judge Woodward, F. W. Hughes, of Pennsylvania, Price of New Jersey, all distinguished men, were among those who favored adherence to the South.

Not until after Lincoln and Seward held in their grip all the machinery of Government, and felt certain they could carry out their purpose of conquering the South, did the Republican party begin to use the words: Rebel! Rebellion! Traitor! Treason! The great numbers of the North's people who opposed the war suddenly became traitors; any and every word of opposition became treason; arbitrary arrests and imprisonments began, and a pall of blackest despotism spread over the land. Greeley's *Tribune*, April 15, 1861, had this:

> The day before Sumter was surrendered two-thirds of the newspapers in the North opposed coercion in any shape or form, and sympathized with the South. These papers were the South's allies and champions. Three-fifths of the entire American people sympathized with the South. Over 200,000

voters opposed coercion, and believed the South had the right to secede.

Think of this, men of America! Think how easy it is for an American President elected to serve and carry out the will of the people; how easy it is to make himself the master of the people, and force them to do his will, contrary to their own.

CHAPTER TWENTY-SIX

Why Grant Refused to Exchange Prisoners. Grant Compares Northern and Southern Soldiers. Desertions from Union Army. Riots, Arbitrary Arrests, "Suspects." Thirty-Eight Thousand Innocent Men and Women Fill Northern Prisons. Civil Law Overthrown. Lincoln Unpopular. The People's Indignation in 1861, 1862, 1863. The People's Indictment in 1864. Judiciary Opposes Lincoln.

The *Journal of Commerce* fought coercion until the United States mail refused to carry the papers, in 1861. The New York *Daily News* continued to denounce the Republican party as a blood-thirsty set, advocating wholesale murder, as vultures gloating over carnage, until the freedom of the press was suppressed.

John A. Logan, in *Great Conspiracy*, page 551, describes a gathering at Springfield, Illinois (Lincoln's home), in June of 1863, of nearly 100,000 anti-war Democrats, which utterly repudiated the war. There was open and avowed hostility to Lincoln in Philadelphia, New York, and Boston, and of strong opposition in New Jersey. So violent was the hostility to war in Massachusetts and New York, the call for volunteers was unheeded, and when the Government demanded a draft, the people gathered in crowds and fearful riots ensued. In New York City the opposition was so violent, the rioters so numerous, the city was terrified for days and nights. The houses in which the draft machines were at work were wrecked and then burned to ashes. The police were powerless to restrain the immense gatherings of men and women who walked the streets day and night. The order for the draft was rescinded by the Washington Government, the people urged to disperse and retire to their homes, which they did, as they thought, on the promise that there would be no more drafting. But that treacherous Government, as soon as the people returned to their daily work, sent a large body of soldiers to overawe them, and again the accursed machines were set to work, and again the wheels began to turn, until the required number of men were secured. In this way men were forced to fight a people toward whom they had no animosity, and for a Government they knew was blackly despotic.

Before a Congressional committee Grant testified as follows:

> I refused to exchange prisoners because as soon as the South's soldiers are released from our prisons they rush back into the rebel ranks and begin fighting again. When Northern soldiers return from Southern prisons either they never again enter the ranks, or if they do, not until they go to their homes and have a long furlough.

It is easy enough to see the cause of this difference between soldiers of the North and soldiers of the South. The former were forced into a war they were unwilling to fight, and millions believed unjust. The South's soldiers, every man, felt and knew they were fighting for their lives, their liberties, their homes, all that hearts hold dear. The very souls of the South's men and women were in that fight.

Nicolay and Hay, Vol. VI, tell of violent resistance to the draft in Pennsylvania. Half fed, badly clothed, exposed as they were to the cold of winter and the heat of summer, in no part of the South was manifested any opposition to the war. In Grant's *Memoirs* he draws comparison between the feelings of the people of the North and the people of the South during the war:

> In the South no rear had to be protected. All the troops in the service could be brought to the front to contest every inch of ground threatened with invasion; the press of the South, like the people who stayed at home, were loyal to the Southern cause. Vast numbers in the North were hostile to the war. Troops were necessary in the North to prevent prisoners from the Southern army being released, armed and set free by outside force. Copperheads of the press magnified rebel success and belittled those of the Union army.

Copperheads were Northern Democrats. For the first two years of the war the successes of the South's soldiers were so great and the success of the North so small, the latter could hardly have been belittled. The election of 1862 showed great losses to the Republican party. Nicolay and Hay assert that, "In all strong Republican States the opposition was triumphant and the administration defeated." This falling off of votes resulted from the people's hatred of the war and distrust of Lincoln.

Tarbell, who simply worships Lincoln, in her *Life of Lincoln* says:

> In the winter of 1862-3 many and many a man deserted the army. They refused to fight. Mr. Lincoln knew that hundreds of soldiers were being urged by parents and friends to desert. New York, Pennsylvania, Ohio, Indiana. and Illinois reversed their vote. Under the August call, 1864, for 360,000 militia, the people were very uneasy. They were weary of the war, weary of so much waste of life and money. Their feelings showed itself in an extensive form, in open dissatisfaction in Pennsylvania and Wisconsin, which broke out in violence over the draft for more men.

The numerous arbitrary arrests and imprisonments in dismal and distant fortresses of innocent citizens greatly alarmed the people; murmurs were deep but not loud. A reign of terror existed in the Northern States. Dissatisfaction made itself felt at the polls. The November and October elections in many States opposed the Republican party. To lull this feeling, Lincoln, Seward and Stanton, as usual, resorted to trickery and deception. Stanton became the ready tool to perform the mean and contemptible work of lying to the public. From his official office, 1862, Stanton wrote a letter, which he had published in the newspapers. The object was two-fold; first, to excuse Lincoln's arbitrary arrests, on the ground that a vast amount of treason (opposition to the war was called treason) existed in the Northern States. Second, to make the public believe that the resistance in the South was declining, therefore there was no further necessity to make arbitrary arrests. Therefore President Lincoln intended to order the release of citizens in the jails and forts. To carry out this lying scheme, Stanton wrote his official letter, which, being verbose, I will only give the gist, as follows:

War Department, Washington City, 1862.

Treason in the Northern States astounded the world. [This was utterly false. The world was not astounded, nor did the world call adherence to the South treason.] Every department in the Government was paralyzed. Disaffection was in the Senate, in the Federal Courts, among the Ministers returning from foreign countries, in the Cabinet. Treason was in the revenue and post office services, in the territorial government, in the Indian reserves, ministerial officers, among judges, governors, legislators. Treason was in that portion of the country which was most loyal. Secret societies were found furthering the work of disunion. The judicial machinery seemed as if it had been designed not to sustain the Government, but to embarrass and betray it. The President thought it his duty to suspend the habeas corpus and arrest all suspected persons. The insurrection is believed to be declining. In view of these facts the President *directs that all political or state prisoners now held in military custody be released*, on their subscribing to a parole to render no aid and comfort to the enemy.

Every word in this letter was intended to deceive. First, Stanton makes a big blow over what he called treason (opposition to war) to justify Lincoln's illegal arrests; then he pretends the South's insurrection is declining, in order to make a decent excuse for Lincoln's *pretense* of stopping the illegal arrests; then he falsely states that Lincoln has ordered the prisoners released. To carry out the deception, Stanton issued the following order:

War Department, Washington City, Nov. 22, 1862.

Order First. That all persons now in military custody, etc., be discharged from further military restraint.
By order of Secretary of War.
(Signed)
E.D. Townsend.

Now, mark this mean lie. Lincoln had no intention of directing the prisoners released. Order First was for the people to see, not for jailers to obey. Only two days after issuing the above order Stanton sent a secret order to the jailers, as follows:

> Washington, November 24, 1862.
>
> Commanding Officer, Fort —— :
>
> None of the prisoners confined at your post will be released on orders of the War Department of the 22nd inst., without special instructions from this Department.
> By order of Secretary of War.
>
> E.D. Townsend.
> (*American Bastile*, page 767)

In Rhodes' *History of the United States*, Vol. IV, p. 165, he has this: "One of the results of the elections of November and October was that Stanton issued an order *which, after a formal delay, effected the discharge from military custody of practically all the political prisoners.*" Rhodes makes no mention of Stanton's second order, sent to rescind the first; he makes a mistake when he says the prisoners were practically released from custody on Stanton's first order. Marshall, in *American Bastile*, states that the second order prevented the first being obeyed, and that the greater number of the prisoners in Forts Lafayette and Delaware (if not in all other forts) were not discharged until late in December, and some not until long after.

In explanation of Mr. Lincoln's great unpopularity during his life, General Piatt says: "Lincoln was a minority President, and had no hold on the affections of the people." At no time did the living Lincoln have any hold on the affections of the people. Even before he took his seat the great body of the people distrusted and disliked him. His adorer, Miss Tarbell, testifies to this. In Vol. I, p. 398, Miss Tarbell says:

> Before Mr. Lincoln left Springfield for Washington, the North was desperate and helpless. All the bitterness and confusion centered about Mr. Lincoln. The rapid disintegration which followed Mr. Lincoln's election filled the North with dismay. A furious clamor broke over Mr. Lincoln's head. His election had caused the trouble. What could he do to stop it?

Had Lincoln been true to the Constitution and the principles of '76, he could have stopped it in 24 hours. The people were afraid Lincoln meant war. Had he told them, as Buchanan did, that he had no intention of inaugurating a war of conquest. the uneasiness of the people would have vanished into thin air. Over two-thirds of the people greatly disliked and distrusted the Republican party, which was chiefly known by its fierce, vindictive hate of the Union, of the South, and of the United States Constitution. The majority of the Republican party distrusted Lincoln. They wanted Seward or Chase. The latter would have made a far more humane, honest President than either Seward or Lincoln.

In Vol. II, page 65, Tarbell says: "In 1861 a perfect storm of denunciation broke over Mr. Lincoln's head. The whole North was angry; impeachment was threatened. Fremont was talked of to put in his place." This dissatisfaction did not cease or abate during Mr. Lincoln's term in office. Even the dread of arbitrary arrest and imprisonment did not wholly quell the people into silence. In the army great dissatisfaction prevailed. In *McClure's Magazine*, January, 1893, p. 165, Tarbell says:

> Many and many a man deserted in the winter of 1862-3 because of Lincoln's emancipation proclamation. The soldiers did not believe that Lincoln had the right to issue it. They refused to fight. Lincoln knew that hundreds of the soldiers were being urged by parents and friends, hostile to him and his administration, to desert.

In 1864 the opposition to the war and to Lincoln was violent and bitter, and almost universal. Tarbell describes the people's feelings of that year as follows:

> In 1864 the awful brutality of the war came upon the people as never before. There was a revolution of feeling against the sacrifice going on. All the complaints that had been urged against Mr. Lincoln broke out afresh; the draft was talked of as if it were the arbitrary freak of a tyrant. It was declared that Lincoln had violated constitutional rights, declared that he had violated personal liberty, and the liberty of the press. It was said that Lincoln had been guilty of all the abuses of a military dictatorship. Much bitter criticism was made of his treatment of the South's peace commissioners. It

was declared that the Confederates were anxious to make peace. It was declared that Lincoln was so blood-thirsty he was unwilling to use any means but force. The despair, the indignation of the country in this dreadful time was all centered on Mr. Lincoln.

Republican writers give positive evidence that every one of the above charges was true. President Lincoln –
Had violated personal liberty.
Had violated constitutional rights.
Had violated the liberty of the press.
Had been guilty of all the abuses of a military dictator.
Had repulsed the Confederate peace commissioners.
Had refused to use any means except bloody force to attain peace.
No man who reads Republican history can deny one of the above charges.
At that time the people of the North did not know that Lincoln himself had confessed to Medill, as related by Tarbell, that he, Lincoln, had begun the war at the demand of Medill. Though not having this evidence, the people felt in their hearts that Lincoln was responsible for the awful war. Not until Miss Tarbell. in 1895, related Medill's confession of his part in the wicked work of deluging the land with blood was it known that Lincoln had knowingly, deliberately, of set purpose, plunged the country into war at Medill's request. Never should Lincoln's words to Medill be forgotten: "*You* asked for war; I have given you what you asked for. *You* demanded war. I have given you what you demanded. *You* are chiefly responsible for all the blood that has flowed."

CHAPTER TWENTY-SEVEN

What a Battle Meant to Lincoln. Greeley Prays Lincoln for Peace. Rosecrans, Grant, Hallack on the People's Hatred of the War. Soldiers Dislike Lincoln. Judge Curtis on Lincoln's Usurpation. Republican Writers, Rhodes, Morse, Hapgood, Bancroft and Others Laud Despotism.

As illustrative of Lincoln's character, General Piatt says: "A battle to Lincoln meant the killing and wounding of a certain number of men, the consequences to be counted like a sum in arithmetic. *Lincoln faced and lived through the awful responsibility of the war with the courage that came from indifference.*" Piatt does not mean indifference as to the result of the war; that Lincoln was certain of, if only the Northern people would not force him to end it too soon, but indifference to the suffering caused by the war. Piatt says Lincoln was by nature incapable of sympathy. Greeley, on the contrary, seemed to have possessed the capacity to feel pity and sympathy for the agonies the war caused the people of the North, and even gave some little thought to the suffering South. When Lincoln refused to see or to hear the Confederate commissioners, Clement Clay and James P. Holcomb, Greeley wrote Lincoln a letter protesting against that refusal, in which he painted a heart-rending picture of the bleeding, bankrupt, almost dying country. Greeley said he shuddered at the prospect of more conscriptions, of further wholesale devastations and more rivers of human blood. He said to Lincoln: "There is a widespread conviction that the administration is not anxious for peace, and does not improve proffered opportunities to achieve it." So far as I can learn Greeley was the only prominent man in the Republican party who, during that dreadful war, and that still more dreadful reconstruction period, manifested the least desire to stop the devastation suffered by the South.

As further evidence of opposition to Lincoln may be stated the following: "General Rosecrans reported to Washington the existence in the Western States of secret organizations of men bound by oath to co-operate with the Confederates, to the number of 400,000. Nicolay and Hay put the number at 350,000." And the following in Grant's *Memoirs*, Vol. II, p. 323, is significant: "During August, 1864, Halleck informed me that there was an organized scheme on foot to resist the draft, and that it might be necessary to withdraw troops from the field to put it down."

McClure says : "There was no period from January, 1864, until September 3 when McClellan would not have defeated Lincoln for President." Secretary of War Stanton, when at death's door, said to General Piatt: "When Lincoln visited the camps fears were felt at headquarters that the soldiers would insult him, and orders were issued to cheer the President when he appeared." Yet it now suits Republicans to pretend that Lincoln was almost adored during his life.

The soldiers must have had very bitter feelings toward Lincoln, if in a time like that they felt like insulting him. Though half fed, though ragged, though many were shoeless and nearly all tentless, the soldiers of the South would have received their President at any time with acclamations of joy.

Stanton also said to Piatt: "All the time our huge army lay coiled about Washington, a distrust of the Lincoln Government was insidiously cultivated among the men." Private soldiers are not fools; while in the ranks under the rule of officers, they dare not talk aloud, but they talk to each other freely. The men in the ranks were not ignorant of Lincoln's treachery. They knew that in New York the conscripting machines had been put in quarters where working men are most numerous; they knew that these machines had been put in these districts where the Democratic votes went largely against the administration; they knew how the working men revolted against this injustice, how they rose and wrecked the houses in which the cursed drafting machines were at work. The private soldiers had enough to resent and did resent. The millions paid in pensions have sealed their lips. Money seals the lips of the G.A.R. on the wrongs of the war.

B.F. Butler, whose very soul delighted in despotic measures, in his book says: "During the whole war the Lincoln Government was rarely aided, but was usually impeded by the decisions of the Supreme Court, so that President Lincoln was obliged to suspend the writ of habeas corpus in order to relieve himself of the rulings of the court."

In 1862 Benjamin R. Curtis, of the Supreme Court, wrote and published a little work showing Lincoln's usurpations, entitled *Executive Power*. Judge Curtis said:

> The President has made himself a legislator. He has enacted penal laws governing citizens of the United States. He has superadded to his rights as commander the power of a usurper. He has established a military despotism. He can now use the authority he has assumed to make himself master of our lives, our liberties, our properties, with power to delegate his mastership to such satraps as he may select.

If this be true, and no man has or can deny it, Lincoln was guilty of a crime blacker than Benedict Arnold's. Yet, mark how mildly Judge Curtis talks of that crime. He says, "President Lincoln can now use the authority he has usurped." Curtis, as every man in the Northern States, well knew that Lincoln at that time was using his usurped powers every day of his life. Lalor's *Encyclopedia* states that the records of the Provost Marshal's office in Washington show that 38,000 political prisoners filled the bastiles of America. These men were accused of no crime, of no offense known to the law of the land. They were Democrats. All Democrats were *"suspects."* Stanton and Seward were commissioned by Lincoln to arrest and imprison *"suspects."* Rhodes thinks Lalor's estimate of 38,000 is exaggerated, but when one considers it was the nature of Seward and Stanton to revel in the use of power, and that neither of these men ever gave one sign of possessing the quality of mercy, pity or justice, one can more easily believe that Lalor underrates more than overrates the number of victims. To show how strangely a worship of dead or living despots demoralizes the human mind, I offer the following comments on Judge Curtis' little work, *Executive Power*, made by John T. Morse, author of *Lincoln* in one of the *American Statesmen* "series," published in 1892: "It was unfortunate," says Mr. Morse, "that the country should hear such phrases launched by a Chief Justice against deeds' done under the order of the President." Had it come to this, that an American President's illegal deeds shall not be criticised? Does Mr. Morse think it right to conceal Presidential acts from the country, from the people? This is indeed imperial practice.

In reply to the people's outcry against illegal arrests, Lincoln argued that he had the right. His arguments were as fallacious and as shallow as any second rate lawyer's hired to defend a bad case. Lincoln's defense of his crime only made it the more odious. Some daring man had the courage to criticise. Of this, Morse coolly remarks: "It was undesirable to confute the President's logic on this question."

In his *History of the United States*, Rhodes frankly says: "Mr. Lincoln stands responsible for the casting into prisons citizens of the United States on orders as arbitrary as the *letres de cachet* of Louis XIV. of France, instead of their arrest, as in Great Britain in her crisis, on legal warrants." Lincoln himself boasted that he was responsible for all arbitrary arrests and imprisonments. He alone was the foundation of power. On page 232, Vol. III, of Rhodes' *History*, he remarks: "Mr. Lincoln's extra judicial proceedings were inexpedient, unnecessary, wrong, yet the great principles of liberty up to the present time have not been invalidated."

The despotism of that time has so demoralized men's minds, many men seem now ready to welcome the advent of any coming despot. In an article published February, 1903, in *Scribner's Magazine*, Mr. Rhodes too plainly shows the deep demoralization of his own mind on the question of human liberty. Rhodes says: "Mr. Lincoln assumed extra legal powers, at the same time trying to give to those illegal acts the color of legality. Lincoln has made a precedent which future riders will imitate. What Lincoln excused and defended will be assumed as the right for rulers to follow."

Mr. Rhodes' judgment is so demoralized by the worship of a despot he sees no danger in the precedent set by Lincoln of usurping power. Not so with wiser heads. The Supreme Court saw and bemoaned the danger. "Wicked men," said that court, when rendering its decision on the *Milligan* case, "ambitious of power, with contempt of law in their hearts, may fill the place once occupied by Washington and Lincoln, and if the right of arbitrary arrests and other extra judicial acts is conceded, the dangers to human liberty are frightful to contemplate." Why did that court couple the names Washington and Lincoln together? The one a respecter of law, the other a law-breaker of the most unscrupulous stripe? Was that court truckling to the despotism that ruled the land? Was it *afraid* to speak out boldly, and denounce Lincoln as the most dangerous law breaker America has produced? To laud, to condone the crime of breaking laws, of usurping authority, is to invite the recurrence of despotism, is to encourage wicked men to follow in Lincoln's footsteps, and make themselves, as Judge Curtis said, "the masters of our lives, our liberties, our properties."

Rhodes remarks:

> It is an interesting fact that the ruler [Mr. Rhodes seems to be fond of the word ruler] of a Republic which sprang from a resistance to the English King and Parliament, should exercise more arbitrary power than any Englishman since Oliver Cromwell, and that many of his acts should be worthy of a Tudor.

Many were worthy of the most despotic Caesar that ever ruled Rome. To the lovers of freedom, the fact Mr. Rhodes calls *"interesting"* is more alarming than interesting. It shows how easy wicked men, if in high office in this country, can overthrow civil law and rob the people of every right they possess. It further shows how men are prone to fall at the feet of usurpers and worship.

Even in the darkest days of Lincoln's rule there were men of his own party who were less tolerant of despotism than modern Republican writers. The New York *Post*, a Republican paper, had the courage to disapprove of and to denounce arbitrary arrests and imprisonments of men for criticizing Lincoln's despotic acts. "No government," said the *Post*, "and no authorities are to be held as above criticism, or even denunciation. We know of no other way of correcting their faults, of restraining their tyrannies, than by open and bold discussion."

There was no lack in the '60s of mean and contemptible souls eager and ready with open arms to embrace despotism, as there is now no lack of despot-loving men to beckon on the coming of despotism. E.C. Ingersoll, candidate for Congress during Lincoln's life, in a public speech, joyously announced the advent of despotism and the overthrow of American liberty, using the following words: "President Lincoln is now clothed with power as full as that of the Czar of Russia. It is now necessary for the people of this country to become familiar with that power and with Lincoln's right to use it."

The Rev. Henry Ward Beecher welcomed despotism with a broad, smiling face and open arms. In a public address this so-called follower of the Christ, who taught the Democratic doctrine of equal rights, spoke as follows:

I know it is said President Lincoln is not the Government, that the Constitution is the Government. What! A sheep-skin parchment a government! President Lincoln and his Cabinet are now the Government, and men have now got to take their choice whether they will go with their Government or against it.

It would have been more correct had Beecher said, "Men have now to choose whether they will go with Mr. Lincoln or to some dungeon cell." Before Lincoln established despotic rule, how differently men felt and spoke of American liberty, of the danger of losing it. Daniel Webster warned the people against executive power:

> The contest for ages has been to rescue liberty from executive power. On the long list of the champions of human freedom, there is not one name dimmed by the reproach of advocating the extension of executive authority. Through all the histories of the contests for liberty, executive power has been regarded as the lion that must be caged, it has always been dreaded as the great object of danger. Our security lies in our watchfulness of executive power. I will not trust executive power to keep the vigils of liberty. Encroachments must be resisted at every step. We are not to wait till great mischief comes, till the Government is overthrown or liberty put in extreme jeopardy. We would be unworthy sons of our fathers were we to so regard questions affecting freedom.

Where were the worthy sons of our fathers in the '60s? Many were immured in the Northern bastiles. Those in the South were in the ranks bravely fighting to drive back Lincoln's invading legions – legions sent down on a free people to kill, conquer or annihilate.

Before Lincoln rushed on carnage, while Greeley in the columns of his *Tribune* was doing his best to prevent that awful crime, the Boston *Atlas* was doing its best to spur Lincoln on to make the rush. The following is a specimen of the *Atlas'* tone, temper and ferocity: "Draw the sword! Throw away the scabbard! Hurl 100,000 men on the South to subjugate. Let us never cease until South Carolina is a desert, a desolate land sown with salt, that every passer-by shall wag his head." Why this worse than human hate? Why this fiercer than tiger's rage? Carolina had only done what the Republican party had long wanted her to do, had invited her to do. Soon after Carolina's secession, in a speech, Wendell Phillips said: "No man has a right to be surprised at this state of things. It is just what we disunionists have attempted to bring about. Thank God disunion has come at last!" Was it possible as the war progressed that these men forgot their own advocacy of disunion? If they remembered how could they justify their insane hate of a people whose only crime was defending themselves against armed invaders?

It has been said a thousand times that had Mr. Lincoln lived through his second term there would have been for the conquered South no horrors of the so-called reconstruction period. A careful study of Mr. Lincoln's *real*, not his apotheosized, character will not warrant that conclusion. Let the reader consider the following facts and judge for himself:

1st. *Before* Mr. Lincoln came into Presidential power he had openly, from the floor of Congress, declared the right of secession and the right of the South to secede and to form an independent government of her own.

2nd. *After* Mr. Lincoln became President and held in his hands the reins of all the government machinery, at the instigation of such soulless men as Medill of Chicago, Senator Chandler of Michigan, Seward of New York, and the urgency of such South-hating journals as the Chicago *Tribune* and Boston *Atlas*, he not only turned his back on his own publicly proclaimed principles of right, but turned his back on the principles and issues of his own party, which had been delivered from a thousand rostrums since the organization of his party in 1854.

3rd. Yielding to the influence of bloody-minded men and journals, Mr. Lincoln inaugurated the most unnecessary, cruel, wicked war of the Nineteenth Century.

Never will it be forgotten that Medill of the Chicago *Tribune* bears witness to the awful fact that Mr. Lincoln began the war of conquest on the South. Never will it be forgotten that Medill of the Chicago *Tribune*, as stated in Tarbell's *Life of Lincoln*, testifies that in 1864 Abraham Lincoln said to him, in the presence of Stanton, Secretary of War, and other public men in high office: "After Boston, Chicago has been the chief instrument in bringing this war on the country. It is *you*, Medill, who is largely responsible for making blood flow as it has. *You* called for war until you got it. *I* have given it to you."

Great God! What a confession is this! In all the black and bloody calendar of crime did ever man before confess himself openly of so stupendous a crime as this? *"You, Medill, called for war until you got it. I have given it to you."* And this when these very men had proclaimed and promulgated the lie that the South began the war; this when the South had prayed for peace and an equitable settlement of their partnership affairs. When this confession issued from Lincoln's lips blood was still flowing like water on battlefields, the rivers in the South were still running red with the heart's blood of brave men of the North and of the South. A thousand hospitals in both lands were filled with wounded, mutilated, dying, pain-racked soldiers, and the air all over America was thick and sick with the wailings of war-made widows and war-made orphans. Oh, if the men who so wantonly begun that war had human hearts in their breasts, what anguish of remorse must have wrung and stung their consciences! Yet nowhere have I found any evidence that remorse touched them for their awful crime. It is recorded that Lincoln suffered intense anxiety when the success of his wicked scheme of conquest seemed doubtful, but when victory appeared in sight his joy was unalloyed by any thought of the awful price paid for it. The men who best knew Lincoln testify that the suffering of his own soldiers gave him little or no personal concern. In Lamon's *Life of Lincoln*, page 344, he says: "Lincoln's compassion could be stirred deeply by an object present, but never by an object absent and unseen. Mr. Lincoln was not an ardent sympathizer with suffering of any sort which he did not witness with the eye of the flesh."

In view of the fact that Mr. Lincoln was of so plastic a nature as to be easily induced to plunge the country into war by such men as Medill and Chandler of Michigan, is it not likely had he lived through his second term the Medills and Chandlers would as easily have induced him to pursue their vindictive and tigerish policy toward the South? President Johnson was in favor of the pacific policy it is said that Lincoln intended, but the Republican leaders in a body opposed him, and came near deposing him from power. Though impeachment failed, the Presidential authority was so curtailed, Johnson's administration was crippled, but in spite of the leaders, Johnson showed some mercy to the South. He made himself in some degree a break-water to hold back the malignant tide of hate which the remorseless Republican leaders were almost frantic to roll over the people of the South. Their plan to confiscate the land of the Southern whites and divide it into forty-acre lots, and give a lot to every negro man in the South, was never carried out.

When the people in the Northern States became alarmed at President Lincoln's bold usurpation of power and began to loudly murmur at his arbitrary arrests of influential citizens and their imprisonment in distant forts, John W. Forney, Secretary of the Senate and close friend of Lincoln's, through the Philadelphia *Press*, spurred on Lincoln to further outrages on the people's liberties. As a sample of Forney's advice, I give the following from the Philadelphia *Press*: "Silence every tongue; seal every mouth that does not speak with respect of our cause [conquest of the South] and of our flag. Let us cease to talk of safeguards, of laws and restrictions, of dangers to liberty."

In Bancroft's *Life of Seward*, published in 1899, he gives some account of Mr. Seward's illegal arrests. On page 276, Bancroft says: "Arbitrary arrests and imprisonments were made to *prevent*, rather than to *punish* treason. *Of course it would have been unsafe to be frank about such a thing."* Despots never think it safe to be frank about their deeds of despotism. Men were not arrested and imprisoned for what they *had* done, but for what possibly they *might* do. On this Mr. Bancroft complacently remarks: "There is no occasion, however, to apologize for arbitrary arrests." None in the world. Nobody wants apologies. What is wanted is hatred, deep, deadly, undying, ineradicable, red-hot, *holy* hatred of despotism, not apologies.

Mr. Bancroft says:

> The least excusable feature of these arrests was the treatment of the prisoners. Month after month they were crowded together in gloomy, damp casemates, where even the dangerous pirates captured on the South's privateers [the South had no pirates] and the soldiers taken in battle ought not to have remained long. Many had committed no overt act. Many were editors and politicians of good character and honor. It [the power to make illegal arrests] offered rare opportunities for the gratification of personal enmity and the display of power by United States Marshals and military officers. Seward cannot be blamed for this.

Bancroft here assumes that Seward, Stanton and Lincoln were not as likely to abuse the power of arrest as United States Marshals and military officers. The assumption is worthy of a simpleton. Every arrest ordered by Seward. Stanton and Lincoln was inspired by personal or political spite. These three men were peculiarly vindictive toward any man they even suspected of opposing their cruel war policy. General Piatt, who well knew this triumvirate of despots, said of two of them: "Seward and Stanton fairly rioted in the enjoyment of power. They reveled in the use of power. Stanton was more vindictive in his dislikes than any man ever called to public station." Were men of this pagan nature fit to hold absolute power over the liberties and lives of their fellow creatures? Yet to these two unscrupulous, unfeeling men, Lincoln deputed the rule he had usurped over the people of the Northern States.

"No man," remarks the simple Bancroft, in his *Life of Seward*, "will deny that Mr. Seward sought and was given too much responsibility." This is exactly what the writer of this does deny. Responsibility means the state of being answerable for a trust. Neither Lincoln, Seward or Stanton sought to be or desired to be answerable to any person or power for any trust they assumed. They were not answerable. On the contrary, they sought and desired to exercise the powers they wrested from the people without accountability to mortal or immortal being.

In Vol. 2, page 254, of Mr. Bancroft's *Life of Seward*, he sagely says: "Some of the features of these arbitrary arrests bore a striking resemblance to the odious institution of the ancient regime in France – the bastile and the *letres de cachet*." Were Mr. Bancroft called on to describe two peas as like each other as peas can be, he would look from one to the other, gravely reflect, then solemnly say: "Some of the features of this pea bear a striking resemblance to some of the features of this other pea." He further says:

> The person arrested was usually seized at night. It was found best to take prominent men far from friends and sympathizers. They were usually taken to Fort Warren or other remote places. In some cases from one to three months elapsed before the case of the arrested man was looked at. As a rule prisoners were not told why they were arrested. The arrested men were deprived of their valuables, money, watches, rings, etc., and locked up in casemates usually crowded with men who had similar experiences. If any prisoner wished to send for relatives, friends, or an attorney, they were told that any prisoner who sought the aid of an attorney would greatly prejudice his case. Appeals to Seward, Lincoln or

Stanton a second, third or fourth time were all useless.

In conclusion, Mr. Bancroft naively remarks: "There is, however, nothing to indicate that Mr. Seward was fond of keeping men in prison." It would be interesting to know what facts and acts would afford such indication to men of the Bancroft sort.

Roman history relates that after a long life spent in evil deeds, in his sullen old age, the Emperor Tiberius left Rome and secluded himself in the Island of Capri, off the coast of Southern Italy. Either to relieve the tedium of time or to keep up the practice of cruelty, the Emperor would order his guard to seize any fisherman or peasant, or other passer-by, and summarily pitch him from the highest cliff into the deep sea below. The unfortunate man was either drowned in the sea or torn to pieces on the jutting and jagged rocks as he fell. This done, the Emperor would placidly return to the privacy of his palace, and the next day as he took his morning constitutional, if he happened to see another unfortunate man passing by, the kind-hearted old Emperor would gently order him pitched over the cliff in the same way. Were Mr. Bancroft writing the life of Tiberius, after relating the above little incidents, after describing the cries of the poor wretches as they fell from one jutting rock to another, down to the deep sea, Mr. Bancroft would amiably remark: "There is nothing, however, to indicate that Tiberius was fond of ordering men thrown over steep cliffs to certain death."

On August 8, 1862, Stanton issued an order under which many thousand men were kidnaped, hurried off to the nearest military post or depot, and placed on military duty. The expense of the arrest, the conveyance to such post, also the sum of five dollars reward to the men who made the arrest, were deducted from the arrested man's poor pay while serving in the ranks. Is it any wonder that, as Stanton told Piatt, there was great dissatisfaction in the Union army, and great dislike of Lincoln among the common soldiers?

CHAPTER TWENTY-EIGHT

Lincoln's Eagerness for Second Term. He is Elected by the Use of the Army. B. F. Butler's Story. The Crime of the Century. Republican Writers Unfit Teachers of American Boys. The Fox's Skin.

Many men of this day fancy Lincoln's election to a second term proves that he was the people's choice, and was trusted and beloved by the people. In this busy age few men have the time to look below the surface and find facts. Some of Lincoln's apotheosis biographers boldly assert that Lincoln was indifferent about his re-election. Others deem it better to tell the plain truth on this question. Lamon says during his first term he was all the time anxious to secure re-election.

In his *Life of Lincoln*, McClure says: "Lincoln's desire for re-nomination was the one thing uppermost in his mind during the third year of his first term." In *Our Presidents*, page 184, McClure says: "A more anxious candidate I have never seen. I could hardly treat with respect Lincoln's anxiety about his re-nomination." After Lincoln's nomination for the second term, but before election, the prospects of his re-election became very gloomy. Many of Lincoln's friends predicted the success of McClellan. Mr. Lincoln himself was almost in despair of re-election. In Vol. I, on this subject, Morse has this:

> In Lincoln's party the foremost men, as the time approached for a second term, so strongly opposed Lincoln they determined to prevent his re-election. They called a convention to be held May 21, 1864, in Cincinnati, Ohio. The call said: "Republican Liberty is in danger. The object of this call

is to arouse the people, and make them realize that while we are saturating Southern soil with the best blood of the country in the name of Liberty, we have really parted with it at home.

Nicolay and Hay's *Life of Lincoln*, Vol. II, page 249, says: "By August, 1864, Weed, Raymond and everyone, even Lincoln himself, despaired of his re-election. Raymond, Chairman of the Republican National Executive Committee, August 22, 1864, wrote Lincoln: 'I hear but one report. The tide is setting against us.'"

In *Our Presidents*, page 183, McClure says:

> Three months after Lincoln's renomination in Baltimore, his defeat by General McClellan was feared by his friends and conceded by Lincoln himself. Wade of Ohio, and Winter Davis, aided by Greeley, published in Greeley's *Tribune*, August 5, 1864, their bitter manifesto against Lincoln, in which they charged him with having committed a more studied outrage on the authority of the people than had ever before been perpetrated.

In Holland's *Life of Lincoln*, he says:

> After Mr. Lincoln's nomination for a second term, a peculiar change came over the spirit of Mr. Lincoln's friends; the thought became prevalent that a mistake had been made; simultaneously and universally the friends of the Administration felt he ought not to have been nominated for a second term.

Morse, in Vol. II, says: "Recent local elections in New York and Massachusetts showed a striking reduction of Republican strength." In *The True Story of a Great Life,* Weik states that Wendell Phillips made stump speeches over New England denouncing Lincoln, and holding him up to public ridicule. At Cooper Institute, 1864, before an immense audience, Phillips said: "Lincoln has overthrown Liberty. I call on the people to rise in their might and see to it that Lincoln is not elected to a second term."

On August 14, Greeley wrote: "Mr. Lincoln is already beaten. He cannot be re-elected. We must have another ticket to save us from utter overthrow. Grant, Butler or Sherman would do for President."

Chase, Winter Davis, Wade of Ohio, Governor Andrew of Massachusetts, were in sympathy with the movement to prevent Lincoln's re-election. The editor of the Cincinnati *Gazette* wrote: "The people regard Mr. Lincoln's candidacy as a misfortune. I do not know a Lincoln man. In all our correspondence, which is large and varied, are few letters from Lincoln men." The New York *Sun* said: "The withdrawal of Lincoln and Fremont, and the nomination of a man who would inspire confidence, would be hailed with delight." In his apotheosized *Life of Lincoln*, Holland bears witness to the strong and general dissatisfaction of the people in 1864, and their desire for a change. Fremont's name was the rallying cry with dissatisfied Republicans. Fremont boldly denounced Lincoln:

> Had Mr. Lincoln remained faithful to the principles he was elected to defend, no schism could have been created, and no contest against him could have been possible. The ordinary rights secured under the Constitution have been violated. *The Administration has managed the war for personal ends, and with incapacity and selfish disregard for constitutional rights, with violation of personal liberty and liberty of the press.*

Miss Tarbell, who seems to have written her *Life of Lincoln* while on her knees before his image in a sacred shrine, says:

> In the spring of 1863 a plot was formed and favored by all the most prominent Republican leaders to *force* President Lincoln to abdicate, and to put Vice-President Hamlin in his place. Greeley thought he could use such pressure on Lincoln as would force him to step down and out. Lincoln knew of this plot. Mr. Enos Clark states that in the interview President Lincoln had with the committee of seventy men from Missouri in 1863, at the moment the committee was about to leave he saw tears streaming down Lincoln's face. On getting to the door Mr. Clark looked back, and instead of tears, Lincoln was laughing heartily and joking (Tarbell, Vol. II, p. 176).

This committee of seventy was anti-Lincoln. Next day Secretary of the Treasury Chase gave the committee a reception, and told them he was heartily in sympathy with their mission. The committee went to New York and was given a great and enthusiastic meeting at Cooper Institute. William Cullen Bryant made a speech, and various distinguished men indulged in violent denunciation of the Administration and threatened Lincoln with revolution (Tarbell, Vol. II., p. 178).

In 1863 the New York *Herald* advocated Grant for the Presidency. The great majority of the Republican leaders wanted a change. Lincoln knew of all these efforts:

> The despair, the indignation of the country in this dreadful year [1863] all centered on Lincoln. The Republicans were hopeless of re-electing him. Amid this dreadful uproar of discontent, one cry alarmed Lincoln – the cry that Grant should be presented for the Presidency (Tarbell, Vol. II, p. 199).

Leonard Sweet, a loving friend of Lincoln, August, 1864, in a letter from New York City to his wife, wrote:

> The fearful things in relation to this country induced me to stay a week. The malicious foes of Lincoln are getting up a Buffalo convention to supplant him. They are Sumner, Wade, Henry Winter Davis, Chase, Fremont, Wilson, etc. The most fearful things are probable. Democrats preparing to resist the draft. There is not much hope; unless material changes, Lincoln's re-election is beyond any possible hope, and is probably clear gone now.

Lincoln himself believed he would be defeated. On August 23, 1864, Lincoln, fully understanding the danger, put on record his belief that he would be defeated. In a speech bitterly denouncing Lincoln at a Republican meeting in Boston, Wendell Phillips went so far as to say, "Lincoln and his Cabinet are treasonable. Lincoln and Stanton should be impeached." The Chicago *Tribune* denounced Lincoln as the author of the negro riots. So eager was Lincoln for a second term, so intense his anxiety, it showed in his face. Miss Tarbell describes his looks during that period, 1863-4:

> Day by day he grew more haggard, the lines in his face deepened, it became ghastly gray in color. Sometimes he

would say, "I shall never be glad again." When victory was assured a change came at once. His form straightened up, his face cleared; never had he seemed so glad.

Yet in the face of all this evidence of Lincoln's unpopularity, it now suits Republicans to assert that Lincoln was trusted and beloved during his lifetime.

Such being the gloomy outlook for the Republican party immediately preceding the Presidential election of 1864, what brought about the change? What lifted from Lincoln's heart its load of despair, and filled it with hope? The answer is easy. First came a few Union victories, which indicated that the poor Confederates were failing for want of numbers. Farragut captured Mobile, Sherman was taking a holiday march over the South, burning and pillaging to his heart's delight, no armed men to impede his progress; Sherman's unresisted entrance into Atlanta, Ga., his brilliant victory over the 15,000 unarmed women and children of that unfortunate city, his splendid strategic feat in driving at the point of the bayonet the 15,000 Atlanta women and children out of their homes, out of the city – out into the pathless woods to wander about shelterless, foodless, and after Atlanta was tenantless, its streets all silent save where armed men trampled over them, Sherman's magnificent success in burning every house in the city, private as well as public – these valiant deeds of Sherman's army served to expel the despair from Lincoln's head and let in fresh breezes of hope. In addition he had General B.F. Butler and others of that calibre ready and willing to do his bidding, regardless of honor or honesty. In his book Butler relates how he obeyed orders, and, by the use of soldiers, secured Lincoln's election for a second term.

Oh, if the souls of liberty-loving men of '76 take cognizance of the workings of affairs in the land they loved, and many died to free, how must they mourn over the decadence of the men of this age – the men who glorify the shameful fact that an American President procured his re-election to office by the use of the United States army at the polls! Hapgood's *Life of Lincoln* contains the following unblushing paragraph:

> Charles A. Dana testifies that the whole power of the War Department was used to secure Lincoln's re-election in 1864. There is no doubt but this is true. *Purists may turn*

pale at such things, but the world wants no prettified portrait of Mr. Lincoln. Lincoln's Jesuitical ability to use the fox's skin when the lion's proves too short was one part of his enormous value.

Think of it, men of America! "Jesuitical ability" to trick, to deceive, to rob the people of their right to the ballot is, by a modern Republican historian, not only condoned, but commended as of *"enormous value."* And any honest man, shocked at so infamous an outrage on the rights of freemen, the Republican, Hapgood, sarcastically terms *"purist." "Purists may turn pale,"* etc.

In his book, published in 1892, General Butler proudly relates his part in the infamous work of using the army at the polls. The story is this: The election day was November 8, 1864. Lincoln had sent agents to New York City to spy out and report how the election would go. The report boded ill for Lincoln's success; in fact, indicated that New York would give a large majority for General McClellan. Lincoln, Seward and Stanton were alarmed. The latter instantly telegraphed General Butler to report to him at once. Butler rushed to Washington, and Stanton explained the situation at New York.

"What do you want me to do?" asked Butler.

"Start at once for New York, take command of the Department of the East, relieving General Dix. I will send you all the troops you need."

"But," returned Butler, "it will not be good politics to relieve General Dix just on the eve of election."

"Dix is a brave man," said Stanton, "but he won't do anything; he is very timid about some matters." This meant that General Dix was too honorable to use the United States Army to control and direct elections.

"Send me," suggested the shrewd Butler, "to New York with President Lincoln's order for me to relieve Dix in my pocket, but I will not use the order until such time as I think safe. I will report to Dix and be his obedient servant, and coddle him up until I see proper to spring on him my order, and take supreme command myself."

"Very well," assented Stanton; "I will send you Massachusetts troops."

"Oh, no!" objected the shrewder Butler, *"it won't do for Massachusetts men to shoot down New Yorkers."*

Stanton saw this also would be bad politics, so Grant was ordered to send Western troops – 5,000 good troops and two batteries of Napoleon guns – for the purpose of shooting down New Yorkers should New Yorkers persist in the evil intention of voting for McClellan.

When the citizens of New York saw Butler and his escort proudly prancing their horses on the streets and saw the arrival of 5,000 Western troops and the Napoleon guns, there was great agitation and uneasiness over the city. Newspapers charged that these warlike preparations were made to overawe citizens and prevent a fair election. Butler was virtuously indignant at such charges. General Sanford, commanding the New York State militia, called on Butler and told him the State militia was strong enough to quell any disturbance that might occur and he intended to call out his militia division on election day. Butler arrogantly informed General Sanford that he (Butler) had no use for New York militia; he did not know which way New York militia would shoot when it came to shooting. General Sanford replied that he would apply to the Governor of the State for orders. "I shall not recognize the authority of your Governor," haughtily returned Butler. "From what I hear of Governor Seymour I may find it necessary to arrest all I know who are proposing to disturb the peace on election day."

Butler well knew he was the only man in the city who intended to disturb the peace on election day. Butler's mean and cowardly soul gleefully gloated over the power he possessed to bully and insult the great State of New York, its Governor and militia officers – power given him by Lincoln, whose orders he had in his pocket to relieve General Dix, and take command of the army under Dix, and hold himself ready on election day to shoot down New York men at the polls to secure the re-election of President Lincoln. On November 5th Butler issued Order No. I, the purpose of which, he said:

> Is to correct misrepresentations, soothe the fears of the weak and timid and allay the nervousness of the ill-advised, silence all false rumors circulated by men for wicked purposes, and to contradict once for all false statements made to injure the Government in the respect and confidence of the people. The Commanding General takes occasion to declare

> that troops have been detailed for duty in this district to preserve the peace of the United States, to protect public property, and insure calm and quiet election.

The citizens of New York well knew that the above was one tissue of falsehood; they knew that Butler and his 5.000 Western troops, his batteries and Napoleon guns, were there to overawe the people and force the re-election of Lincoln. Order No. 1 continues:

> The Commanding General has been pained to see publications by some not too well informed persons, that the presence of the troops of the United States might by possibility have an effect on the free exercise of the duty of voting at the ensuing election. Nothing is further from the truth.

Who, knowing Butler's nature, does not picture to himself the Mephistophelean smile which ornamented his visage as he penned the above, and the following pretty falsehood: "The soldiers of the United States are here especially to see that there is no interference with the election." If the reader cares to see the full text of this lying order he can find it in Butler's book, page 1097.

On Nov. 7th, the day before the election, after Butler had placed his troops and made all arrangements necessary to control the ballot, he wrote to Secretary of War Stanton a letter in which he said:

> I beg leave to report that the troops have all arrived, and dispositions made which will insure quiet. I enclose copy of my order No. 1, and trust it will meet your approbation. I have done all I could to prevent secessionists from voting, and think it will have some effect.

"Secessionists" meant Democrats who chose to vote for McClellan. On page 760 of his book Butler describes how he disposed of the troops to accomplish his purpose. On page 771 Butler gives a joyful account of a reception at Fifth Avenue Hotel tendered him in honor of his signal success in keeping Democrats from voting. Full to bursting with pride, Butler made a speech to his entertainers, explaining how, after the Union army had conquered the South, her people should be treated. "Let us," said this willing and eager tool of despotic power, "take counsel from the Roman method of carrying on war." The Roman

CONCERNING THE WAR ON THE SOUTH   251

method was to make slaves of all prisoners of war; to inflict upon them every cruelty pagan hearts could devise. Butler continued:

> Let us say to our young men, "look to the fair fields of the sunny South for your reward. Go down there in arms; you shall have what you conquer, in fair division of the lands, each man in pay for his military service." We will open new land offices wherever our army marches, dividing the lands of the rebels among our soldiers, to be theirs and their heirs forever. Rebels should no longer be permitted to live in the land of the South, or anywhere in the boundaries of the United States. Let them go to Mexico, or to the islands of the sea, or to a place I do not like to name. I know of no land bad enough to be cursed with their presence. Never should they live here again.

This pagan speech was so rapturously received by Butler's audience, the Rev. Henry Ward Beecher (who a few years later was tried and found guilty by all the world except those interested in whitewashing him, of breaking up the home of one of his parishioners and blasting the reputation of that parishioner's wife), made a speech highly lauding Butler's evil work and pagan principles and naming him for the Presidency in 1868. General Whitmore followed Beecher in the same strain of eulogy, all of which filled Butler to bursting with pride. But he sorrowfully relates that these high laudations proved disastrous to all the hopes he had cherished of promotion in the army. These fine compliments, says Butler, and the grand receptions tendered:

> Were the most unhappy and unfortunate occurrences of my life. I should at once have repudiated the honor intended. I should promptly have said: "Gentlemen, you do me too much honor. General Grant ought to be our next President after Lincoln retires." That would have taken the sting out of the whole affair. I could then have been put in command of the Army of the Potomac, if I wished.

Butler no doubt thought his service in New York in keeping Democrats from voting would be rewarded by promotion. As a salve to his vanity he tries to have it appear that Grant's jealousy interfered. Butler's vanity was immense. It shines out from every page of his book.

In the year 1903, in the city of St. Louis, Mo., two men of foreign birth and from the lower ranks of life were found guilty of having procured fraudulent naturalization papers for some of their countrymen just arrived from Italy. These two men were sentenced to serve a term of five years in the penitentiary. The St. Louis *Globe-Democrat*, a stanch Republican journal, in an editorial called the offense of which these two men were found guilty, "A horribly atrocious crime against the ballot box and American citizenship." Reader, compare the magnitude of the crime these two men committed in 1903 with the magnitude of the crime committed in 1864 by the President of the United States. Is not the one as a molehill to the mountain of the other? Yet the criminals of 1903 were condemned to wear the stripes of infamy in a State penitentiary for five years. The criminal of 1864 is held up as a model for American youths to imitate.

The following are samples of telegraphic orders sent by Seward and Stanton to arrest innocent men:

Telegram. Washington City, Sept. 14, 1861.
United States Marshal:

Arrest Leonard Sturtivant and send him to Ft. Lafayette, New York. Deliver him into the custody of Col. Martin Burk.

W. H Seward.

Telegram. War Department. Washington. Oct. 19, 1861.
Richard H. Dana, U. S. District Attorney:

Send Wm. Pierce to Fort Lafayette.

W. H. Seward.

Telegram. Washington, Sept. 2, 1864.
United States Marshal:

John W. Watson is in Boston, No. 2 Olive street. He will to-day or to-night receive goods from Lawrence. New York, probably nautical instruments, care of Winer & Son, also clothes and letters from St. Denis Hotel. Watch him. Look out for the clothes. Seize them. Arrest him at the right time. [The right time was in the dead of night.] When he is arrested don't let him see or communicate with anyone. Bring him at once to Washington. The letters and goods must be seized by all means.

E.M. Stanton.

In Rhodes' *History of United States*, page 468, is this item:

The New York *World and Journal of Commerce* published, innocently, a forged proclamation, purporting to be Lincoln's. As soon as they discovered the mistake they made adequate and apparently satisfactory explanations to the authorities, but President Lincoln ordered the editor arrested and imprisoned and the paper suppressed. A file of soldiers seized the officers and held them until the order for arrest was rescinded.

CHAPTER TWENTY-NINE

Mr. Vallandingham's Case. Unhappy Conditions of Northern Democrats. Lincoln's Public Declaration of Despotic Doctrines.

In 1863 Mr. Clement L. Vallandingham was the Democratic nominee for Governor of the State of Ohio. Vallandingham was an eloquent speaker and very popular in his own party. Being a Democrat he naturally opposed despotism, and frequently commented on Lincoln's illegal arrests and imprisonments. He also censured Lincoln for refusing to permit the South's commissioners, Mr. Holcomb and Mr. Clement C. Clay, to enter Washington and make some effort to end the war by diplomacy. This greatly irritated Lincoln, Seward and Stanton. They became eager to have Vallandingham arrested and cast into prison. For some time the people had been greatly agitated and alarmed about illegal arrests, but as the exercise of power was the soul's delight of that triumvirate of despots, they could not deny themselves such pleasure. General Burnside was commander of a large military force in Southern Ohio. It was made known to him that the President would be much pleased if Vallandingham was put where his voice could not be heard. Of course, Burnside was eager to please the President, who held the power of promotion and dismissal from the army. A mass meeting of Democrats was to be held May 1, 1863, at Mount Vernon, Ohio. It was widely advertised that Vallandingham would be the orator of the day. Burnside sent two of his soldiers in citizen's clothes to hear Vallandingham's speech, and to bring back a report on which he could be arrested.

Of course, Burnside's two spies got what they were sent for. That night, or rather the next morning at half past two o'clock, one hundred armed men stole silently along the deserted streets of Dayton, Ohio, toward the house in which Vallandingham lodged. Armed men were deployed around the house to stand guard at every exit. Knocking on the front door with the butt end of his pistol, the captain of the company demanded admittance. On entering, a score or more men tramped through halls and rooms until they came to Vallandingham's bedchamber, where he lay fast asleep.

"Get up and dress," ordered the captain of the company, shaking the sleeping man.

"What's wanted?" asked Vallandingham, starting up and rubbing his eyes.

"*You!* Hurry! We take the next train to Cincinnati."

When dressed, one soldier seized Vallandingham's right arm, another his left, and hurried him down to the front door, where a carriage waited. He was rapidly driven to the depot and soon on his way to Cincinnati, where he was closely confined until May 6, then taken before a military court, put through the farce of a trial, found guilty and sent to Fort Warren, Boston Harbor.

Arrests of this arbitrary nature were made every day, or rather every night, but this of Vallandingham aroused more than ordinary indignation and alarm. Mass meetings were held, eloquent speeches made in Ohio, New York and other States. In the history of the long and woeful contest between Despotism and Democracy I know of no more pitiable condition to which the latter has ever been reduced than that in which the Democrats of the North found themselves under the rule of the Republican party in the '60s. Sympathizing as they did with the South, believing as they did that her cause was just, hating as they did the War of Conquest, yet feeling themselves unable openly to oppose and fight the mighty machinery of the Republican Government, during all the four years' war Democrats were subject to the insults, scoffs, gibes and taunts of Republicans. They were denounced as disloyal, as rebels, as traitors, as copperheads. They were liable any night to arrest and imprisonment. Thousands of their friends and relatives languished in jails, and many died there. Some Democrats, hoping to escape persecution, paid a half-hearted homage to Lincoln, refrained from criticism, affected to rejoice at Republican successes; but no professions of loyalty to Lincoln and his measures saved them from the scorn and contempt of the Republican party. Too well that party knew it was not possible for any man with one particle of Democracy in his heart to believe in the conquest and subjugation of free men, or free States. In the very beginning of the war the Republican rulers had cast a lasso over the head of Northern Democracy and tied it fast to the tail end of the great juggernaut car, which, loaded with munitions of war, was sent crashing over the Southern States, grinding under its wheels every living thing in its pathway. Not until after Lee's surrender and after Lincoln's death did Northern Democracy shake from its neck that humiliating thralldom.

All during the war the State of New York remained Democratic, yet was forced to render its full quota to aid a war it knew was iniquitous. Nevertheless, having a Democratic Governor, the people of New York felt that the air of their State was somewhat less oppressive to free men than in some other States. Hence, New York men were more outspoken. A mass meeting was held in Albany, New York, to discuss the Vallandingham outrage. Eloquent speeches were made denouncing Burnside's actions, and an able address to President Lincoln was drawn up, setting forth the fact that Burnside had violated the law of the land; that his arrest and trial of a civilian in a military court when the civil courts of Ohio were in full and unrestrained operation, was an outrage, and deserved the severest reprehension, and requested Lincoln to rescind Burnside's order to imprison Vallandingham, release him from military custody and restore him to freedom. The Albany address and President Lincoln's reply thereto being too lengthy for the limits of this work, I can only give a few extracts from Mr. Lincoln's written reply to show the men of this age with what cool, self-complacent confidence the first American despot propounded the Caesarian doctrine of absolute rule. Twenty of the first citizens of Albany were appointed to go to Washington and present the address to the President. If the reader desires to see the address and Lincoln's reply he can find it in Carpenter's *Logic of History*.

In reply to the statement that the citizens of Ohio were amenable to the laws of that State, and if charged with any violations of law Mr. Vallandingham should have been tried in a civil court, President Lincoln wrote: "Civil courts are organized for trials on charges of crime well defined by law. A jury of the civil courts too frequently has at least *one* member more ready to hang a panel than to hang the traitor." Men of America! consider these words written by an American President. Daniel Webster objected to military courts because, as he said, "military courts are organized to convict." The so-called *humane* Lincoln objected to *civil* courts because *one* member of the jury might be more ready to hang the panel than to hang the man! Lincoln seems to assume that men arrested by military officials must be guilty, therefore should have no chance of escaping conviction by trial in a civil court. Lincoln also objects to civil courts because they only convict on charges of crime *well defined* by law. Military courts convict on the most frivolous pretexts, or no pretext at all. The chief thing necessary to military conviction is that some man in high place should desire the man to be convicted and put out of his way.

In the Albany address reference was made to the suspension of the habeas corpus. To this Mr. Lincoln replied as follows: "The suspension of the habeas corpus was for the purpose that men may be arrested and held in prison who cannot be proved guilty of any defined crime." Reflect on these words, O, you men of America! You who forget that "eternal vigilance is the price of liberty." You who, with child-like innocence, rest in the belief that the future has no dangers for American liberties. But even the above declaration of Lincoln's is not the worst.

"Arrests," wrote President Lincoln to that Albany committee of Democrats, "are not made so much for what has been done as for what possibly might be done. The man who stands by and says nothing when the peril of his Government is discussed cannot be misunderstood. If not hindered [by arrest, imprisonment, or death] he is sure to help the enemy." Is it any wonder under rulings like this that 38,000 arbitrary arrests threw 38,000 innocent men and women into American bastiles to languish for months or years, and many therein to die?

Under the above definition of treason as given by Lincoln, what man was safe? Is it any wonder a reign of terror existed in the Northern States? Under Lincoln's definition *silence* became an act of treason. A man with a sore throat, unable to talk aloud, if he happened to be present when the Lincoln Government was discussed, was liable to arrest and imprisonment in the most distant fortress in the land. Strange as this may appear to the people of this age, blackly despotic as it certainly was, there was still a lower deep of despotism, and President Lincoln fell into that lower deep and dragged down with him the last shred of freedom left to the people of the Northern States:

> Much more [wrote the President of the United States] if a man talks ambiguously, talks with "buts" and "ifs" and "ands" he cannot be misunderstood. If not hindered [by im-

prisonment or death] this man will actively commit treason. Arbitrary arrests are not made for the treason defined in the Constitution, but to prevent treason.

That is to prevent the sort of treason never before known on earth – the treason of "ifs" and "'buts" and "ands" – the treason made and invented by Abraham Lincoln, the first President of the Republican party. In *Recollections of the War*, page 236, Charles A. Dana records the arbitrary arrest, by order of President Lincoln, in one day, of ninety-seven of the leading citizens of Baltimore, and their imprisonment, mostly in solitary confinement. Not one of these men had committed or was charged with having committed any offense known to the law of the land. Nor is there the least evidence showing that any one of the ninety-seven men had used the "ifs" and "ands" and "buts" so offensive to Mr. Lincoln's sensitive soul. The fear that they *might* possibly at some future time mutter or speak aloud the dangerous "ifs" and "buts" and "ands" caused the arrest and imprisonment of the ninety-seven men of Baltimore. In the darkest days of President Lincoln's despotic rule, Governor Seymour, of New York, had the courage to condemn and denounce that rule. In a speech referring to arbitrary arrests and imprisonments, Seymour said: "In Great Britain the humblest hut is to its occupant a castle impregnable to the monarch. In our country the most unworthy underling of power is licensed to break within the sacred precincts of our homes and drag men out and cast them in dungeon cells."

The men who wielded this power reveled in its possession. Seward is the man who, with a sardonic smile, said to Lord Lyons. "My Lord, I can touch the bell at my right and order the arrest of a man in Ohio; I can again touch the bell and order the arrest of a man in New York, and no power on earth save that of the President can release them. Can the Queen of England do as much?"

"No," replied the astonished Englishman. "Were she to attempt such an act her head would roll from her shoulders."

These three men – Lincoln, Seward and Stanton – proudly boasted that they held more power over the people of America than any monarch since the reign of the Stuarts had wielded over the English people. No man need be surprised at the Republican party's open and insolent usurpation of power. A thousand times had the speakers of that party publicly declared their contempt and hatred of the Union, of the

Constitution, of the laws of the land.

The New York *Evening Post* reported that the great Republican preacher, Henry Ward Beecher, in a speech, said to his audience: "I believe that Sharp's rifle is a truly moral agency. There is more moral power in one of these instruments than in a hundred Bibles." It was also reported that this same Beecher, on bidding farewell to some of his protégés about to start off for Kansas, told them that to shoot at a Southern man and miss killing him would be a crime.

Of such inestimable value to liberty did Daniel Webster esteem free speech, in an oration he said:

> Free speech is a home-bred right, a fireside privilege. It is not to be drawn into any controversy. It is as undoubted as the right of breathing the air and walking the earth. It is a right to be maintained in peace and in war. It is a right which cannot be invaded without destroying constitutional liberty. This right should be protected and guarded by the freemen of this country with a jealous care unless they are prepared for chains and anarchy.

To prevent honorable men from using this sacred and God-given right Abraham Lincoln, the first American despot, caused the illegal arrest and imprisonment of 38,000 free born men and women. Thomas Jefferson said: "Those to whom power is delegated should be held to a strict accountability to their constitutional oath of office. The plea of necessity is no excuse for a violation of such oath."

The "plea of necessity" is always put forward to excuse the evil deeds of despots. Modern Republican writers laud Lincoln's violation of law and affect to hold him as a god above all human laws. Even John Adams, Federal though he was, opposed the use of arbitrary power. "The nature of encroachments on liberty and law," said Adams, "is to grow every day more and more encroaching; like a cancer, it eats faster and faster every hour."

Yet modern Republican writers admire and applaud Lincoln's encroachments. The conscience of the conquering party has become so dulled, its reasoning faculties so befogged, its love of liberty so weak, it sees no danger in the precedent set by Mr. Lincoln. Yet that party well knows that no monarch of England since the reign of the Tudors has dared play the despot as Lincoln did. Charles the First lost his head and James the Second his throne for lesser crimes than the despot of the '60s was guilty of.

As illustrative of Mr. Lincoln's peculiar character I give the following story: When almost in despair of re-election Lincoln wrote General McClellan an autograph letter, which he sent by Mr. Blair, proposing to pay him (McClellan) roundly if he would withdraw from the canvass and leave the field clear for Lincoln's running. The compensation Lincoln offered was the immediate appointment of McClellan General of the army, and the appointment of McClellan's father-in-law, Mr. Marcy, Major General, and the substantial recognition of the Democratic party. This was a brilliant bait, but the fish did not bite. General McClellan promptly refused. The story of the affair is related in Lamon's *Recollections of Lincoln*, edited by his daughter Dorothy. McClellan was the chosen nominee of the Democratic party at that time; the times boded success to Democracy. Neither Lincoln or Lamon seemed to perceive the baseness involved in the transaction which Lincoln proposed. If Lincoln believed that McClellan was the best man to be at the head of the army, was it not *base* to make his appointment a matter of bargain and sale? Was not Lincoln's offer to *bribe* McClellan to betray the trust his own party had put in him when it nominated him for the Presidency as gross an insult as one man could offer another? Instead of seeing this, poor Lamon laments that General McClellan had not the patriotism to accept Lincoln's offer.

Patriotism! These men had ceased to know, if they ever had known, the meaning of the word. To them it no longer meant love of country. It only meant approbation of Lincoln's war of conquest on the South. Lamon seems to have thought that Lincoln had as much right to divide the power he wielded over the country as he had to divide an apple he was eating; as much right to bestow one-half of the power he had usurped as he would have to give away half an apple he had bought. Lamon looked on Lincoln's offer as most generous. He says:

> The division of the Roman world between the members of the triumvirate was not comparable to the proposal of Lincoln to McClellan, because the Roman was a smaller world than the American, and it [the Roman world] was partitioned among *three,* while the American world was only to be halved.

Think of it, gentle reader! Think of any man outside of a lunatic asylum fancying he had the right to look upon this great country as his to divide and give away as he liked! Poor Lamon blamed General McClellan for not accepting "Lincoln's generous offer." Before this occurred, Lincoln had tried to make a deal with Governor Seymour. Lamon tells the story thus:

> The affairs of the country were in a very precarious condition, and were daily and hourly growing worse, and time was imperative. Mr. Lincoln had a telegram sent from Washington to Governor Seymour requesting him to come to Washington on very important business. Seymour declined, and added that the "distance from Washington to Albany was precisely the same as from Albany to Washington." Lincoln then sent Thurlow Weed to Albany empowered to make Seymour the following proposal:
> "If Governor Seymour will withdraw his opposition to the draft, and use his authority and influence as Governor in putting down the riots in New York, and will co-operate in all reasonable ways with the administration in the suppression of the Southern rebellion, President Lincoln, on his part, will agree fully and honestly to renounce all claims to the Presidency for the second term, and will decline under any circumstances to be a candidate for re-election, and will further agree to throw his entire influence, in so far as he can control it, in behalf of Horatio Seymour for President of the United States" (Lamon's *Recollections of Lincoln*, page 213).

Governor Seymour promptly declined. Was Lincoln's proposal a trap to catch Seymour? Did Seymour remember the nursery rhyme: "'Will you walk into my parlor?' said the spider to the fly. 'It's the prettiest little parlor you ever did spy.'" Did Seymour remember Vallandingham's case? Vallandingham had been arrested, tried and condemned for far less offense to President Lincoln than Seymour had been guilty of. Was it to arrest and silence Seymour that he was invited to visit Washington? At any rate Seymour was too prudent to be caught in a trap like that; his answer to Lincoln's invitation, that "the distance to and from Washington to Albany was precisely the same," shows he was not without suspicion.

CHAPTER THIRTY

*Was the War Waged to Free Slaves? Lincoln on the Negro.
Van Buren. Lamon's Testimony. Wendell Phillips.
Lincoln's Letter to Greeley. Seward's Indifference.
Grant's Feeling. Conway's Evidence.*

Those who best knew Mr. Lincoln assert that he not only was indifferent to the future of the African race, but disliked negroes as a race, and had little or no faith in their capability of development. At no period of his life was he in favor of bestowing upon them political or social equality with the white race. General Donn Piatt, a fervent Abolitionist, sounded Mr. Lincoln on this question: "I found," says Piatt, "that Mr. Lincoln could no more feel sympathy for that wretched race than he could for the horse he worked or the hog he killed. Descended from the poor whites of the South, he inherited the contempt, if not the hatred, held by that class for the negro." In his *Life of Lincoln*, page 236, Lamon says, in 1846, in a speech, Mr. Lincoln "imputed to Van Buren, a Democrat, the great sin of having voted in the New York State Convention for negro suffrage with a property qualification. Douglas denied the imputation, but Lincoln proved it to the injury of Van Buren." On page 334 of Lamon's *Life of Lincoln* is this:

> None of Mr. Lincoln's public acts, either before or after he became President, exhibit any special tenderness for the African race, or commiseration of their lot. On the contrary he invariably, in words and deeds, postponed the interest of the negro to the interest of the whites. When from political and military considerations he was forced to declare the freedom of the enemy's slaves, he did so with avowed reluc-

tance; he took pains to have it known he was in no wise affected by sentiment. He never at any time favored the admission of negroes into the body of the electors in his State, or in the States of the South. He claimed that those negroes set free by the army were poor spirited, lazy and slothful; that they could only be made soldiers by force, and would not be ever willing laborers at all; that they seemed to have no interest in the cause of their own race, but were as docile in the service of the rebellion as the mule that ploughed the fields or drew the baggage trains. As a people, Lincoln thought negroes would only be useful to those who were at the same time their masters, and the foes of those who sought their good. He wanted the negro protected as women and children are. He had no notion of extending the privilege of governing to the negro. Lincoln always contended that the cheapest way of getting rid of the negro was for the Nation to buy the slaves and send them out of the country.

General Donn Piatt says: "Lincoln well knew that the North was not fighting to free slaves, nor was the South fighting to preserve slavery. In that awful conflict slavery went to pieces." Lincoln himself gives testimony on this slavery question. Herndon said when Lincoln issued the Emancipation Proclamation there was no heart in it. Every one remembers Lincoln's letter to Greeley, in which he frankly declared that whatever he did for or with negroes, he did to help him save the Union; that is, to conquer the South. He wrote:

> My paramount object is to save the Union, and not either destroy or save slavery. If I could save the Union without freeing the slaves, I would do it. If I could save the Union by freeing some and leaving others in slavery, I would do it. If I could save it by freeing all, I would do that. What I do about slavery and the colored race, I do because I believe it helps to save the Union.

Yet this man had been put in office by a party which hated and despised the Union. On another occasion Lincoln wrote:

> I have no purpose to introduce political or social equality between the white and black race. There is a physical

difference between the two which probably will forever forbid their living together on the same footing of equality. I, as well as any other man, am in favor of the race to which I belong having the superior position. I have never said anything to the contrary.

Simon Cameron, Lincoln's first Secretary of War, wrote General Butler, then in New Orleans: "President Lincoln desires the right to hold slaves to be fully recognized. The war is prosecuted for the Union, hence no question concerning slavery will arise." In his inauguration Lincoln said: "I have no lawful right to interfere with slavery directly or indirectly; I have no inclination to do so." Mr. Wendell Phillips said that Lincoln was badgered into issuing the Emancipation Proclamation, and that after it was issued, Lincoln said it was the greatest folly of his life. That much lauded instrument speaks for itself. It plainly proves that its writer had not the least heart in the business of freeing slaves. Had he taken any joy in the work, would he have bestowed the boon of freedom only on those negroes still under the rule of the Confederacy, leaving the large number in those States and parts of States under his own control in the bondage they were born in?

When General Grant was Colonel of the Twenty-First Illinois Infantry he expressed himself plainly on the negro question:

> The sole object of this war is to restore the Union. Should I become convinced it has any other object, or that the Government designs using its soldiers to execute the wishes of the Abolitionists, I pledge you my honor as a man and a soldier I would resign my commission and carry my sword to the other side (*Democratic Speaker's Handbook*, p. 33).

On May 29, 1863, Mr. F.A. Conway, Congressman from Kansas, wrote to the New York *Tribune*, as follows:

> The independence of the South is now an established fact. The war for the future becomes simply an instrument in the hands of the political managers to effect results to their own personal ends unfavorable to the cause of freedom. It is now assumed that the Union is the object paramount over every other consideration. Every institution is now of small importance. Slavery must give way, or not give way; must be

strangled, or given new lease of life with increased power, just as the exigencies of the North may require. This has now become the doctrine of life-long Abolitionists. Gerritt Smith, Raymond and other men want power and care for nothing else. *For the sake of power they would kill all the white people in the South, or take than to their arms. They would free all the slaves or make their bondage still more helpless; they would do anything wicked for the sake of power.*

Never were truer words spoken or written than these by that zealous Abolition Congressman Conway of Kansas. In Herndon's suppressed *Life of Lincoln*, he said: "When Lincoln issued the proclamation to free the slaves there was no heart in the act." One of the boldest Republican organs, in 1880, the Lemars (Iowa) *Sentinel*, frankly betrays its party's real feeling toward the negro race, as follows:

> As an office seeker, the negro has more brass in a square inch of his face, more rapaciousness for office, than his barbarian masters ever dared to possess. The Southern brigadier wants office and place, but he is willing to fight for them, or vote for them; at the drop of the hat he will shoot and cut for them; he does not whine like a whipped cur, or demand like a beggar on horseback, as the nigger does. Let the nigger first learn to vote before he asks for office. The brazen-jawed nigger is but a trifle less assuming, insolent and imperious in his demands than the lantern-jawed brigadiers; the educated nigger is a more capacious liar than his barbarian masters ever were, or dared to be.
>
> The greatest mistake the Republican party ever made was taking the nigger at a single bound and placing on his impenetrable skull the crown of suffrage. It is a wrong to him and to us to let him wield the ballot. The nigger is necessarily an ignoramus. The free nigger, we repeat, is a fraud.

CHAPTER THIRTY-ONE

The Reconstruction Period. Hate and Cruelty.

The full horrors of this dreadful period have never been portrayed. God knows the South was hated enough before and during the war, but after the conquest, as she lay disarmed at the feet of her conquerors, wounded almost unto death, the vengeful ferocity of Republicans was something to wonder at. The events of that period deserve a volume to themselves. I shall only say a few words on the subject. Wendell Phillips, insane hater of the South though he was, sometimes had the honesty to speak plainly of his own party. Witness the following:

> The Republican party is not inspired with any humane desire to protect the negro. It uses the bloody shirt for office, and once there, only laughs at it. Today our greatest danger is the Republican party. Wolves in sheep's clothing! Hypocrites! I hail their coming defeat, looking forward to it as the dawning of a glorious day.

From early manhood General Grant was afflicted with the drink disease. Phillips said: "Grant can never stand before a bottle of whiskey without falling down." General Piatt, in *Memories of the Men Who Saved the Union*, says: "Grant's habit of drink lost us thousands and thousands of patriotic lives. The attempt to conceal this is not only pitiable, but hopeless." The terrible slaughter of Union soldiers at Cold Harbor was charged to Grant's drunkenness. Major-General William F. Smith, in a confidential letter to Senator Foote, July 30, 1864, states that soon after Grant had taken a pledge to drink nothing intoxicating, he (Grant) called at his (Smith's) headquarters, and asked for whiskey, and drank so often he went away drunk, *and General Butler saw him.* A short while before this Grant had written to Washington asking that General Butler be relieved from that department, because he (Grant) *"could not trust Butler with the command of the troops in the movements about to be made."* Instructions were sent to Grant to remove Butler. Butler heard of this and hurried to see Grant. General Smith wrote Senator Foote that he heard direct from Grant's headquarters, and also from another source, that General Butler threatened Grant that he would expose his drunken habits if the order was not revoked. The order *was* revoked, and Butler remained in command, although Grant had said he was unfit to be trusted.

General Piatt says: "Grant has his monument in the hearts of Republicans; for that he lent his name to secure the perpetuation of Republican power." Grant did not lend his name to secure the perpetuation of Republican power, but to secure the Presidency for himself. When Grant came to believe that the Republicans who opposed Johnson and his policy would succeed in deposing Johnson, he abandoned Johnson and his policy (the very policy he himself had recommended to Johnson), rushed into the camp of Johnson's bitter foes, and became the tool and agent of the Republican leaders to carry out their cruel policy toward the people of the South.

General Piatt testifies concerning Grant thus:

> Secretary Stanton had no hesitation in expressing his contempt for Grant – contempt caused by the following event: When the army of the Cumberland was cooped up in Chattanooga, with starvation or surrender staring them in the face, Stanton hurried to meet Grant at Louisville and consult with him as to the best means of relieving our forces. The day on which the two men met was given to these considerations, and the wire between Chattanooga and Louisville trembled with continuous messages. When night came the two men separated with the understanding that after an hour's rest and refreshment they should again meet and continue their labor. Grant was to leave next morning for Chattanooga. When the time came for the meeting Grant did not appear. Stanton waited impatiently, receiving the telegrams that continued to pour in, and at last sent for Grant, who could not be found.

CONCERNING THE WAR ON THE SOUTH 269

Annoyed and disgusted, Stanton had the theatres searched without success. At last, long after midnight. General Grant was found *in a place and under such circumstances not necessary to relate to those who knew his habits.* Had Grant been of a sensitive nature, under Stanton's savage reprimand, he would have then and there disappeared from history.

Grant came near being arrested by Halleck more than once. In a telegram to McClellan, Halleck said: "A rumor has reached me that Grant has resumed his former bad habits. If so it will account for his oft repeated neglect of my oft repeated orders. I do not deem it advisable to arrest him at present." In a telegram to Grant, Halleck said:

> Your neglect of repeated orders has caused great dissatisfaction and seriously interfered with military plans. Your going to Nashville without authority, and when your presence with your troops was of the greatest importance, was a matter of serious complaint at Washington, so much so that I was advised to arrest you on your return.

Yet to this alcohol-soaked man – this man who could not see a bottle of whiskey without falling down – a Republican Congress gave absolute power over the Southern States. There was no escape from any decree issued from Grant's whiskey-soaked brain. He had power to delegate his rule to any man under him. Grant said to the military commanders under him: "The law makes the district commanders their own interpreters of their power under it." This drunken despot wielded absolute and irresponsible power over the unarmed people of the South. A few samples of the methods Grant's sub-despots used will illustrate the South's condition:

Headquarters Fourth Military District of Mississippi.
Vicksburg, Miss., June 15, 1868.

General Order No. 123.

First. – Major-Gen. Adelbert Ames is appointed Governor of the State of Mississippi, vice Benjamin G. Humphreys, hereby removed.

Second. – Captain Jasper Myers is appointed Attorney General of the State of Mississippi, vice C. Hooker, hereby removed.

Third. – The officers appointed above will repair without delay to Jackson, and enter immediately upon the duties of their respective offices.

> Headquarters Third Military District
> Georgia, Alabama and Florida.
> Atlanta, Ga., January 13, 1868.

Charles J. Jenkins, Milledgeville, Ga.

Sir: – I have no alternative but to remove you from your office, as you will see by the enclosed order. I do not deem myself called upon to answer the arguments in your letter.

> George Mead, *Major-General Commanding.*

No despot ever felt called upon to answer arguments. Force is the only argument despots use or can understand. Mr. John Imes was the Treasurer of Georgia. Meade wrote him as follows:

Mr. John Imes:

Sir: – I am compelled to remove you from office, as you will see I have done by the enclosed order.

> George Meade, *Major-General Commanding.*

Grant's sub-despot over South Carolina wrote as follows:

> Headquarters.
> Charleston, S.C, Oct. 16, 1867.

Judge Aldrich has been suspended, and will not be permitted to hold any court in his circuit. See special Order No. 183, of this date.
By command of

> Brevet Major General E.R.C. Canby.

Does the reader want to know how the sub-despots appointed by Grant ruled the people of the South? To this day that rule is referred to as the "horrors of the reconstruction period." After the military had full possession of all the offices of the civil courts, from the highest down, malignant bullies everywhere in power, a reign of terror set in almost equal to the awful days of the French Revolution. Every day numbers of the best citizens arrested on the most frivolous charges, or no charge whatever, hands and feet fettered as felons, dragged hundreds of miles away from homes and friends, were thrown into dungeon cells, in which they lay months or years in solitary confinement unless death ended their suffering. These prisoners were not permitted to see friends, relatives or counselor-at-law. During their long imprisonment, miserably fed, cursed, abused by jailers, tried by military commissioners, many died, many were condemned and sentenced for life to the Dry Tortugas – condemned on evidence no court of justice would have received. It was noticed that the military courts seemed to feel special antipathy to young men, to beardless boys – sons of the best citizens. The suffering of these youths in prison, their tortures in the Dry Tortugas, they knew would inflict the keenest anguish on the hearts of parents and relatives. The Montgomery (Ala.) *Mail*, speaking of the large number of innocent young men sent to the Dry Tortugas, thus describes that place of torment:

> At the Dry Tortugas the prisoners' heads are shaved. They have to labor under a torrid sun upon a sand bank in the midst of the ocean, with balls and chains about their legs. The men who command the prisoners are amenable to the laws of neither God or man. Col. Grental, a soldier, was tied up by his thumbs, and treated with every species of cruelty and barbarity. The laws are silent and newspapers dumb. The prisoner who enters the Dry Tortugas leaves liberty, justice, hope, behind him. Large numbers of young Southern men, for any or no offense, in what is called the reconstruction period, are arrested, go through the farce of a drumhead trial, presided over by men who take a fiendish delight in torturing any Southern man or woman, nearly always found guilty, and sentenced for life to the Dry Tortugas. The lips of the Alabama journals are pinned together with bayonets. Our hands are fastened in iron cuffs. We dare not speak the whole truth. If we did our paper would be suppressed, our business ruined, our wives and children brought to want.

Neither the despot Grant nor his sub-despots ever forgot the press. Every officer and private in that army of despotism kept a sharp eye on newspapers, and were quick to apply the muzzle if any paper dared make public their evil deeds. Despotism is a noxious plant, which hates the light and flourishes only in dark places. A few samples will show how despots muzzled the press in the South: On November 15, 1867, a file of soldiers entered the office of the Vicksburg *Times*, arrested the editor, dragged him to jail. McArdle's offense was having reported in the paper a despotic order made by General Ord, and comparing the situation of the South with that of Poland. McArdle was tried by a military commission (always organized to convict) and condemned. Being a man of talent he took an appeal, but all the influence of the military was against him. The case dragged on for years before a final decision, which I have failed to find.

Early on the morning of August 8, 1867, a body of soldiers forced their way into the office of the *Constitutional Eagle*, published at Camden, Ark., seized, carried off and destroyed all the material of the office. Col. C.C. Gilbert, the small despot commanding the Union soldiers at Camden, justified the acts of his men, saying to the editor:

> An article in your paper unnecessarily exasperated my soldiers. The press may censure the servants of the people, but the military are not the servants of the people, but their masters. It is a great impertinence for a newspaper in this State to comment on the military under any circumstances (*Democratic Speaker's Handbook*).

The comment which unnecessarily exasperated the soldiers was a statement that when drunk the soldiers were in the habit of indecently exposing their persons on the street when ladies were passing. The *National Intelligencer* of Washington City commented on the rule of the military satraps in the South, as follows:

> Without any proof whatever four respectable citizens were arrested and confined in separate cells in Atlanta, denied all communication with friends, save under military surveillance, denied all opportunity to confer with legal counsel. Two white men in Fort Pulaski were confined in cells and denied all access to friends or legal counsel. These six men were

brought out of their dungeons, hurried to trial for their lives before a military commission, one of those institutions, Mr. Webster said, always organized to convict. The statement of facts is sufficiently horrible and damnable to every officer and agent concerned in it. But this is only a part of the infamous record. While these men are immured in dungeons, cut off from all access to friends or counsel, their enemies, with artful and incessant malice, have been busy in procuring false testimony, and the uniform of the nation is degraded by the military arrest of ignorant negroes, dragging them by force before a military board, and then by threats and curses, starvation and solitary confinement, endeavor to extort from them false testimony upon which the lives of innocent men may be taken away. The testimony we publish to-day establishes these facts, and shows the character of the government under which the people of the South now live *(Democratic Speaker's Handbook*, page 162).

These military lords permitted the farce of elections, if carried on under military control. Armed battalions of negroes and Federal white men surrounded the voting places. In vain Democrats issued protests against these outrages. In the House of Congress Mr. Brooks, in behalf of the Democratic members, offered a powerful protest:

The military have been used to destroy States. The General of the army [Grant], representing the sword, and only the sword [he represented a whiskey bottle also], has been exalted by acts of Congress above the constitutional Commander in Chief [the President] of the Army and Navy, in order to execute these military decrees and root out every vestige of constitutional law and liberty. To prolong and perpetuate this military rule in the North and West, as well as the South, this same General of the army [Grant] has been elected at the Chicago Convention to head the electoral votes for the Presidency in ten States of this Union, which are as much under his feet as Turkey is under the Sultan's, or Poland under the Czar of Russia.

If the protests from Northern Democrats did not stem the tide of despotism, they at least showed that a spark of the old fire of liberty yet existed in this corrupted Union. At one stroke of the pen Sheridan, Grant's sub-despot, disfranchised thirty thousand white men in Louisiana. Grant was responsible for every criminal act done by the military. The New York *Herald* said of Grant's brutality in the South:

> Every personal right of the citizen is invaded at once. Without any process of law whatever, a man is deprived of his liberty and thrust into a cell at the mere bidding of a political or military bully. The secrecy of the telegraph and post office is violated as no man would dare violate them in despotic France.

At that time France was ruled by an Emperor. The South was ruled by the despotism of hate. No Christian Emperor, King or Kaiser was ever so cruel, so bitter, so vindictive as the hate despotism imposed by Grant upon the people of the South. By bogus elections carpetbaggers went to Congress. It seemed that the chief aim of these bogus Congressmen was to obtain additional power to rob, oppress and torment the people of the South. The excuse for seeking Congressional aid was the ready lie that the people of the South were on the eve of another rebellion. On the 23d of July a bill to send more soldiers and munitions of war to the Southern States was up for discussion. A man by the name of Stokes, who claimed to represent a Tennessee Congressional district, spoke as follows:

> If you do not send us guns and powder and bayonets and cannon, and send 'em quick, Forrest and his rebel crew of Democrats will be down on us like – like a thousand devils! I want ten thousand stand of arms for my own district. Unless you send on these arms all the truly loyal negroes will be overrun and the Republican party killed in Tennessee.

Mr. Washburn, of Illinois, seemed to be very anxious to send guns and bayonets down to the loyal negroes and carpetbaggers, but he was afraid. "Sir," said Mr. Washburn, "I believe that in most of the States not ten days after these arms are sent South to the loyal negroes they will be in the hands of the rebels." Congress saw the danger. Never before was any Congress in so painful a quandary. Anxious, yet afraid, to arm loyal negroes and carpetbaggers. A man named Dewees, claiming to represent the people of North Carolina (he might as well have claimed to represent the people in the moon or the farthest star), added to the distress and perplexity of Congress. "If you don't give us arms," cried Mr. Dewees, pale and anxious, "before six months the Ku-Klux-Klan, the Rebels and the Copperheads will be ruling the whole South."

Ku-Klux, Rebels and Copperheads were a trinity of devils. Hades had no worse. Still, Congress was afraid to send to the loyal negroes and carpetbaggers munitions of war, which seems a little strange to us of this generation, knowing, as all now know, that the Ku-Klux or Rebels in the South had no arms or munitions of war, while the loyal negroes and carpetbaggers were well armed. A Democrat named Woodward ventured to ask if the reconstruction government in the South could be maintained in no other way than by the bayonet. This question aroused Mr. Dewees' indignation. "No!" he roared. "We can only sustain our Government by arms! Arms we must have, or Ku-Klux, Rebels and Copperheads will wipe us out and rule the South." At this one or two Copperheads (Northern Democrats) were imprudent enough to laugh, which had the effect of stirring Mr. Dewees up to the very highest flight of oratory. Mr. Dewees was short, thick set, and very ruddy, so to speak; every pore of his body broke out into a glow and gush and roar of eloquence, and the whole House on both sides became convulsed with laughter. The man claiming to represent North Carolina shouted:

> Come on! I say, come on when you feel disposed! Stretch out your traitorous hands to touch again one fold of the old flag, and representatives of four million of men with black skins, but loyal hearts, will dash themselves a bulwark between you and the loyal governments in the South, and you will only live in sad memories of bad events. Come on! Come on!

No one seemed disposed to come on, though entreated so fervently. Never before was Congress in such a higgledy-piggledy state of mind. If they sent arms to negroes and carpetbaggers the rebels would get every gun within ten days. Mr. Washburn said so. If they didn't send arms the rebels would get every negro and carpetbagger in ten days. Mr. Dewees said so.

CHAPTER THIRTY-TWO
☆ ☆ ☆ ☆

Republican Hate.

Forgiveness to the injured does belong;
But they ne'er pardon, who have done the wrong.

On reading over the preceding pages of this work, I find the word hate often recurs. In the absence of evidence the men of this generation will not be able to form any adequate conception of the vast volume of virulence which, like an empoisoned stream bubbling up from hell itself, continually flowed downward on the people of the South. This stream was started in 1796, and continued until, swollen to enormous proportions, it culminated in a deluge of blood in 1861-1865. For four cruel years that deluge spread itself over the States of the South, and at the end of four years the men of the South laid down their arms and peace was declared, but there was no peace. In 1898 the Republican party inaugurated war on Spain to rescue Cuba from Spanish oppression. As soon as this purpose was accomplished the victorious Republican party made haste to resume friendly relations with Spain, and when Spanish army officers visited this country they were courteously treated, not one unkind word spoken or written of them or of their country. How differently did the conquering Republicans treat the conquered people of the South after peace was declared between the two sections! If anything, Republican hate became more intense. The whole reconstruction period was a deadly war on Southern people, and the more base and cowardly because waged on unarmed men and women. The Republican party declared it waged the war of the '60s to restore the Union. The Union was restored precisely to suit their ideas. Every negro in the land was freed. Why, then, was not the Republican party satisfied with its success, as it was satisfied with its success in 1898? The answer is plain. Because the war of the '60s was not fought to restore the Union or to free negroes; these were the pretexts, not the true purpose, of that war. Republicans hated the Union, and had little love for any enslaved people. Republicans waged that war of the '60s to down, crush, kill the Democratic party. When the South surrendered and peace was proclaimed, Northern Democracy took courage, lifted up its head, fronted and faced its old enemy and prepared itself to resist any further torture and persecutions of Southern Democracy. All the old fear of Democracy awakened in Republican hearts, hence its increased intensity of hate. The people of the South were talked of as though they were wild beasts, which it were virtue to exterminate from the face of the earth. This feeling suffered no abatement until after Garfield's death. During Garfield's campaign Republican hate amounted to insanity.

The Cincinnati *Enquirer*, January 15, 1881, said: "Republican hate has blasted the fair heritage of our fathers." It certainly had blasted that heritage, and for a time seemed to have killed liberty itself. Two years before Daniel Webster's death, he foresaw and predicted the evil deeds that party would commit should it ever ascend to power: "If these fanatics ever get the power in their own hands they will override the Constitution, set the Supreme Court at defiance, change and make laws to suit themselves, lay violent hands on them who differ in opinion or who dare to question their fidelity, and finally deluge the country with blood." Every word of this prediction came to pass. The Constitution *was* overridden. The Supreme Court *was* set at defiance. Violent hands *were* laid on those who differed in opinion. The country *was* deluged in blood.

Samples of Republican Hate.

In 1859, at a meeting in Natick, Massachusetts, Senator Wilson, of Massachusetts, offered the following: *"Resolved,* That it is the right and duty of Northern men to incite and aid negroes in the South to rise in insurrection."

Seward said: "I would like to see the negroes of the South rise in blackest insurrection."

In 1859 the New York *Herald* said: "Not only the Republican clergy encourage the insurrection of negroes in the South to bring on a civil war, but the gentler sex also." Hate like this came well from the descendants of men on whose souls rested and still rests the horrors of the "Middle Passage."

In a speech delivered by Mr. Joshua R. Giddings, in Kansas, he said:

> I look for the day when I shall see a negro insurrection in the South, when the negroes will be supplied with British bayonets and commanded by British officers, and shall wage a war of extermination against the whites, when every white man shall see his dwelling in flames and his hearth polluted; and though I may not mock at their calamity, yet I shall hail it as the dawn of the millennium (Carpenter's *Logic of History*).

It was the hope of witnessing horrors such as Giddings wished to see that made Seward, Medill, Chandler and others, so eager to inaugurate war on the South. Republicans confidently believed that at the first tap of the drum the negroes would rise in "blackest insurrection" and set to work killing white women and children. The amiable conduct of the negroes, their docile obedience to the white women of the South while husbands, brothers and fathers were at the front battling for freedom, was a sore disappointment to hating hearts. During that trying time not a white woman on the great plantations was afraid of negroes; not a white woman was outraged or afraid of outrage. The mistress of the "gret-us," as the negroes called the great house, or the family mansion, never locked their doors at night. The negroes on the place were their protectors, not their enemies. Rapes of young matrons and maidens and little girl children were not known in the South until *after* the savage but slumbering instincts of negro nature had been awakened by instructions of and companionship with those who hated the Southern people so insanely. During Buchanan's administration the Rev. William Duvall, unable to attend in person and address a convention of Republicans, sent a letter to be read to the convention. A short extract will show the spirit of the writer and of the convention to which he wrote:

> Long before this an army of 20,000 men should have expelled from Washington City the Goths and Vandals of this administration [President Buchanan and his Cabinet]. The people of the North are ready to do this work – only let the

capitalists of the North furnish the money – and the men are ready to fight this propagandizing government. I sincerely hope that a civil war may soon burst upon this country. I want to see it. My most fervent prayer is that England, France and Spain may speedily take this accursed nation into their special consideration and when the time arrives, for the streets and cities of this land to run with blood to the horses' bridles. If this writer be living there will be one heart to rejoice (See Carpenter's *Logic of History*).

The Rev. Charles E. Hodges wrote a little work widely circulated. The following extract will show its spirit:

> He is not a traitor to his country, but a true patriot, as well as a Christian, who labors for the dissolution of the Union. We do not expect to dissolve the Union alone; we simply ask co-operation, and for this appeal to the people. This is not the time to lay out the plan of a campaign, to open trenches, dispose of forces and besiege the citadel. The thing to be *now* done is to urge upon every man this question: Are you ready?

James Watson Webb said in a speech: "If we fail at the ballot we will drive back the South with fire and sword – so help me God!"

At a public meeting held in Buffalo, New York, some years before the South seceded, Governor Reeder, of Kansas, spoke as follows:

> When I am on the trail of the enemy against whom I have a deadly hate, I will follow him with cat-like tread; I will not strike until I can strike him dead. I do not wish to give the South notice of our intentions. When the time comes to strike I want the South to have the first notice of the blow in the blow itself.

Hate blinded this man Reeder and his hearers to the baseness involved in the declaration that he would steal upon the object of his hate as the tiger steals upon his prey, and strike as tigers and assassins strike – in the dark and without warning. Before the first blow of war was struck the Chicago *Tribune* jauntily said to the Eastern States: "Get out of the way; we of Illinois can fight this battle. In three months Illinois can whip the South."

Before a battle was fought the New York *Tribune*, which time and again had declared the South's right to secede, right to independence, said: "The hanging of traitors is sure to begin before the month is over. The nations of Europe may rest assured that Jeff Davis will be swinging from the battlements of Washington at least by the Fourth of July. We spit upon a later and longer deferred justice."

The New York *Times* said: "Let us make quick work. The rebellion is an unborn tadpole. A strong pull will do our work effectively in thirty days."

The Philadelphia *Press* said: "No man of sense can for a moment doubt that the war will end in a month. The rebels, a mere band of ragamuffins, will fly on our approach like chaff before the wind. The Northern people are simply invincible."

Seward said: "It is erroneous to suppose any war exists in the United States. There is only an ephemeral insurrection."

The battle of Bull Run was fought July 21, 1861. Prominent Republicans, having no doubt of victory, boastingly invited friends, Senators, Congressmen, their wives and daughters to go out and "see the rebels run." "This," they gleefully said, "will be your only chance to see anything like a battle." Accordingly, long strings of carriages filled with fine ladies escorted by gentlemen on horseback, drove out of Washington City that 21st day of July, 1861, followed by express wagons loaded with eatables for luncheon, baskets of champagne, bottles of brandy, beer, etc. They prepared for a pleasant picnic, but their return was not quite so joyous. However, there were some loaded wagons that went from Washington that morning which never returned. They were captured by Confederates, driven southward, and their contents divided among the women of Virginia as mementoes showing the spirit of Republicans at that time. Some of these mementoes which escaped the pillaging and burning by the Union armies now hang in Southern halls for Southern children to wonder at – iron shackles and iron balls "for rebel feet, and ropes and handcuffs for rebel hands." Republicans confidently expected to see long strings of Southern soldiers driven into Washington, painfully dragging iron balls on their fettered feet, handcuffs on their hands.

Republicans often declared that the negro "would be delighted to get a chance to cut their masters' throats." They confidently expected negroes to rise in "blackest insurrection" and help them burn houses and barns and kill Southern whites. When B.F. Butler, surnamed the Beast, was commander of New Orleans, he was anxious to see negroes rise and kill white women and children in La Fourche Parish, in which were only a few old white men and many thousand blacks. Butler unfolded these views to General Weitzel, who commanded that parish, and that officer refused to engage in the work. "The idea," wrote Weitzel to Butler, "of a negro insurrection is heartrending. I will resign my command rather than induce negroes to outrage and murder the helpless whites." In 1863 Morrow B. Lowry, Republican Senator in Pennsylvania, in a public speech stated that he had declared that if any negro would bring him his "Rebel" master's head he would give him one hundred and sixty acres of his master's plantation. Not a "Rebel" head did any negro take to Mr. Lowry.

Russell, correspondent of the London *Times*, was in Washington when the battle of Bull Run was fought. On page 176 of his diary Russell says:

> The first Confederate soldiers captured were taken to the station and mobbed in the streets. Men dressed as Union soldiers hurled every kind of missile they could lay their hands on at the prisoners, pelting them with mud and filthy words. It was with difficulty the guard could save the prisoners from being killed.

The unfortunate Confederate soldiers shut up in Northern prisons describe the various cruelties, the tortures perpetrated on helpless Southern soldiers. Many were killed wantonly by brutal negro guards, who were rewarded, never punished, for such deeds. Many died of starvation and cold. To cover up their own cruelty, Republicans were eternally accusing the South of cruelty. On page 163 of Russell's diary he says:

> The stories which have been so sedulously spread of the barbarity and cruelty of the Confederates to all the wounded Union men ought to be set at rest by the printed statement of the eleven Union surgeons, just released, who have come back from Richmond, where they were sent after their capture on the field of Bull Run, with the most distinct testimony that the Confederates treated their prisoners with

humanity. Who are the miscreants who try to make the evil feeling, quite strong enough as it is, perfectly fiendish by asserting that the rebels burned the wounded in hospitals and bayoneted them as they lay helpless on the battlefield?

Who were they? Russell did not know that lies of this nature were only part of the gospel of hate so long preached by the Republican party and its progenitors, the Federalists of New England. Never for a moment did those lies cease to be told. The testimony of the eleven surgeons was blown away on the wind and the lies went on. Lies of this sort were credited by the prison guards, hence their cruel treatment of Southern soldiers.

On page 152 Russell says of Republican lies told in Washington: "Such capacity for enormous lying, both in creation and absorption, the world never before witnessed." Even at the early stage of the war Seward, the vindictive, gloated over the prospect of the South's sufferings. In the Union army were large numbers of the lowest class of men from European kingdoms. Of these Seward said to Russell: "Thousands of half savage Germans come over, enlist in our army and plunder and destroy as if they were living in the days of Agricola" (Russell's *Diary*, page 211).

Well informed Englishmen well knew how savage was the hate Republicans felt toward the South. The London *Telegraph* tersely put it thus: "The North simply demands blood, blood, blood. Dominion, spoliation, confiscation." At a Republican meeting in Cadiz, Wisconsin, March 26, 1863, the following was unanimously passed: *"Resolved, That we hail any policy of our Government toward the South, be it annihilation, extermination, starvation or damnation."* What virulence of hate lies in these words!

Cassius Clay said in a public speech: "I find fault with Lincoln, not because he suspended the habeas corpus, but instead of doing it by a dash of the pen, he did not do it by 'ropes around the necks of the rebels.'"

"We'll hang 'em yet!" cried out a voice from the crowd.

"Yes," rejoined Clay, "the hanging of such men as Seymour and Wood will be true philanthropy." Seymour was the Democratic Governor of New York. Wood was a distinguished Democrat of New York. All through the history of the Republican party may be seen evidence that the basic foundation of Republican animosity toward the

South was hatred of Democracy and Democrats. McClellan was only a half-hearted Democrat, but Republican hatred of McClellan was intense. Witness this from the Chicago *Tribune*: "Give us rebel victories, let our armies be defeated; let Maryland be conquered, Washington captured, the President exiled, our Government destroyed. Give us these and any other calamity that can result from war and ruin sooner than a victory with McClellan as General" (Carpenter's *Logic of History*).

Wendell Phillips, who, before blood began to flow, eloquently declared that the South was in the right, that Lincoln had no right to send armed men to coerce her, after battles began seemed to become drunk on the fumes of blood and mad for more than battlefields afforded. In a speech delivered in Beecher's church, to a large and presumably a Christian congregation, Phillips made the following remarkable declaration:

> I do not believe in battles ending this war. You may plant a fort in every district of the South, you may take possession of her capitals and hold them with your armies, but you have not begun to subdue her people. I know it seems something like absolute barbarian conquest, I allow it, but *I do not believe there will be any peace until 347,000 men of the South are either hanged or exiled.* (Cheers).

Why the precise number, 347,000, does not appear. If the hanging at one fell swoop of 347,000 men and women seemed to Phillips something like barbarian conquest, it would be interesting to know what would have appeared truly barbarian. History records some crimes of such stupendous magnitude, even to this day men shudder at their mention. In the Thirteenth Century, within two hours, while Sicilian priests were chanting vesper songs in Christian churches, 8,000 men were slaughtered. In the Eighth Century, Charlemagne hanged 4,000 men in one batch. In the Sixteenth Century, on St. Bartholomew's Day, if we take the lowest estimate, 30,000, if we take the highest, 70,000, innocent men and women were butchered as fast as human hands could do the work. In France, during the revolution, one fine September day, 1,000 men were put to death. During the Reign of Terror, some estimate 2,000, others 4,000, human heads were chopped off by the guillotine; but these 4,000 were killed day by day. Was Mr. Phillips and his party ambitious to overtop all of these stupendous crimes and win for himself and his party the highest record in the calendar of crime? Marat was the monster of the Reign of Terror. Becoming impatient at the killing daily done by the guillotine, Marat demanded it be given at one batch an extra 250,000 heads. Was it Mr. Phillips' ambition to reach a higher pinnacle of infamy than Marat had attained? Is it indeed true that the heart in a human breast sometimes ceases to be human, and a wolf's ramps in its place?

While the war was fiercely raging a meeting was called in New York City for the relief of the sick and wounded Union soldiers. Parson Brownlow made a speech which elicited from the Republicans frequent and loud applause. The following extract will show the spirit of hate that ruled the hour. Brownlow said:

> If I had the power I would arm and uniform in the Federal habiliments every wolf and panther and catamount and tiger and bear in the mountains of America; every crocodile in the swamps of Florida and South Carolina; every negro in the Southern Confederacy, and every devil in hell, and turn them on the rebels in the South, if it exterminated every rebel from the face of God's green earth – every man, woman and child south of Mason and Dixon's line. I would like to see Richmond and Charleston captured by negro troops commanded by Butler, the beast. We will crowd the rebels into the Gulf of Mexico, and drown the entire race, as the devil did the hogs in the Sea of Galilee. (Long and loud applause.)

After this fine burst of ferocity Lincoln, Seward and Stanton thought it would be a good thing to have Parson Brownlow Governor of Tennessee, from which vantage ground he could harass and torture the white people of that State at his leisure. By Federal aid the negroes and carpetbaggers in Tennessee put Brownlow in the Governor's office, which he abused by cruelties, rascalities and oppressions of every sort.

English writers make frequent mention of the bitter hate Republicans felt toward the conquered South. From an English work, published in 1891, called *Black America*, I take the following:

> In spite of the fact that all resistance to Federal authority had ceased, and that according to Mr. Justice Nelson of the Supreme Court, the States in which the civil government had been restored under the pacific Presidential plan

were entitled to all the rights of States in the Union, in spite of these facts Congress solemnly decided that the war was not over, and in March, 1867, Congress passed the reconstruction act, over President Johnson's veto. These acts annulled the States' government, then in peaceful operation, divided the States into military districts, and placed them under martial law; enfranchised the negroes, disfranchised all white men, whether pardoned or not, who had participated in the war against the Union, if they had previously held any executive, legislative or judicial office under the State or Federal Government.

So bitter, blinding venomous was Republican hate, high men in that party openly and gleefully exulted in the cruelty of the so-called reconstruction acts. Garfield was one of this sort. "This bill," said Garfield joyfully, "first sets out by laying its hand on the rebel States' governments, and taking the very breath of life out of them. In the next place it puts a bayonet at the breast of every rebel in the South. In the next it leaves in the hands of Congress utter and absolute power over the people of the South." Percy Gregg, the English historian, in his history of the United States, says:

> The reconstruction policy was at once dishonest and vindictive. The Congressional majority [Republican] were animated not merely by selfish designs, but by rabid hatred of the South's people which had fought so gallantly for what the best jurists of America believed to be their moral and constitutional right.

For what the foremost men in the Republican party had declared their right. Another English writer of great eminence, Anthony Trollope, was in this country during the reconstruction period, and wrote of it thus:

> I hold that tyranny never went beyond this. Never has there been a more terrible condition imposed upon a fallen people. For an Italian to feel an Austrian over him, for a Pole to feel a Russian over him, has been bad indeed, but it has been left for the political animosity of the Republicans of the North – men who themselves reject all contact with the negro

– to subject the Southern people to dominance from the African who yesterday was their slave. The dungeon chains were knocked off the captive in order that he may be harnessed as a beast of burden to the captive's chariot.

We will give another passage from Gregg, the English historian:

> The devastation of the Pallatine hardly exceeded the desolation and misery wrought by the Republican invasion and conquest of the South. No conquered nation of modern days, not Poland under the heel of Nicholas, not Spain or Russia under that of Napoleon, suffered from such individual and collective ruin, or saw before them so frightful a prospect as the States dragged by force, in April, 1865, under the "best government in the world" (page 375, Gregg's *History of United States*).

When the bill to confiscate land in the South was before Congress, the English language seemed to be inadequate to convey the insane hate of the Republican party toward the people of the South. A short extract from Thaddeus Stevens' speech will show something of the spirit of that time:

> Why [cried Stevens, his face livid, his lips flecked with foam], why all the carnage and devastation we have had? It was that treason might be put down and traitors punished. I say, the traitor has ceased to be a citizen; he has become a public enemy. The South's land must be seized and divided and conveyed to loyal men, black or white. This confiscation bill can be condemned only by the criminals and their friends, and by that unmanly kind of men whose mental and moral vigor has melted into a fluent weakness, which they mistake for mercy, and by those religionists who mistake meanness for Christianity.

Conventions were called in different States to arouse the people to the fury of another war on the crushed, conquered, disarmed South. A convention was held in Philadelphia in 1866, the purpose of which seemed to stir up hate toward President Johnson, and to fire the old soldiers with a desire to march down on the South and "finish the war." General B.F. Butler was a big man in that convention, and made venomous speeches. With one blood-streaked eye turned Southward toward the land he hated, and the other downward toward the hot home bad souls are doomed to dwell in, Butler shouted out: "By their rebellion the men of the South forfeited their property, their liberty, their lives, every right they possessed. Unfortunately they were not hanged, but we will march on them once more, and woe to him who opposes us! I say," Butler shouted, his terrifying eyes still turned in different directions, "I say, keep the men of the South out of the Union until the heavens melt! And if that should not come to pass in our day, we will swear our sons to keep them out." (Long and loud applause).

Zack Chandler made a fierce attack on President Johnson, whom leading Republicans had come fiercely to hate, because Johnson's policy toward the South was less cruel than theirs: "Who is Andy Johnson?" wrathfully demanded Chandler. "What is Andy Johnson's policy? Andy Johnson has no more right to a policy than my horse has. If Johnson does not stop about now he will learn that treason is a crime, and that it shall be punished."

Brownlow was a very big man at that convention. Brownlow, like Johnson, had fled from the South and entered the camp of her foes. Lincoln had disliked Johnson, but had held Brownlow in much favor. Before going to the Philadelphia convention Brownlow made a speech to the carpetbaggers and negroes of Nashville, Tennessee. The following extract will show its spirit. He said:

> I am one of those who believe the war has ended too soon. We have whipped the rebels, but not enough. The loyal masses constitute an overwhelming majority of the people of this country, and they intend to march again on the South, and intend this second war shall be no child's play. The second army of invasion will, as they ought to, make the entire South as God found the earth, without form and void. They will not, and ought not to, leave one rebel fence-rail, outhouse, one dwelling, in the eleven seceded States. As for the rebel population, let them be exterminated. When the second war is wound up, which should be done with swift destruction, let the land be surveyed and sold out to pay expenses.

This speech so highly pleased Republicans that the Philadelphia convention gave Brownlow a boisterous welcome. The following extract is from Brownlow's address to the convention:

> I mean to have something to say about the division of your forces the next time you march on the South. I would divide your army into three grand divisions. Let the first be armed and equipped as the law requires, with small arms and artillery. Let them be the largest division, and do the killing. Let the second division be armed with pine torches and spirits of turpentine, and let them do the burning! Let the third and last division be armed with surveyors' compasses and chains, that will survey the land and settle it with loyal people.

Brownlow's speech so much pleased Republicans they invited him to go about repeating his speech to stir up the old soldiers to the fury of a second war on the South. Governor Yates of Illinois was at that convention, also eager for a second war on the South. In his speech Yates said: "Illinois raised 250,000 troops to fight the South, and now we are ready to raise 500,000 more to finish the good work."

In another speech Brownlow exhorted the soldiers to march down on the South, to "burn and kill! burn and kill!" until the whole rebel race was exterminated. These sentiments were praised as "truly loyal." These two words, "truly loyal," were so prostituted by Republicans during the war. and for years after, not for a thousand years will they regain their purity of meaning. Not a man of the Republican party, not a paper condemned (so far as I can discover) these rabid utterances. On the contrary, the more rabid and malignant a man was, the higher he rose in Republican favor. Richard Busted, a carpetbagger from New York, who was playing the part of Judge in Alabama "Territory," in a speech made in New York City, spoke as follows:

> I would keep the rebels out in the cold till their teeth chattered to the music of the Union. (Applause). Keep them out in the cold till they learn that treason is the greatest crime of the century! I would keep them there till the last trumpet sounded! I say, better a boundless waste of territory, filled with owls and bats, than that the Southern States should be occupied with such men! (Cheers). I tell you, although there may be forgiveness before God for the crime of the South,

there can be no forgiveness before men. (Long applause).

The carpetbagger, Hamilton, who was playing the part of despot-governor over Texas, was eager to have another army sent down on the devastated South. In his speech at the Philadelphia convention, the carpetbagger, Hamilton, said: "Prepare your hearts, and your guns, and your swords, for another conflict. It is bound to come. Get yourselves ready."

"We are ready," shouted back a blood-thirsty Republican.

"We are ready! We'll march down and finish the Rebs!"

About the same time a convention was held in Syracuse, New York, in which a second war on the South was urged. Lyman Tremaine was president. In his address Mr. Tremaine said of that second war: "At the very first tap of the drum an army of veteran troops capable of overwhelming all opposition will come to the rescue." Rescue of what? Of whom? Who, *what* was in danger? Were these men absolutely insane with hate? Was it possible they still apprehended danger from the disarmed South? They well knew if they sent another army on the South it would not be against armed men; they knew, as Brownlow had declared, all their army would have to do would be to "kill and burn ! kill and burn!" to the dreadful end.

"Traitors," continued President Tremaine, "must be punished. Our soldiers will proceed to punish them. This time it will be effectually done by our soldiers without the intervention of President Johnston, or Congress, judge or jury." Yet this man Tremaine had once possessed a fair share of reason and some sense of justice. In the early days of the war, while speaking of the Southern people's resistance to the armed invasion of their country, Tremaine said to his audience:

> But, gentlemen, while I do not justify secession in the abstract, we must not forget that the South has had the most terrible provocation to which civilized men have ever been subjected. When they found the Government turned into an engine of war and oppression – make the case your own, and then make proper allowance for our Southern friends – I ask whether they are doing very differently from what human nature would do under such circumstances?

It seemed as if Republicans lay awake at night devising new ways of manifesting hate toward the people of the South. On May 25,

1866, a man by the name of Bond, in the House of Representatives, gave notice as follows: "I will introduce a bill to adopt the gray uniform of the so-called Confederate States to be the uniform of the convicts in the State penitentiaries, and that the prisoner convicted of manslaughter be entitled to wear the ensign of rank of a Colonel, and so on down to the lowest grade in crime."

In the summer of 1863 the Washington *Chronicle* reported a speech made by Jim Lane, Republican Senator from Kansas, in Washington City. Senator Lane said:

> I would like to live long enough to see every white man in South Carolina in hell, and the negroes inheriting their territory. (Loud applause.) It would not any day wound my feelings to find the dead bodies of every rebel sympathizer pierced with bullet holes, in every street and alley in Washington City. (Applause.) Yes; I would regret the waste of powder and lead. I would rather have these Copperheads hung and the ropes saved for future use. (Loud applause.) I would like to see them dangle until their stinking bodies would rot and fall to the ground piece by piece. (Applause and laughter.)

Nothing done by the Republicans after the war ended manifested more malignant hatred than the way they treated and lied on the President of the Southern Confederacy. This western continent has introduced no man of whom it has more reason to be proud than Jefferson Davis. Brave, gentle, kindly, a true Christian in every walk of life, a patriot of the truest type, an ardent lover of the liberty which inspired the men of '76, Davis should be held up before the youth of America as deserving esteem, reverence, emulation. When the war ended the Republicans selected Mr. Davis as the chief object on which to pour foul streams of hate. The English language was ransacked in search of vile epithets to throw upon him; human ingenuity was taxed to invent base falsehoods to defame him. The murder of Mr. Lincoln was seized as a pretext to charge him with the crime of assassination. Without the faintest shadow of evidence Republicans made haste to proclaim to the world that in their bureau of military justice they had proof that Mr. Davis was guilty of the assassination of Lincoln. $100,000 were offered for his arrest. When arrested he was cast into prison and treated as a felon. Every species of indignity and insult was heaped upon him. Though old, feeble, sick, and strictly guarded, brutal men were ordered to enter his cell, throw him down and weld iron chains and balls on his ankles, ordered by the present Lieutenant-General Nelson A. Miles. In vain Mr. Davis requested to be taken into open court and tried on the charges made. They dared not try him in any court. They knew they had no particle of evidence on which to convict him. Were he tried for Lincoln's murder, *they* would be proved guilty of lying, not Mr. Davis of murder. Were he tried for treason, not Mr. Davis, but the whole Republican party, would be proved guilty of treason – treason to the Constitution – treason to the principles of '76. Not daring to try Mr. Davis, too venomously cruel to restore him to freedom, they kept him in prison two years and every day of those two years, and almost every day afterward for more than a dozen years, Republicans continued to pour out on Mr. Davis' name streams of sulphuric hate.

When Republicans proclaimed that Mr. Davis and other distinguished men of the South had assassinated Lincoln, there was not a human on earth outside of the hate-crazed Republican party who believed that charge. Earl Russell, from the floor of Parliament, voiced the sentiment of all England when he said: "It is not possible that men who have borne themselves so nobly in their struggle for independence could be guilty of assassination." To this *Harper's Weekly* replied with the hate-born lie: "If it seems too incredible to be true that the rebel leaders were guilty of Lincoln's assassination, it must be remembered that Lincoln's murder is no more atrocious than many crimes of which Davis is notoriously guilty."

From the floor of Congress Mr. Thaddeus Stevens, March 19, 1867, poured out Republican hate in this fashion:

> While I would not be bloody-minded, yet if I had my way I would long ago have organized a military tribunal under military power, and I would have put Jefferson Davis and all the members of his Cabinet on trial for the murders at Andersonville and Salisbury, for the shooting down of our prisoners of war in cold blood – this man who has murdered a thousand men, robbed a thousand widows and orphans, and burned down a thousand houses.

In *Harper's Weekly* of June, 1865 is this little burst of hate:

"The murder of President Lincoln furnished the final proof of the ghastly spirit of the rebellion. Davis inspired the murder of Lincoln." If the murder of Mr. Lincoln furnished the proof of any one thing, it is proof of the truth of Christ's saying: "They that take the sword shall perish by the sword."

Boutwell of Massachusetts introduced a resolution into Congress as follows: "Be it resolved, That Jefferson Davis shall be held and tried on the charge of killing prisoners and murdering Abraham Lincoln."

John Forney, Clerk of the Senate, in the Washington *Chronicle*, said: "The judiciary has ample evidence of Davis' guilt of Lincoln's murder, and of the murder of our soldiers in his prisons." Not one particle of such evidence was in existence.

In *Harper's Weekly* of June 17, 1865, we find this hate-born lie: "Davis is as guilty of Lincoln's murder as Booth. Davis was conspicuous for every extreme of ferocity, inhumanity and malignity. He was responsible for untold and unimaginable cruelties practiced on loyal citizens in the South." Mr. Davis was conspicuous for Christian mercy and gentleness of character, as well as for wide culture. He was morally and physically one of the bravest men this country has produced.

In *Harper's Weekly* of June 10, we find this: "In its last struggle the South's expiring force was concentrated into one crime [the murder of Lincoln] so black the shuddering world everywhere recognizes the devilish spirit of rebellion." The shuddering world today will recognize in Harper's raving the insanity of hate. The history of man's struggle for freedom shows that rebellions have won for mankind all the freedom they possess. Did ever any ruler on earth, of his own will, loosen his grip on the liberties of those he ruled? Every inch of liberty the English-speaking people now have was gained by rebellions. The colonies of '76 won freedom by rebellion. Rebellion means resistance to lawful rule. George III. was the lawful King of the Colonies. At no period in the existence of this Union has one State or group of States held lawful rule over any other State or group of States. The most stupendous falsehood ever told on this continent is the falsehood that the Southern people rebelled. There can be no rebellion except against lawful rulers. The Republican party of the '60s was guilty of the monstrous crime of usurping the power to rule the Southern States.

Not only did Republicans pour out the virulence of hate on the South's men, her women came in for a share, and a large share they received. A few specimens will show the women of this generation how their mothers were hated in the past. *Harper's Weekly*, October 12th, 1861, has this: "The ladies of the South ought to be sent to the almshouses and made to nurse pauper babies, and put to wash tubs under Irish Biddies." In the year 1865, June 4th, *Harper's* had this little nugget of pure hate: "The women of the South are lovely and accomplished to look at, but their bold barbarity has de-humanized them; they are like the smooth-skinned wives and daughters of the ogres in fairy tales – hyenas and wolves in woman's shape."

The lies of hate are not all dead yet; as late as June, 1894, a little paper called the *Picket Guard*, run in the interest of the Grand Army of the Republic of St. Louis, published the following wanton falsehood on the women of the South: "The mothers of the South," said the *Picket Guard*, "systematically taught their children to be cruel. During the war it was the custom of Southern ladies, accompanied by their little boys and girls, to walk through the prison hospitals and tear bandages from the wounds of the Union prisoners, to exult in the pain they witnessed." Not a paper in St. Louis denounced this hate-born lie. On the contrary, a Republican daily paper, the *Star*, of that city, reproduced the lie in its columns, as a warning to the Society of the Daughters of the Confederacy to keep silent on the war of the '60s.

On June 8th, 1866, Mr. Shellabarger of Ohio, from the floor of Congress, poured out a stream of hate-born lies, of which the following is a sample: "They [the people of the South] framed iniquity and universal murder into law – their pirates burned your commerce on every sea [the South had no pirates]. They planned one universal bonfire of the North. They murdered by systems of starvation and exposure 60,000 of your sons in their prisons." Of the malignant as well as foolish lies in this extract, it is only necessary to notice the biggest of them all, the assertion that the South murdered 60,000 Union soldiers in her prisons. Secretary of War Stanton left on record the number of men on both sides who were made prisoners during the war, and the number who died in prison.

In Northern prisons were Southern soldiers: 220,000
Of those died in Northern prisons: 26,000
In the South's prisons were Union soldiers: 270,000
Of those who died in Southern prisons: 23,576

These figures show that Mr. Shellabarger's figures exceed Stanton's by 36,424. If only 23,576 Union soldiers died in the South's prisons, how did it happen that she starved to death 60,000 in her prisons?

"And," continued Mr. Shellabarger, in a final burst of mendacity, "to concentrate into one crime all that is criminal in crime, all that is barbarian, they [the people of the South] killed the President of the United States."

Five days later Mr. Windom of Minnesota undertook to rival if not surpass Mr. Shellabarger in mendacity. Standing on the floor of Congress, Mr. Windom spoke as follows:

> The people of the South waged a diabolical four-years' war; they murdered our soldiers in cold blood; they fired our hotels filled with women and children; they starved our soldiers to death in their prisons, within sight of storehouses groaning with Confederate supplies. They polluted the fountain of life. They only laid down their arms when our victorious bayonets were at their throats; and, while professing to accept the issues of the war, they assassinated the Nation's President.

In 1876, eleven years after the South surrendered, Mr. James G. Blaine of Maine stood up in Congress and poured out a lot of hate-born lies as malignant as human tongue ever uttered or human brain ever concocted:

> Mr. Davis was the author, knowingly, deliberately, guiltily, and willfully, of the gigantic murders and crimes at Andersonville. And I here, before God, measuring my words, knowing their full extent and import, declare that neither the deeds of the Duke of Alva in the Low Country, nor the massacre of St. Bartholomew, nor the thumb-screws and other engines of torture of the Spanish Inquisition, began to compare in atrocity with the hideous crimes of Andersonville.

When his speech was concluded Mr. Blaine's admirers rushed up to congratulate him. Mr. B. H. Hill of Georgia rose to his feet and confronted them with Stanton's figures:

> If [said Mr. Hill] cruelty killed the 23,500 Union soldiers who died in the South's prisons, *what* killed the 26,000 Confederate soldiers who died in the North's prisons? In other words, if the nine per cent. of men in the South's prisons were starved and tortured to death by Mr. Jefferson Davis, *who* tortured to death the twelve per cent. of the South's men who died in the North's prisons?

Mr. Blaine and his friends were dumfounded. Stanton was an authority whose figures they dared not assail; they, as Shellabarger, had not chanced to see Stanton's figures. Mr. Blaine made no reply to Hill for several days. Finding the figures had been quoted correctly, he did not venture to deny their accuracy, but attempted to weaken their force; he had not magnanimity enough to admit an error, to regret a wrong. His explanation was lame, but it was the best he could frame: "Our men," said Mr. Blaine, "when captured were in full health; they came back wasted and worn. The rebel prisoners in large numbers were emaciated and reduced from having been ill-fed, ill-clothed, so they died rapidly in our prisons – died like sheep." This excuse was accepted by Republicans, and the lie that the South starved prisoners to death was kept alive, and to this day is often told.

In 1892, B. F. Butler, surnamed the Beast, wrote a book he called *Butler's Book*. No one will fancy that Butler would willingly speak one kind word of man or woman in the South. Butler was a renegade from the Democratic party, therefore, like all renegades, hoped to win favor with the party he had joined by vilifying the party he had abandoned. Butler wrote his book twenty-seven years after the South surrendered. During all those twenty-seven years the lie that Mr. Davis had willfully starved and tortured Union soldiers to death was told and retold a hundred thousand times. All that time Butler knew the statement was false, but he did not choose to say so until he wrote his book in 1892. In that book, page 610, Butler says:

> In the matter of starvation of prisoners the fact is incontestible that a soldier of our army would easily have starved on the rations which in the latter days of the war were served out to the Confederate soldiers before Petersburg. I examined the haversacks of many Confederate soldiers captured on picket during the summer of 1864, and found there-

in, as their rations for three days, scarcely more than a pint of kernels of corn, none of which were broken, but only parched to blackness by the camp fires, and a piece of raw bacon about three inches long by an inch and a half wide, and less than half an inch thick. No Northern soldier could have lived three days on that. With regard to clothing, it was simply impossible for the Confederates, at that time and months before, to have any sufficient clothing on the bodies of their own soldiers. Many went bare-footed all winter. Necessity compelled the condition of food and clothes given by them to our men in their prisons. It was not possible for the Confederate authorities to supply clothes and food (*Butler's Book*, page 610).

Yet Windom had the gall to assert that the South starved her prisoners to death within sight of granaries groaning with Confederate supplies.

While Mr. Davis lay in a dungeon cell in Fortress Monroe, and while the whole air of the North was thick with the cries, "Hang him! Hang him! Hang him!" a number of the leading men of the Republican party consulted together, and decided to settle the question decisively, was Davis guilty, as charged, of cruelty to the Union soldiers in prison? Gov. Jno. A. Andrew of Massachusetts, Horace Greeley, Thaddeus Stevens, Henry Wilson, then Vice-President of the United States, and Gerritt Smith were of the number who were willing *secretly* to admit they did not believe Mr. Davis guilty as charged – *secretly*, not one had the fairness to say so openly. However, in the first week of Congress, 1866, these men sent Chief Justice George Shea of the Marine Court to Canada to inspect the official records of the Confederate Government. Judge Shea saw General John C. Breckenridge, then in Canada, and through his influence was placed in Judge Shea's hands the official records of the Confederate Government, which Judge Shea carefully examined, especially all the messages and acts of the Executive and Senate in secret sessions, concerning the care and exchange of prisoners. Judge Shea found that the inhuman and unwarlike treatment of the South's soldiers in Northern prisons was a most prominent and frequent topic during those secret sessions. From those documents, not meant to meet the public eye, it was manifest that the people of the South had reports of the cruel treatment of their loved ones in Northern prisons, and through representatives in Richmond had pressed Mr. Davis, as the Executive and the Commander-in-Chief of the South's Army and Navy, instantly to try active measures of retaliation, to the end that the cruelties to prisoners should be stopped. Judge Shea, in his report of the investigation, said:

> It was decisively manifest that Mr. Davis steadily and unflinchingly set himself in opposition to the demands made for retaliation, and this impaired his personal influence and brought much censure upon him from Southern people. These secret sessions show that Mr. Davis strongly desired to do something which would secure better treatment to his men in Northern prisons, and would place the war on the footing of wars waged by people in modern times, and divest it of a savage character; and to this end Mr. Davis commissioned Alexander Stevens, vice-President of the Confederacy, to proceed to Washington as military commissioner. This project was prevented by Lincoln and Seward, who denied permission for Mr. Stevens to approach Washington. After this effort to produce a mutual kindness in the treatment of prisoners failed, the Southern people became more unquiet on the matter, yet the secret records show that Mr. Davis did not yield to the continual demand for retaliation (*Southern Historical Papers*).

Although this report, made in 1866, completely exonerated Mr. Davis from the vile charge of having tortured and starved prisoners to death, such was the despotism of the party in power, such was the bitter hate Republicans in the North felt toward the South, this report was not given to the public until nearly eleven years after Judge Shea's report was made. All these eleven years every Republican engine, newspapers, magazines, lecturers, politicians, were hard at work vilifying Mr. Davis and repeating the lie that he was guilty of torturing and starving prisoners to death; and this, although Horace Greeley, Senator Wilson, Gov. Jno. A. Andrew of Massachusetts, Gerritt Smith and other high Republicans knew these charges were absolutely false. *Was this Shea investigation kept secret from Blaine?* While in a Fortress Monroe cell, sick, feeble, unable to rise from his cot because of the iron shackles and heavy iron balls on his ankles, Republican cartoonists were using all the ingenuity of their art to picture Mr. Davis, not only as contemptibly weak, but as ferocious as a wild beast. In the collection of the New York Historical Society are preserved a number of these malignant productions. One, entitled the "Confederacy in Petticoats," shows Mr. Davis dressed as a poor old woman, feebly climbing a fence to escape the Union soldiers which pursue him with pointed pistols and drawn swords. Another cartoon, entitled "Uncle Sam's Menagerie," shows Mr. Davis as a hyena in an iron cage playing with a human skull. A noose is around his neck connected with a high gallows, and the rope about to be drawn taut. Above the iron cage, in the shape of birds perched on little gallows of their own, each with a noose around his neck, are figures of other Confederate leaders. Uncle Sam, in his usual red and white striped breeches, acting the showman, stands by the iron cage, a long stick in his hand, pointing up to the gallows.

In Toledo, Ohio, October, 1879, fourteen years after the war had ended, about four thousand five hundred ex-Union soldiers held a meeting. The object of the meeting, it seems, was to vilify the South, and especially to iterate and reiterate the lies that Union soldiers were willfully starved to death in her prisons. A man named Moody made the welcoming address. A few extracts from the different speeches will show the spirit of hate that ruled the crowd. Mr. Moody said:

> And now, ladies and gentlemen, in behalf of the thousands that starved and rotted and died in the damnable hells controlled by that accursed traitor, Jeff Davis (loud applause), assisted by imps like Puppy Ross, Captain Wertz and others; in behalf of every one that lies in graves where they were put by traitors, accursed traitors, to their Government, the best in the world; in behalf of the God above, we thank you for this grand reception.

Col. Streight made a speech, in which he said:

> I am called on by Copperheads [Northern Democrats] to smoke the pipe of peace with Ben Hill of Georgia, and with men who stand up in Congress and deny that the Union soldiers had been starved and tortured in their prisons. Men who lied like traitors, as they are, to get out of it, when they say rebel prisoners were abused in Northern prisons. (Applause). And now Hill wants to smoke the pipe of peace with me. He fills that pipe with

rebel lies, with infamy. He fills it with self-conceit and self-glory. It makes me sick. Hill stands up there in Congress and says the rebels took the best care they could of our men in their prisons. He lies! He lies deep down in his throat! He knows he lies! Yet we have some persons in this country anxious to forget and forgive. (Long and loud applause).

Garfield was a speaker at that meeting. Garfield's speech and Colonel Streight's had been cast in the same mould. The following is an extract from Garfield's reported speech:

> The Southern Senators lie like traitors, as they are! when they say our men were treated as well in their prisons as the rebels were treated in our prisons. Hill of Georgia stands up in Congress and lies when he says the rebel chiefs took as good care of our men in their prisons as they could. Yes, deep down in his throat he lies. They were human fiends. Hill is a liar. There is no peace with rebels! They are very anxious to forget and forgive. Are *we* to be friends with traitors? No! No! Never! We have proof that Jefferson Davis was guilty of torturing our men in his prisons to death! It was his policy to make idiots of our men by tortures. Southern cruelty never before in all the world had its parallel for atrocity. Never can we forgive them! Never will I be willing to imitate the loving kindness of Him who planted the green grass on the battlefields.

And all this, twelve years after Judge Shea had made his report! Garfield seldom missed an opportunity to give vent to his animosity. In a speech in Chicago he said: "Never will I consent to shake hands with the South until she admits she was wrong, eternally wrong, and the North was right, eternally right."

In 1879 and 1880, during the Garfield campaign, Republican hate became a howling insanity. Judge Yaples, in the Cincinnati *Enquirer* of 1880, said: "Republican hate is grounded on the fact that the people of the South will not join the Republican party." How could they be expected to join a party which, from its birth, had wronged and hated them? Garfield's champions boldly declared that when he was elected the South would be territorialized, so that the whole country could be Africanized, and negroes put in rule over whites and upheld by military power.

A Washington correspondent of the Louisville *Courier-Journal*, 1879, wrote this:

> At no time since the war has the rancor of the Republican press been fiercer than it is at this time. No epithet is too vile to be applied to the people of the South. They are held up as barbarous ruffians, outlaws, murderers, thieves. The New York *Tribune* the other day compared them to hyenas, and begged pardon of those beasts for the comparison. The speeches of Conkling, Blaine, Edmonds and the rest are pitched in the same key.

In December of 1883 the Cincinnati *Commercial Gazette* contained this gem of pure hate and pure lie:

> If the actual state of things South of the Ohio were set before the Northern people they would have no sympathy to spare for cruelty in any other part of the world. No other land can furnish a parallel to such barbarity as our own. From Zululand and Congo, Ashantee and Abysinnia, through the Nomadic Bedouins, the Bashi Bazouks, the half-civilized tribes of Western Asia, to the savage rule of the Czar, with his endless procession of political prisoners to Siberia, not one can equal the reign of the savagery which exists in the South.

When this was written the Southern people were hard at "work increasing their crops, multiplying their industries, enlarging their school facilities, teaching the older and richer portions of the country lessons in manufacturing, renewing the soil of their fields, and offering the world an example of two widely differing races living in harmony together."

A Republican paper, the Lemars (Iowa) *Sentinel*, during Garfield's campaign, said:

> On the Fourth of July, 1881, the pig-headed brigadiers of Massasip and Kaintuck, Arkansas, Alabam, and the whole barbarian Southland, will see their State Constitutions, and State sovereignties, and State lines, their ignorance and

their cowardice, torn up by the roots from their blood-soaked soil. Garfield's Presidency is to be the Regency of Stalwartism; after that – *Rex*.

During Mr. Hayes' campaign, Mr. Howard Kutchins, editor of the Fon-du-lac (Wis.) *Commonwealth*, two weeks before election day inserted in his paper the following address to Republican voters:

To Arms, Republicans!

Men! Work in every town in Wisconsin for men not afraid of fire-arms, of blood, or dead bodies. To preserve peace and prevent the administration of public affairs from falling into the hands of obnoxious men, every Republican in Wisconsin should go armed to the polls on next election day. The grain stacks, houses and barns of all active Democrats should be burned to the ground, their children burned with them, their wives outraged, that they may understand the Republican party is the one which is bound to rule, and the one which they should vote for or keep their stinking carcasses away from the polls. If they persist in going to the polls and voting for Jenkins [Democrat], meet them on the road, in the bush, on the hill, anywhere, night or day, and shoot every one of the base cowards and agitators. If they are too strong in any locality and succeed in putting their opposition votes into the ballot boxes, break open the boxes, tear to shreds their discord-breeding ballots, and burn them to ashes. This is the time for effective work. These agitators must be put down. Whoever opposes us does so at his peril. Republicans, be at the polls in accordance with the above directions, and do not stop for a little blood.

Hayes became President; in reward for so much party zeal he nominated the bloodthirsty Kutchins for the Internal Revenue Collectorship in the Third District of Wisconsin. So far as I can learn, not a man or woman in the Republican party made any objection to Kutchins' savage advice to voters. Yet this is the party which to this day weeps tears of sympathy over any negro man whose vote is not cast and counted in the South.

It seems that Mr. Wendell Phillips never fully recovered from the gangrene of heart caused by the fumes of blood continually rising from battlefields. An article by him in the *American Review* of March, 1879, shows that a wolf's, not a human, heart still ramped in his breast. He wrote:

> Treason should have been punished more severely. We all now see that magnanimity went as far as it safely could when it granted the traitor his life. His land should have been taken from him, and before Andrew Johnson's treachery, every traitor would have been too glad to be let off so easily. His land should have been divided among the negroes, forty acres to each family. Every rebel State should have been held as a territory under the direct rule of the Government, without troublesome questions. Henry Wilson, Vice-President, confessed to me that this was the greatest mistake of our party. His excuse for the mistake was that the Republican party did not dare to risk any other course in the face of Democratic opposition.

Only a heart gangrened with hate, only a judgment distorted by hate, could call the South's resistance to invasion treason. Before hate-insanity got in its work on Phillips' brain he declared that the South acted on the principles of '76, and that no one standing with these principles behind him could deny the South's right to independence. The smallest affairs of life Republicans slimed all over with the poison of hate.

Articles like the following adorned Republican newspapers. The Topeka (Kansas) *Citizen*, a Republican paper, in 1879 had this:

> By allowing the worthless scoundrels of the South to live, their contemptible seed was perpetuated. They are a set of demons, both by nature and practice, and while one of the breed is left they will remain the same. As well try to hatch chickens from snake eggs as to raise a decent race of human beings from the offscouring of the miserable, heartless murderers and robbers of the South.

A Chicago paper had this: "In their houses, their persons, their food, their habits, Southern men and women, as a rule, are unclean. They have dogs and hogs and other unclean animals for their nearest neighbors, and share their houses with these animals and vermin of a different sort." Another Chicago paper kindly served notice as follows: "When Southern men come North, whether for business or pleasure, they must understand they will not be received as equals."

Robert Ingersoll, the favorite infidel lecturer of the Republican party, made loud pretense of loving liberty. The following is a sample of the kind of liberty Ingersoll loved: "When a man," said Ingersoll, "talks of *despotism* you may be sure he wants to steal, or be up to some devilment. *I* am not afraid of centralization; *I* want the power where somebody can use it. I want the ear of the Federal Government acute enough, its arms long enough, to reach a man in any State."

In 1879 the Quincy (Illinois) *Whig* had this:

> Every Republican knows that nothing so good could happen to this country, nothing that would be of such advantage, as a general and judicious slaughter of Democrats at the polls. Every Republican ought to take a bayonet to the polls for the purpose of assisting the Federal army in the work of killing the Democrats.

The reader must never forget that all the hate Republicans felt originated in hate of Democrats. Hate of Thomas Jefferson's principles is as inherent and ineradicable in Republican hearts as it is in the open and avowed monarchists. In 1879 the Lemars (Iowa) *Sentinel*, a true-blue Republican paper, published in its columns Republican opinions of Southern people as follows:

> The South is not and never was aught else but pusillanimous, perfidious, cowardly. We ask, nay challenge, all the Brigadiers in Yah-Hoo land [the South] to show one instance, one solitary instance in all her history, of either honor or courage. We could fill the *Sentinel* ten thousand times with deeds of Southern infamy, treachery, blood-thirstiness, mendacity, malevolence, barbarity, ingratitude, ruffianism, dishonor, cowardice, rapine, and general hellishness. That so infamous, base, sinister, indecent, corrupt, and demoniacal people should ever have enjoyed the reputation of chivalry or of courage, is bad enough, but that such spawns of hell should be rehabilitated with political rights, and made political equals of the brave, loyal, true Northern men, is the cham-

pion crime of the Nineteenth Century.

Brevet Major George W. Nichols, aide-de-camp to General Sherman when he made that vainglorious march to the sea, wrote a book called *The Story of the Great March*. Hate so warped Major Nichols' mind he made statements so absurd no one outside of imbecile asylums could possibly believe them. Instance this from page 173:

> A characteristic feature of South Carolina has impressed itself upon all of us. I refer to the *whining, helpless, craven spirit* of the men. These fellows are more cowardly than children; they whine like whipped boys. There is not an officer or soldier in all our army who does not feel the most supreme disgust and contempt for those chivalric creatures.

On page 193 Major Nichols has this: "The white people of South Carolina are among the most degraded specimens of humanity I ever saw – lazy, shiftless; only energy to whine. The higher classes in South Carolina represents the scum, the lower, the dregs of civilization. They are not Americans; they are merely South Carolinians." On page 213 is this: "What strikes me most is the evidence of intellectual decay. They so want in energy and vitality as to approach senility." The imbecility of North Carolina's people did not escape this sharp-sighted Major. On page 293 he tells of his visit to an insane asylum: "I found," said the Major, "that the inmates were more idiotic than insane. *The only inmate who gave evidence of ever having intellect was a man from Massachusetts."*

So completely did the devilish spirit of hate dominate the hearts and brains of Sherman and his officers, they had not as much kind feeling for the unfortunate women living on the line of that march as humane men would have felt for dumb cattle. The divine quality of mercy, of pity, had no lodgment in their breasts. Major Nichols' book proves this. Soon after entering Atlanta, Ga., Sherman ordered every inhabitant (fifteen thousand in number) driven from the city. Not a single armed man was among them; they were mostly women and children, with a few old men. Of this unnecessary measure, Major Nichols says: *"The order was firmly but kindly executed. They were allowed to choose which way to go."* Was it this allowance that constituted the kindness? Think of it, Christian people! 15,000 women and children, at the point of bayonets, driven from their homes into the pathless woods, in the bleak November month, shelterless, foodless, to wander about as they might. In his report of this to General Halleck, Sherman says: "They [the women and children] *did not suffer, unless for want of food.*" Picture to yourselves, Christian people of this age, the suffering of 15,000 women and children in such a condition! Of this act General J. B. Hood wrote Sherman: "Your unprecedented measure transcends in studied and ingenious cruelty all acts ever before brought to my attention in the dark history of war." Hood's letter greatly angered the irascible and self-inflated Sherman, who wrote to Halleck: "I cannot tamely submit to such impertinence. But as long as my Government is satisfied I do not care what rebels say."

Sherman's government was highly satisfied. Every act of cruelty to Southern people greatly pleased that cruel and pitiless government. Had Sherman ordered the women of Atlanta to be prodded by bayonets out of their homes, along their streets bleeding, fainting, to the woods, or had he ordered them hanged by the dozens until dead on the boughs of the trees, that government would have been fully as well pleased. There is nothing in the history of that government to show that it ever manifested the slightest disapprobation of the atrocities its armies perpetrated. After Atlanta was empty of its citizens, every woman and child in the woods, Major Nichols cheerfully informs us that, *"The soldiers are now resting and enjoying themselves thoroughly."* Resting from the labor of driving women and children out of their homes into the woods, and enjoying themselves over the suffering caused. After resting the soldiers were ordered to burn down the city.

Major Nichols says: "The houses are now all vacant. The streets are empty. A terrible stillness and solitude depresses even those who are glad to destroy all. In the gardens beautiful roses bloom, the homes are all in flames. In the peaceful homes of the North there can be no conception how these people suffer for their crimes." What crimes? Only hate-poisoned hearts, only hate-distorted brains could or can call a war of defense a crime. Remember, oh posterity, from the first to the last of the war, the South fought in self-defense. The Republican party fought a war of conquest.

On page 37 Major Nichols says:

> We are leaving Atlanta. Behind we leave a track of smoke and flame. Yesterday we saw in the distance pillows of smoke; the bridges were all in flames.

"I say!" said a soldier, "I believe Sherman has set the very river on fire."

"If he has, its all right," replied his comrade.

The rebel inhabitants are in an agony. The soldiers are as hearty and jolly as men can be.

All through his book Major Nichols seems to be anxious to show that the greater the sufferings inflicted on Southern people, the healthier and jollier were his soldiers. On page 38 Major Nichols made the following record:

> Atlanta.
> Night of the 15th of November, 1864.
>
> A grand and awful spectacle is presented to the beholders of this beautiful city now in flames. The Heaven is one expanse of lurid fire. The air is filled with flying, burning cinders. Buildings covering 200 acres are in ruins or in flames.

For 2,000 years the name of Nero has been execrated as that of a monster. The burning of Rome was the work of a moral monster. Sherman's crime of burning Atlanta proves him to have been the greater monster of the two, inasmuch as Sherman had been born and reared under the merciful light of Christianity. Nero was descended from a line of pagan ancestry on which the divine light of Christ's teachings had never fallen.

On page 39 is a picture of Atlanta in ruins. On page 112 is a picture which should today, thirty-eight years after that war ended, bring the blush of shame to every Republican cheek. This picture represents a little cottage on the wayside of Sherman's march. In the open door stands a sorrowful woman, a babe in her arms; four frightened children cling to her skirt. Nine or ten men in blue are in the yard prodding the earth with bayonets and sabres in search of the little trifles, trinkets, the sorrowful woman had hoped to save from army robbers by burying in the ground. Of scenes like this Major Nichols says:

> It is possible that some property thus hidden may have escaped the keen search of our men, but if so it was not for want of diligent exploration. With untiring zeal the sol-

diers hunted the concealed things whenever the army halted. Almost every inch of ground in the vicinity of the dwellings was prodded by ramrods, pierced by sabres, upturned by spades. The result was very distressing to rebel women who saw their little properties taken.

What can be more contemptible than this? Armed men, officers and privates, robbing helpless, poverty-stricken women of the poor little trinkets they had hoped to save by burying in the ground! And these contemptible deeds are related in a boasting way! Our fine Major continued:

It was comical to see a group of these veterans punching the unoffending earth. When they "struck a vein" the coveted wealth was speedily unearthed. Nothing escaped the observation of these sharp-witted soldiers. The woman watching these proceedings was closely watched, her face, her movements, giving the men a clue.

"These searches," cheerfully remarks the Major, *"made one of the pleasant excitements of oar march."* Yes, *one*; but by no means the only one. Robbing the women of rings, pins, silver cups, looting their houses, carrying off all they could; destroying what they could not appropriate, immensely added to the "pleasant excitements of that march." Even the poor little garments, which expectant mothers, with patient toil, carding, spinning the thread, weaving the cloth, cutting and sewing, had prepared for unborn babes, even these poor little things were seized by rude hands, held up to the rude jokes and laughter of the jubilant men in blue, then torn into strips, thrown on the ground and trampled under foot.

So useless as a military measure was this vainglorious march of Sherman's, even Union officers (General Piatt for one) condemn that march. Piatt says: "Sherman could just as well have disbanded his army (60,000 strong) as have been guilty of the folly of that march."

On page 207 of Major Nichols' book, I take the following:

It was usual to hear among soldiers conversations like this: "Where did you get that splendid meerschaum?" or "Where did you get that fine cameo?"

"Oh," was the reply, "a lady presented me this for

saving her house from being burned."

The wit of this lies in the fact that the trinkets had been taken from the ladies and their houses burned also. Our valiant Major comments:

> This style of answer became the common explanation of the possession of all sorts of property. An officer taking a punch from an elegant chased silver cup, was saluted thus:
> "Hello, Captain! that's a gem of a cup; where did you get it?'
> "Oh," returned the Captain, "this was given me by a lady for saving her household things from burning up."
> An enterprising officer came into camp one day with a family coach filled with hams, flour, and other things, and cried out, "Elegant carriage, isn't it? This is a gift from a lady whose house was in flames." [Set in flames by the order of the officer who had the carriage.]
> Gold watches, boxes, chains, rings, etc., were got in this way.

"This," complacently remarks our Major, "was one of the humors of the camp." What do the people of this age think of such humor? These men in blue first robbed defenseless women of their small trinkets and other little things, set fire to their houses, then lied to their comrades, saying the trinkets had been presented to them by the women they had robbed. What devilish humor was this?

Major Nichols, page 161, says: "The Mayor of Columbia, S.C., came out to surrender the city, but this did not entitle its citizens to protection." Who could expect protection from men whose hearts were as devoid of mercy, of pity, of kindness, as wolves or tigers? These only rend and kill to satisfy the keen pangs of hunger; the men on that march pillaged, robbed and burned to satisfy the devilish demands of hate.

After descanting on the beauty of Columbia, its flowering vines and shrubs, its gardens of roses and fragrant flowers, the Major sagely and solemnly says: "I could but reflect on how utterly these cowardly South Carolinians have lost all pride of nationality." If the Republican party, its officers and armies of the '60s represented the real nationality of this country in that time, forever and forever would that false, unjust, cruel and blood-soaked nationality be detested, despised, scorned, hated by every humane and freedom-loving heart in America!

As the reader knows (from evidence given in preceding pages of this book), the large majority of the Northern people disliked and opposed Lincoln's war of conquest on the South. From the first to the last day of that war they opposed it. Nichols is fond of telling falsehoods which only idiots could accept as truths. Instance this: "The failure of Jeff Davis has brought down on him the hatred and abuse of his own people. Were he here today nothing but execration would have been showered upon him." And this: "The people of Raleigh, N.C, were astonished to find that Sherman's army were Christian gentlemen."

Is it possible that Major Nichols himself for one moment believed Sherman's army were Christian gentlemen? Would any *"gentleman,"* Christian or not, have engaged in the mean work of robbing poor women of their small trinkets, the gifts of love or friendship? Would any man with one particle of gentlemanly feeling have manifested so much pleasure in the sufferings their cruelties caused. Both Major Nichols and General Sherman gleefully parade their wanton wickedness, and gleefully wind up such stories by boasting of their soldiers' great enjoyment of such work. Nichols says:

> History will in vain be searched for a parallel to the scathing and destructive effect of the invasion of the Carolinas. Aside from the destruction of military things, there were destructions overwhelming, overleaping the present generation – even if peace speedily come, agriculture, commerce cannot be revived in our day. Day by day our legions of armed men surged over the land, over a region forty miles wide, burning everything we could not take away. On every side, the head, center and rear of our columns might be traced by columns of smoke by day and the glare of flames by night. The burning hand of war pressed on these people, blasting, withering.

In Sherman's report to Halleck he evidently takes great pride in the wanton destruction he has wrought: "I estimate," writes Sherman, "that the damage to Georgia alone is $100,000,000 – $98,000,000 was simple destruction – two millions have inured to our advantage. *Our soldiers have done the work with alacrity and cheerfulness unsur-*

passed."

In Sherman's report to Halleck of the burning of Columbia, in 1865, Sherman charged that crime to General Wade Hampton. That lie went traveling over the Northern States for ten years. In 1875, Appleton & Co. published Sherman's *Memoirs*, written by himself. In Volume II, page 287, Sherman, without a blush of shame, admits the lie, using the following words: "In my official report of the conflagration of Columbia, I distinctly charged it to General Wade Hampton, and confess I did so pointedly to shake the faith of his people in him." What an old silly Sherman must have been to think anything *he* could say on any subject would shake any Southern man's faith one way or the other! Sherman's sense of honor was too dull to permit his feeling ashamed of lying, ashamed of publicly proclaiming he had lied on an honorable man, and from the mean motive of injuring him in the esteem of his friends.

Shortly after the South surrendered, Salmon P. Chase, Lincoln's Secretary of the Treasury, made a flying visit down the Atlantic States. On his return, newspapers reported Mr. Chase's opinion of the whites and blacks in these States: "I found," said Chase, "the whites a worn-out, effete race, without vigor, mental or physical. On the contrary, negroes are alive, alert, full of energy. *I predict in twenty-five years the negroes of the South will be at the head of all affairs, political, religious, the arts and sciences."*

Though an undisputed and indisputable fact that Guiteau, who assassinated Garfield, was a Northern man, a member of the Republican party, such was the New York *Tribune's* blind and bitter hate of the South, it promptly accused her people of that crime. The Republican paper, the Lemars (Iowa) *Sentinel*, was so filled with the imperial spirit during the Hayes administration, it addressed that mild President in the following rampant style:

> Rutherford! are you a man? If you are, issue a proclamation! Proclaim the States of Mississippi and Louisiana in open rebellion against the Nation! Declare every State of the old Rebel Confederacy in a state of siege. Call an extra session of Congress, exclude every so-called Senator and Representative from the rebellious territory, and with a loyal legislature begin the great work of moulding a plastic Nation into form. Disfranchise the rebel States for a generation, at least. This is the heroic method and requires a hero in the van.

If there is anyone in the North or the South who believes this strange hatred of Southern people has died out, let him look over the columns of modern daily papers, let him observe the tone of modern Republican politicians; especially let him take a glance at modern Republican histories, biographies, lectures, etc.

On this day, October 14, 1903, a telegram from Louisville, Ky., states that the members of the Union Veterans Union, at a public reception given them in a large hall in that city, sang, "We'll Hang Jeff Davis on a Sour Apple Tree." Next day a delegate offered a resolution disclaiming any intention to wound the feelings of Southerners by singing that song. The resolution was voted down.

A few years ago a convention of educators met in Nashville, Tennessee. The delegates were hospitably received and entertained, free of cost to them. One of these delegates, a woman, from the State of Kansas, was entertained in the best hotel in the city. While occupying an elegant room, eating and drinking of the best the State afforded, this woman wrote a letter for publication to one of her own State's newspapers. The Kansas paper promptly published it, and the Nashville *American* reproduced it before the writer left the city and the people she so hated. That woman delegate's malignant hatred of the South found vent in the following sentiment: "I hope and pray when I pass away from earth I will be able to look down from the heavenly blue above and see the black heel set on the white necks of these people."

As a sample of the way Republican writers do not hesitate to tell untruths, I give a few lines from a little history published in 1894, written by a woman named Mrs. Emma Cheney. Speaking of the attempt to reinforce Fort Sumter, Mrs. Cheney says: "The rebels had meant to starve the little garrison out of Fort Sumter." This is not only untruthful, it is ungrateful. Every day the people of Charleston sent to Sumter a boat load of food supplies, fresh meat, fowls, fruits, vegetables, etc. "After Lee's surrender," says Mrs. Emma Cheney, "Jefferson Davis lived in a box car because no man honored him enough to give him hospitality." This is pure fiction. There was not a man in the South who would not have felt honored by having Mr. Davis a guest in his house. There was not a woman who would not willingly have knelt at his feet and reverently kissed his hand in recognition of his high and lofty character, as well as with deep and tender affection and sympathy for the man on whose pure and stainless name so much malignancy had been poured by his unworthy enemies.

Mrs. Emma Cheney says: "Davis disguised himself as a woman and carried a tin pail." This also is pure fiction; but what if he had disguised himself as a woman? A claimant to the English crown, when hunted by his enemies, disguised himself in a woman's garments. As he was going to Washington City, Lincoln disguised himself, and yet there was no danger except what his own imagination conjured up.

As late as 1902, thirty-seven years after the war ended, a life of Abraham Lincoln was published in Chicago, which reproduces, as facts, many malignant lies which have not even a shadow of truth to rest on. Instance the following, on page 798:

> The assassination of Abraham Lincoln was the culmination of a series of fiendish schemes in aid of an infamous rebellion. It was the deadly flower of the rank and poisonous weed of treason. The guiding and impelling spirit of secession nerved and aimed the blow struck by the cowardly assassin.

On page 799 is this:

> The conspiracy [to assassinate Lincoln] was clearly traceable to a higher source than Booth and his wretched accomplices. In the course of the trial positive evidence was furnished connecting Jacob Thompson, Jefferson Davis and their associates with President Lincoln's assassination. This direct evidence is only the keystone of an arch of circumstances strong as adamant.

On page 802 is the following:

> They [the Southern men] had taken a form congenial to their "chivalrous" interests, instigating and aiding piratical seizure on Lake Erie, robbing a St. Alban's hotel, burning and wholesale murder at New York, and in broadcast diffusion of pestilence and death throughout Northern cities. Dr. Blackburn assiduously labored to spread malignant diseases. What further depth of iniquity needed these men before organizing the conspiracy to kill Mr. Lincoln? That they did enter the scheme is proved beyond a doubt. That Jefferson Davis, in whose confidential employment all this while they were, was consulted as to the plan of assassination, and gave it his

approval, is shown by direct testimony.

On page 803 is the following: "The expedient of assassination of Mr. Lincoln had long been a favorite one, beyond doubt, with many of the Southern traitors." On page 806 is this:

> The assassination was not the freak of a madcap or a fanatic; it was the natural outgrowth of the spirit which led to rebellion. The barbarous and upstart autocrat who had deliberately starved thousands of Union prisoners could have no compunction at seeing a chosen emissary stealthily murder the ruler of the Nation.

As long as such lies are told it is criminal for the South to remain silent.

CHAPTER THIRTY-THREE

New England's Two Insanities.

We cannot close this work without some special notice of the singular mental malady New England brought upon herself, and which, being contagious, was caught by large numbers of the Republican party in the '60s. It is known to all that the Creator has implanted in the very atoms of the human being, as well as in the being of animals, certain instincts for the preservation of life and the perpetuity of the race. Among these instincts is that of kinship. Our affections first go out to our parents, our children, our relatives. Next they go out to the people of our own country, our own color and blood. The white race loves white people more than it does the yellow, the red or the black. Negroes prefer their own color; they naturally affiliate with negroes in preference to whites, Chinese or Japanese. This is the law of kinship. Any reverse of this law is perversion – perversion is a species of insanity. We have shown that in the year 1796 certain New England Federalists, to attain a certain object they had in view, set themselves to work to promulgate the gospel of hate toward the people of the South. By dint of teaching hate the teachers developed that feeling in their own hearts. As the teaching went on, the feeling increased in intensity until it became an insanity, a monomania utterly beyond the control or the influence of reason. Finally it came to pass that from this insanity of hate there sprung an insanity of love. The former was directed toward the white people of the South, the latter toward the negroes. Without evidence from the papers and publications of that day, the white men of this generation will not be able to believe that New England, as well as large numbers of the Republican party, came to admire and respect the negro race as morally and mentally superior to the white. At first this strange insanity only held that the negroes in the South were far superior in every way to Southern whites; but as time passed the insanity took on a more violent form, and those so afflicted believed and taught that as a race the negro was greatly superior, morally and mentally, to the whole Caucasian race, and not only this, they came to admire every peculiar quality of the negro, the blackness of their skins, their woolly hair. Their whole makeup New England orators and writers dwelt on with a sort of worshiping rapture and urged intermarriage between blacks and whites, not to elevate the former, but the latter.

Extracts from speeches and papers will throw light on this subject. In the early stages of his insanity Wendell Phillips was fond of announcing to his audiences that "negroes are our acknowledged equals. They are our brothers and sisters." As time went on Mr. Phillips' distemper became more heated. He was not satisfied with asserting that "negroes are our equals;" he made the startling announcement that "Negroes are our Nobility!" and began to clamor that special privileges be granted to "our nobility." He wanted all the land in the Southern States divided and bestowed on "our nobility" and their heirs forever. What "our nobility" had done to deserve this rich reward Mr. Phillips did not explain. Perhaps he thought the fact that negroes had been brought from Africa in a savage state, and had acquired in the hard school of slavery some of the arts of civilization, fitted them to become a noble class.

Governor Stone of Iowa, in a speech made at Keokuk, August 3, 1863, was certainly in the first stages of this insanity when he said to his audience: "I hold the Democracy in the utmost contempt. I would rather eat with a negro, drink with a negro, and sleep with a negro than with a Copperhead" (meaning a Democrat).

The disease certainly had struck Mr. Morrow B. Lowry, State Senator of Pennsylvania, when at a large meeting in Philadelphia, in 1863, he said to his audience: "For all I know the Napoleon of this war may be done up in a black package. We have no evidence of his being done up in a white one. The man who talks of elevating a negro would not have to elevate him very much to make him equal to himself."

The faithful old New York *Independent* sorrowfully wailed over the long delayed coming of the Black Napoleon, which all the insane negro-worshipers confidently looked for:

God and negroes are to save the country. For two years the white soldiers of this country have been trying to find a path to victory. The negroes are the final reliance of our Government. Negroes are the keepers and the saviors of our cause. Negroes are the forlorn hope of our Republican party.

James Parton, the noted biographer, was strongly touched with the prevailing disease – insane love of negroes. "Many a negro," wrote James Parton, in 1863, "stands in the same kind of moral relation to his master as that in which Jesus Christ stood to the Jews, and not morally only, for he stands above his master at a height which the master can neither see nor understand."

J. W. Phelps, General in the Republican army, thought the negro race much better adapted to receive Christianity than the white. "Christianity," said Phelps, "is planted in the dark rich soil of the African nature. Negroes are as intelligent and far more moral than the whites. The slaves appeal to the moral law, clinging to it as to the very horns of the altar; he bears no resentment, he asks for no punishment for his master."

A little work, ably written, titled *Miscegenation*, was published in 1863 or 1864. Before this work was out a white woman, Miss Annie Dickinson, called by Republicans "The Modern Joan of Arc," became a convert to the doctrine of intermarriage between whites and blacks and an eloquent expounder of the same. Miss Dickinson lectured over the Northern States. It was said at the time that President Lincoln and his Cabinet attended her lectures in Washington City. Miss Dickinson wrote a novel called *What Answer?* the purpose of which was to illustrate the beauty and utility of marriage between negro men and white women, and negro women and white men. The characters in *What Answer?* are negroes and whites. They fall in love and marry in a way to affright and disgust people not up to date on such doctrines. The title, *What Answer?* was supposed to indicate that the author's argument could not be refuted. On the night Miss Dickinson was to lecture at Cooper Institute, New York City, she was late in appearing; the impatient audience was quieted by the distribution of circulars advertising the new work, *Miscegenation*, just published.

George Sala, correspondent of the London *Telegraph*, was then in Washington City, and wrote his paper as follows: "Miss Dickinson comes accredited by persons of high authority. She is handed to the rostrum by the second personage in the North. The Speaker of the House is her gentleman usher. The Chief of the State [Lincoln] and his ministers swell the number of her auditors. She is the goddess of Republican idolatry."

February, 1863, the correspondent of the London *Times* wrote from New York describing Republican love of the negro race:

> It has been discovered here, that in many important respects the negro is superior to the whites; that if the latter do not forget their pride of race, and blood, and color, and amalgamate with the "purer and richer blood" of the blacks, they will die out and wither away in unprolific skinniness. The first to give tongue to the new doctrine were Theodore Tilton and the Rev. Henry Ward Beecher. The latter a few months ago declared that it was good for white women to marry black men, and that the passion and emotional nature of the blacks were needed to improve the white race. Mr. Wendell Phillips has often hinted the same thing.

The London *Times* of February 5, 1862 or 1863, I am not certain which, contained copious extracts from *Miscegenation*, as samples of the love-insanity for the negroes which at that time afflicted the Republican party. I also offer a few extracts from *Miscegenation*:

> All that is needed to make us the finest race on earth is to engraft upon our stock the negro element which Providence has placed by our side upon this continent. [The Providence were New England's slave-stealers who imported negroes from Africa and sold them to the South's planters]. Of all the rich treasures of blood vouchsafed to us, that of the negro is the most precious. By mingling with negroes we will become powerful, progressive and prosperous. By refusing to do so we will become feeble, unhealthy, narrow-minded, unfit of noble offices of freedom and certain of early decay. White people are perishing for want of flesh and blood; they are dry and shriveled, for lack of the healthful juices of life. Their cheeks are sunken, their lips are thin and bloodless, their under jaws narrow and retreating, their noses sharp and cold, their teeth decayed, their eyes small and watery, their

complexion of a blue and yellow hue, their heads and shoulders bent forward, hair dry and straggling. The waists of white women are thin and pinched, telling of sterility and consumption; their whole aspect is gaunt and cadaverous; they wear spectacles and paint their faces. The social intercourse between the sexes is acetic, formal, unemotional. How different is an assembly of negroes! Every cheek is plump, the teeth are white, the eyes large and bright, every form is stalwart, every face wears a smile. American white men need contact with warm-blooded negresses to fill up the interstices of their anatomy. I plead for amalgamation, not for my own individual pleasure, but for my country, for the cause of progress, for the world, for Christianity. It is a mean pride unworthy of an enlightened community that will deny the principle of amalgamation. This principle has touched a chord in humanity that vibrates with a sweet, strange, marvelous music, awakening the slumbering instincts of the Nation and the world. It would be a sad misfortune if this war should end without a black general in command. We want an American *Touisant l'Overture*. It is in the eternal fitness of things that the South should be conquered by black soldiers. After that the land of the South must be divided among negroes.

The London correspondent of the *Times* wrote in that paper that doctrines of this nature were applauded by large audiences of men and women in the North. Time has proved how little the Republican party understood the Caucasian or the African race. No *Touisant l'Overture* appeared on the scene. No black general came forward to "fill the eternal fitness of things." On the contrary, all during the war the negroes in the South were amiable servitors, docile and obedient to their white mistresses while their masters were at the front fighting the armed invaders of their country.

Among the cartoons of that time were a number illustrative of the doctrine of *Miscegenation*. One with that title is now in the collection of the New York Historical Society. The Rev. Henry Ward Beecher is pictured holding the hand of a big black, buxom negress, whom he is presenting to President Lincoln, who is bending his head to her as to a queen. The black "lady" is dressed in the extreme of fashion, showing all her teeth by a happy grin. Near by sits Horace Greeley, treating to ice cream another big black "lady," arrayed in all her finery. Beyond is a horribly ugly black man in a chair, holding in his lap a pretty young white girl, apparently pleased with the situation. Near this couple is another hideous negro man about to kiss a pretty white girl.

The doctrine of *Miscegenation* highly delighted Northern negroes. Frederick Douglas, half white and half black, was especially pleased. Douglas addressed a large Republican meeting in Brooklyn, 1863, on the subject of amalgamation. He said:

> There is not now much prejudice against colored men. A few days ago a white lady asked me to walk down Broadway with her, and insisted on taking my arm; everyone we met stared at us as if we were curious animals. By and by you will get over this nonsense. (Cheers). You ought to see me in London walking down Regent street with a white lady on each arm, and nobody stared at us. And it will soon be so here, and then we will all be the nobler and better.

The London *Times* during the war of the '60s published in its columns extracts from a pamphlet issued in the North, which boldly asserted the lie that – "The first love of the beautiful young daughters of the proud planters of the South was for one of their father's negro slaves. *The mothers and daughters,"* said this insane writer, *"of the Southern aristocracy are thrilled with a strange delight by daily contact with their dusky servitors."* The mothers and daughters of the South, when chancing to see insane stuff of this nature, passed it by as the lunacy of a foul and distempered mind.

With this I rest the case which, ere long, will be tried in Posterity's Court – the South vs. the Republican party of the '60s. And as a last thought, I offer the reader the prophetic lines written by that inspired poet, Father Ryan, of Alabama:

> There is grandeur in graves, there is glory in gloom,
>   For out of the gloom future brightness is born,
>   And after the night comes the sunrise of morn.
> And the graves of the dead, with the grass overgrown.
>   Shall yet form the footstool of Liberty's throne.
>   And each single wreck in the warpath of Might
>   Shall yet be a rock in the Temple of Right.

Postscript.

Numbers of soldiers in the United States armies in different wars:

Revolutionary, 1775-1783 309,781
Northwest Indian War, 1790-95 8,983
Tripoli War – Naval, 1801-5 3,330
England, 1812-15 576,622
First Seminole, Florida, 1817-18 7,911
Second Seminole, Florida, 1835-43 41,122
Third Seminole, Florida, 1856-58 3,681
Black Hawk War, 1831-32 6,465
Creek War, 1836-37 13,418
Aroostook War, 1838-39 1,500
Mexican, April, 1846 to July, 1848 112,230

                                                    1,085,043

War upon the South, 1861-65 2,772,408

        Excess 1,687,365

From above it will be seen the United States employed in its four years' of war upon the South 1,687,365 more soldiers than in all its thirty-six years of war with England, Tripoli, Mexico and the Indian tribes.

www.ingramcontent.com/pod-product-compliance
Lightning Source LLC
Chambersburg PA
CBHW050552170426
43201CB00011B/1661